DAY TRADING

4 BOOKS IN 1:

THE BIBLE OF HOW THE MARKET WORKS FOR OPTIONS, SWING, FOREX AND FUTURES. HOW TO USE PSYCHOLOGY FOR A LIVING WITH THE BEST TACTICS AND STRATEGIES FOR EARNING PASSIVE INCOME

or professional advice. The content within this book has been derived from various sources. Please consult a licensed professional before attempting any techniques outlined in this book.

By reading this document, the reader agrees that under no circumstances is the author responsible for any losses, direct or indirect, which are incurred as a result of the use of information contained within this document, including, but not limited to, — errors, omissions, or inaccuracies.

FOREX TRADING

Description..11

Introduction 15

Chapter 1 Forex Trading Basics.........................33

Chapter 2 Elements Of Forex 45

Chapter 3 Forex Trading On A Budget.................61

Chapter 4 The Position Trading Strategy 75

Chapter 5 Developing Your Trading Plan..............85

Chapter 6 Think Before You Trade 91

Chapter 7 Trading Strategies 95

Chapter 8 Fundamental Analysis 109

Chapter 9 Trading Journals............................ 125

Chapter 10 Engulfing Pattern Trading With 3ms

Principles 147

Chapter 11 Psychology Of Forex Trading 165

Chapter 12 Tips For Success........................... 175

Chapter 13 FAQs On Forex Trading................... 181

Conclusion... 187

DAY TRADING FOR BEGINNERS

Description 191

Introduction 193

Chapter 1 What is day trading? 199

Chapter 2 Dos and Don'ts of Day Trading 201

Chapter 3 Personalizing Your Day Trading Plans .. 207

Chapter 4 Finding and Picking Stocks and Trading

Strategies 211

Chapter 5 Demand and Supply and Market Types 227

Chapter 6 Developing Your Day Trading Strategy 235

Chapter 7 Trading Psychology 255

Chapter 8 Support or Resistance Trading 261

Chapter 9 Fibonacci Trading Strategy 277

Chapter 10 Finding Entry and Exit Points 287

Chapter 11 Portfolio Diversification 291

Chapter 12 Managing Risk in Trading and the Role of

Journaling 315

Chapter 13 Tips and Tricks to Make Your Life Easier

when Using the MT4 Platform 331

Conclusion.. 337

OPTIONS TRADING

Description 345

Introduction 349

Chapter 1 Top Reasons to Trade Options 371

Chapter 2 Ways to Trade 375

Chapter 3 Covered Calls 385

Chapter 4 A Step-By-Step Way to Sell Covered calls

.... 395

Chapter 5 Volatility 403

Chapter 6 Technical Analysis 415

Chapter 7 Vertical Call Spreads 435

Chapter 8 Advanced Strategies and Techniques .. 443

Chapter 9 Make Binary Options Trading Simple

Through a Broker 451

Chapter 10 Options Trading Risk Strategies 467

Chapter 11 Top Mistakes made by New Traders .. 473

Chapter 12 Tips for Success 481

Conclusion 487

SWING TRADING

Description 491

Introducing 493

Chapter 1 Why is Swing Trading Better Than Day
Trading? 499

Chapter 2 The Daily Routine of a Swing Trader 507

Chapter 3 How Greeks Predict Option Pricing 519

Chapter 4 Swing Trading with Call Options 525

Chapter 5 Candlestick Chart Patterns and Technical
Indicators 531

Chapter 6 Fundamental Analysis...........................555

Chapter 7 Technical Analysis..............................559

Chapter 8 Watch for Counter Trends 565

Chapter 9 Breakout & Breakdown trading.................571

Chapter 10 Predicting the Market..........................579

Chapter 11 Having the Right Mindset for Trading........603

Chapter 12 The Secret of Profitable Trading..............611

Chapter 13 Commandments of Swing Trading...........619

Chapter 14 The Top Mistakes That Beginners Make.....631

Conclusion 641

FOREX TRADING

THE PSYCHOLOGICAL BIBLE OF CURRENCY. SIMPLE STRATEGIES FOR BEGINNERS TO ACHIEVE MORE SUCCESS AND PASSIVE INCOME EVERY DAY INVESTING IN FUNDAMENTALS MARKETS (SWING, OPTIONS, FUTURES)

Description

The trading market has no "one-size-fits-all" key. Some traders think they can simply purchase Forex trading programs and similar to an ATM- all that they have to do is input a PIN and they get all their cash. No, this is not how it works. This is an actual market, and it is the biggest financial market worldwide, so you have to regard it like that.

It is your decision if you want to be a part-time trader or you want to do it every day. You can even decide to make it a business - your trading business. If there is any secret actually, it is within your brain, and together with your mental awareness, control and accumulated skills and knowledge that you have acquired and the accordant alignment of your objectives and actions, and expertise that is gained through a quality amount of constant practice till knowledge becomes instinctive wisdom.

It is possible to learn to trade, however, the experience has to be acquired. It is developed personally through individual effort and comprehension. It does not just happen in one day. Like any other profession, trading also requires commitment. The theory is acceptable, but practice perfects your skills and combines all your previously acquired knowledge. One other important thing is to know that it is impossible to stop learning. Every day, there is a change in the market, and the Forex market like its traders, is constantly evolving.

What you put in is what you would get. Certainly, you have to invest in your learning, you have to search for knowledge and someone that can guide you through trading in this market. I believe that after you have read the book, it would not be hard for you to decide that you want me to guide teach you more.

This book gives a comprehensive guide on the following:

- Forex Trading Basics
- Elements Of Forex
- Forex Trading On A Budget
- The Position Trading Strategy
- Developing Your Trading Plan
- Think Before You Trade
- Trading Strategies
- Fundamental Analysis
- Trading Journals
- Engulfing Pattern Trading With 3ms Principles
- Psychology Of Forex Trading

- Tips For Success
- FAQs On Forex Trading... AND MORE!!!

The zeal to learn a minimum of one new thing every day is very crucial. After all these years, I still experience my own "Ah-ha" moments of awareness and I hope it never ends. However, these experiences have to be acquired personally. A few of them will be regarded as intuitive, and apparent to a lot of people, while for other people, they are unable to fully comprehend this.

Introduction

What is Forex?

The term *forex,* or also known as *foreign exchange*, *currency trading*, or simply *FX*, refers to the activity of trading the world's currencies. Trading currencies is important for business and foreign trade. This is what keeps businesses, as well as the world's different currencies in existence. For example, if you are an American tourist and you visit Egypt, you cannot pay the stores in USD as it is not the local currency that is accepted in Egypt. Instead, what you need to do is to exchange your USD for the local currency in Egypt, which is the Egyptian pound at its current exchange rate. Here is another example: Let us say that you live in the US and you want to buy a certain commodity from India, you will need to pay the Indian merchant in Indian rupees. Also, in order for the merchant to acquire the said commodity, then he will also have to pay in Indian rupees if he is buying it within India. However, if the Indian merchant is also going to import the said commodity, then he will have to convert his currency into the acceptable local currency of the seller. This constant need to exchange one currency for another makes the FX market the largest and most liquid financial market in the world.

Forex is also an excellent way to make a profit. As the most liquid financial market, there is a high potential to make a positive profit by trading currencies. In fact, there are professional traders out there who make a living solely from this activity. So, just how much can you make by trading currencies? You can make a few dollars up to thousands and even millions of dollars every month. The amount you can profit depends on your invested capital, as well as the outcome of a trade. It is worth noting that forex is also a type of investment. Hence, just like any other kind of investment, there is also the possibility of losing all your money. The good news is that there are things that you can do and strategies that you can apply that can significantly increase your chances of making a profit. These will be discussed in more detail later in the book. For now, you should first have a good foundation and understanding of what forex is all about.

The Forex Market

The forex market is the place where currencies are traded. So, where is this forex market located? One thing that you should understand is that the forex market is a decentralized market. What this means is that there is no central marketplace where forex is conducted. It does not have a physical place or location. Instead, it is made electronically online across a network of computers around the world. Therefore, if you want to trade cryptocurrency, you only have to use the Internet in order to access the forex market. As for the schedule, you have to consider that the forex market has a worldwide scope and that different countries can have different timezones. The forex market is open round the clock starting from Sunday at 5pm EST up to Friday at 4pm EST. The forex market is a continuously moving market, so you can expect to see how the price quotes of the different currencies change at any time of the day or night.

The forex market has two levels: the interbank market and the over-the-counter market (OTC). The interbank market is where banks trade. The OTC market is where regular traders engage in the FX activity. This is where you will trade using an online platform. Before you can trade currencies online, you will have to make an account with an FX broker. It is

17

your broker who will provide you with the platform that you can use for trading.

Among the different types of currencies, the US dollar is the most traded currency. It comprises more than 80% of all trades. It is followed by the Euro, and then by the Japanese Yen.

The forex market is the most active market in the whole world, which makes it a highly profitable place for professional traders. However, you should keep in mind that it is also a challenging place. It is not a secret that there are a number of investors who have lost a big amount of their invested capital in just a few days; worse, some of them have lost all their invested money. Still, for those who understand what they are doing and give it enough focus, effort, and practice, the forex market is the perfect place where you can continuously rake in serious profits.

Is it for you? Although you are welcome to join and participate in the forex market, it does not always mean that it is also the place that will make you earn money. When you trade foreign currencies, there is only one of two possible outcomes: either you make money or lose it. The unfortunate truth is that not everyone can have success in the forex market. If you are the type who just wants to gamble and rely on luck, if you do not want to take time and efforts to study the market, then you will most likely lose your money in just a few days. However, if you are willing to exert serious efforts, if you can sit for hours and study what is going on in the forex market and make analysis, then you can significantly increase your chances of making a profit. Also, if you get really good at it, then you might even be able to turn the forex market into a path that leads financial freedom.

Forex Pairs

When you trade in the stock market, you need to understand forex pairs. They are composed of currencies that are being traded. The major currency pairs are the most liquid in the market, and they are the following: EUR/USD, GBP/USD, USD/JPY, USD/CHF, USD/CAD, and AUD/USD.

There are also currencies that are not traded with the US dollar, and so their pairs are considered as minor currency pairs. Although they are also considered as liquid, they are notas liquid as the major currency pairs. The minor currencies include the GBP/JPY, EUR/GBP, and EUR/CHF.

As a forex trader, you need to understand how to read forex pairs. Take note that a forex pair involves two different currencies, for example: EUR/USD. Every currency pair is composed of a *base currency* and a *quote currency*. The base currency, also known as the *bid price*, refers to the first currency in a pair; and the second currency, also known as the *ask* price, is the second currency in a pair. Therefore, in our example (EUR/USD), the base currency is the EUR while the quote currency is the USD.

When you trade currencies, you will see a number after pair. For example, you may see something like this: EUR/USD 1.25. Take note that the base currency, which in this case is the EUR, is always equals to 1. Hence, you can view it as EUR 1/USD 1.25. What this simply means is that 1 EUR is equivalent to 1.25 USD.

What if you want to use USD as the base currency? In forex convention, it will then look like this, USD/EUR 0.80. Be careful not to just switch the two currencies and their values. Instead, you have to divide the base currency by the quote currency. Although they may seem different, their mathematical relation remains the same. If you divide 1 by 0.80, you will get back to the value of 1.25.

Ask and Bid

Now that you have a better understanding of a forex currency pair, it is time to understand the two important things about a forex quote: The ask and bid price. Let us use an example:

EUR/USD = 1.3400/07

In a normal situation, the difference between the ask and bid price is just a very small amount, usually less than 1/100th of a unit, it has become a normal part of a forex convention to just show the last two digits. In this case, it is 07. If you write this down in its complete form, it will look like this: EUR/USD = 1.34000/1.3407.

Here is something that you need to realize: The bid price does not refer to the price that you need to bid in order to purchase a currency pair. The bid and ask price should be taken from the perspective of your forex broker. Therefore, in order to make a profit from a transaction, a broker will *ask* higher than the price that he would be willing to *bid* if you were the one selling the currency pair. In our example, since you want to buy the EUR which refers to the base currency, then you will have to pay the *ask* price of the broker which is 1.3407 USD. If you are the one who is selling, then you need to accept your broker's bid of 1.3400. AS you can see, either way, it is in favor of your broker. Now, the difference between the ask price and the bid price is what is referred to as the *spread*. Obviously, it is the commission that your broker receives from a trade.

Forex: Buy and selling

What does it mean to buy and sell currencies in the forex market? Forex is about trading currencies, and it is participated by banks and individuals worldwide. When a trade is made in the forex market, there are always two sides to it: there is someone who buys a currency in a pair, and there is another who sells the other currency in a pair. As an FX trader, you make a profit by predicting whether the value of a currency in a pair will increase or decrease against the value of another currency. For example, let us say that you buy US$5,000 by selling $4,000 euros. In this example, the position that you have is that you predict that the value of the US dollar will appreciate (increase) against the euro. If your prediction is correct, then you will make a profit. Now, in order to realize your profit, you still need to sell your US dollars. In this case, you should sell your US$5,000 into euro. In exchange, you will then receive more than $4,000 euros. Needless to say, the value of US dollar must first increase against the euro before you sell them. As you can see, buying and selling foreign currencies is simple and easy to do. You just have to predict if the value of a currency will increase or decrease against the value of the other currency in a pair.

Percentage in Point

Percentage in point, simply referred to as simply *pip*. This refers to the measure of a *spread*. Take note that the spread refers to the difference between the bid price and the ask price and is the commission that your broker receives. The pip is the change in value the value of a particular currency. You might have heard some traders who say that they want to profit by 500 pips. So, what does a pip exactly mean? To illustrate, let us say that the price of a currency pair changes from 1.6000 to 1.6001, then that is a change by 1 pip. Hence, a pip is a unit of value that is used to show the change in the value of a currency pair. It is important to understand the pip because it signifies how much you can profit or lose. For example, if a trader buys the currency pair EUR/USD, he will profit if the price of EUR increases relative to the USD. To illustrate: Let us say that you buy in the pair EUR/USD, you buy the EUR for $1.7500. If you exit the trade at $1.7600, then that is a profit by 100 pips. Of course, if the value decreases, then the value of the pips would be on the negative, say -100 pips, and that signifies a loss.

So, how many pips should you aim for? There is no hard and fast rule as to the number of pips that you should gain. Of course, the longer you hold on to a currency pair the more significant the pip value may change since the price of the different currencies fluctuates slowly. Of course, there is also the possibility that their prices will go back to their original price, depending on their price movement. For small trades, many are already contented with 50 pips or even 30 pips. The key is to be on a positive profit.

Types of Orders

There are different orders that you can give to your broker as to how you want to trade currencies. These orders may be used to control how you enter and exit the FX market. Hence, they play an important element in building a successful career as a foreign currency trader.

- Market order

A market order is the most common type of order in forex. This order tells the broker to buy or sell a currency pair at the best possible price. This happens instantly and is always executed by the broker. A market order is the best way to enter the market as quickly as possible.

- Entry order

As the name implies, an entry order is a way to enter the market. It is difficult to spend the whole day monitoring the market just to see when you will enter it. In this case, you can just use an entry order and be able to spend your time away from the computer. In an entry order, you get to enter the market once the price reaches a certain point.

- Limit order

A limit order is often used to exit a market at a profit. This order directs your broker to buy or sell a specific number of units of a currency pair at a defined value. If you have a long position, then the limit order should be higher than the current market price. If you are taking a short position, then the limit order would be lower than the market price. This of it as a limiting line where you trade will be automatically closed once it reaches that line. Of course, once this line is reached, then you will receive whatever profit you may have into your account balance.

- Stop order

A stop order is used to exit a trade. It is also referred to as *stop-loss order*. The purpose of this order is to control or limit the possible losses that you may experience. Hence, it closes a trade that reaches a certain level of loss. Although a stop order is not a good sign when its defined limit is reached, it is able to limit your losses and closes a trade in order to prevent you from losing more.

Risk/Reward Ratio

The risk/reward ratio simply refers to the calculation of how much you should risk in a trade as compared to how much you should profit from it. For example, if you are making a trade and you set a stop loss at 15 pips and then set your take-in profit at 25 pips, then your risk reward ratio will be 15:25. This means that you are risking 15 pips in order to earn 25 pips.

When used in Forex, the key is to look for an opportunity where you reward will be much higher than the risk. It will be great if you always find trades where the reward always outweighs the risk but such is not always the case. Although it is commonly advised that a high reward and low risk trade is the most ideal, the contrary may be practical when you notice that the market is highly volatile. There is no strict rule as to the most ideal risk reward ratio should be. It may depend on the type of trader that you are, as well as the trading strategy that you use. Of course, as a professional trader, it is still ideal to make more trades where the reward is much higher than the risk in order to increase your chances of ending up with a positive profit after you sum up all your winnings and losses.

Leverage

One of the reasons why many people like to engage in forex is because it gives them a higher leverage unlike other financial instruments. But what does the term *leverage* mean? A leverage allows you to borrow money that you can invest from your broker. Since you will be able to borrow money, you will be able to invest a higher amount, which means that you will have a higher potential profit since you will be earning a certain percentage of your investment. Forex is known for offering a high leverage, which means that for an initial margin, you can be trading a big amount of money. The leverage can vary from50:1, 100:1, or even 200:1, depending on your broker and the size of your position. Take note that before you can start engaging in forex, you should first open an account with your broker; in this case, you need a margin account. So, what do these leverages mean? A 50:1 leverage signifies that the minimum margin requirement is only 2% (1/50) of the total value of trade in his trading account available as cash. Accordingly, a 1:100 leverage would only require 1%, and so on. The usual leverages used as 1:50 and 1:100. A leverage of 1:200 is used normally for positions that are around $50,000 or less.

In application, what this means is that if you want to trade $100,000 with a 1% margin (100:1 leverage), then you only need to invest $1,000 in your margin account. Obviously, this leverage is so much higher than the 2:1 leverage that you get when you put your money in equities or the 15:1 leverage when you invest in futures market. Now, although a leverage of 100:1 may seem very high and risky, do not forget that foreign currencies do not fluctuate so high in one trading day. Normally, they only fluctuate by less than 1% in a trading day.

An obvious advantage of leveraging is that it allows you to have a decent trading size even if you only have a substantial investment capital to begin with. Many professional traders recommend at a minimum of $1,000 as an initial capital for forex. However, the problem is that not all traders can afford to risk a thousand dollars. Also, risking $1,000 when you are just a beginner might not be the best choice to make. This is where leveraging comes into play.

*But, can you still trade foreign currencies without leveraging?*The answer, of course, is in the affirmative. There are some notable traders who do not leverage their position. Here is an example of how *not* leveraging can be an advantage: Let us say that you purchase 1,000 USD using 800 EUR without any leverage. Let us assume that the price of USD experiences a 50% drop in price, then you will only lose only 50% or just 400 EUR. This means that you are still in the game. Now, consider the same example but let us assume that you are using 100:1 leverage' even if the price changes by less than 1%, then you will lose all your funds. Of course, an obvious disadvantage of not leveraging is that you will earn a much lower amount than you would normally have. After all, if you cannot expect to profit a very high percentage of your invested funds. Normally, a professional investor only makes a decent and reasonable percentage profit. Hence, the bigger your fund is, the more money you can make.

What is a Lot?

A *lot* refers to the smallest size that you can trade in the forex market. Hence, it also has to do with your risk exposure. As a trader, you should find the best lot size that is suitable for you based on your current trading account. The lot size can also have an impact how much you will be affected by the forex market movement. For example, if you only have a small trade, a 100-pip movement would not be too significant. However, if you are holding a huge lot, a 100-pip movement can have a strong impact. In your career as a trader, you will surely encounter different lot sizes. As already stated, it is important that you understand them so that you will know which lot size is suitable for you:

- Micro lot

As the name already implies, this is usually the smallest lot that is offered by most brokers. A micro lot refers to a lot of 1,000 units of a currency that your account is funded with. Hence, if you are using US dollars, then a micro lot is equivalent to $1,000 USD. If you want to trade a pair that is dollar-based, then 1 pip is equivalent to 10 cents. If you are a beginner, then it is advised that you stick to micro lots.

- Mini lots

A mini lot is equal to 10,000 units of the currency in your account. Hence, if you are trading an account that is dollar based, and if you are trading a pair that is also dollar-based, then a single pip in a trade will be equal to $1. Compare this with a micro lot where 1 pip is only 10 cents. It should also be noted that in forex trading, the market can move by more than a hundred pips per day. So, just imagine how much profit or losses you can experience. Obviously, trading mini lots requires a higher capital than trading micro lots.

- Standard lots

A standard lot is 100,000 units of the currency of your funding account. If you are trading in US dollars, that is equal to $100,000 USD. Hence, the average pip size for a standard lot is equal to $10 a pip. Therefore, when it says that you are up by 10 pips, then that is equivalent to $100 profit. However, in the case of losing 10 pips, then that would translate to $100 loss. To make trades using standard lots, you should have at least $25,000 as standard lots are mostly for large accounts. Most traders only trade using micro lots and sometimes mini lots.

Chapter 1 Forex Trading Basics

While the concept of forex trading is easy, executing your trades in the market is difficult. This doesn't mean you won't become successful. What it means is that you will need to educate yourself and work hard. The first step anyone should take is to learn as much as possible about forex trading.

Understanding Pairs

The main difference between the stock market and the forex market is that, in forex, you are essentially trading pairs of currency (that is you buy one currency and sell another), while in the stock market, you buy shares of a company. This is not an option when you are forex trading. Whether you are trading, selling, or buying, you have to use pairs. For example, the Japanese yen is often paired against the Canadian dollar and the Euro against the American dollar.

What's a Pip?

A pip is a 1% movement in the currency value. A pip is a basic unit that is used when talking about currency quotes. It is the last number of the quote, so when you are following the movement of two currencies, you observe from the last two digits so that you can say that a currency moved by the number of pips that differentiates the second from the starting figure. The value of the pip is determined from the size of the trade. You make a decision to buy or sell a currency pair depending on your estimation, which is when you make the market order.

Entry Order

When you use an entry order, you enter your currency pair trade at a specific price. If the price of the currency never reaches the specific price, then your trade is not enforced. If the price is reached, then your trade is completed regardless of your presence at the time.

Stop-Loss Order

A stop-loss order is the price at which you want your dealer to exit the trade when the trade moves against your interests. A stop-loss order prevents losses.

Limit

A limit is the price at which you want the dealer to exit the trade when it's moving in your favor. Knowing when to exit the trade even when things are looking up is useful because you can hardly predict when a currency will start to drop.

Margin

When you are buying or selling at a good margin, that means that you control a large amount of currency for an initial investment that is way smaller in comparison. For example, a 100-by-1 margin means that you invest $1,000 for a trade of $100,000. Buying and selling on a margin is safe and appealing because the only amount you risk to lose is the amount you invested, but you have the opportunity to profit a greater amount.

Leveraging Ratios

You are betting at leveraging ratios. A $1,000 bet on 1,000 value of the currency is considered 1:1 leverage.

Trading platforms allow you to follow and market currency in a way that creates a profit. When you're successful in trading one currency so that its value increases against the currency you used to buy it, you can make a profit. You are speculating whether the currency will rise or drop. Your chances of profiting essentially increase with the success of your predictions.

With forex, you trade using leverage, which means that you only need to invest a portion of your positions. By using stop-losses, you can prevent losing your investment.

When it comes to currency rates, many factors have an influence. Interest rates, unemployment numbers, political events, and many more affect the country's currency value.

Currencies may rise and fall in different values for different reasons, one of them being large companies exchanging currencies for the purpose of international trading. The time and circulation of market information is also a significant factor. False and accurate information circulating the market can influence banks to swiftly market currencies, which additionally affects the changes in currency values.

Diversification

You want to ensure you have diversity within your portfolio to tackle risk. In fact, because the forex market is open 24 hours a day during the weekdays, the market holds more diversity. Therefore, don't just focus on the popular currencies, such as the American dollar and Canadian dollar. You may also trade other pairs such as American dollar/British pound (USD/GBP) or American dollar/Japanese Yen (USD/JPY).

What Are The Risks?

While there are many people trading in forex, there are also those who are facing major financial losses. Since forex trading is essentially all about predictions, one of the biggest risks, obviously, is making a wrong prediction. The following are the many risks of forex trading.

The Wrong Mindset

When it comes to any market, you always need to have the right mindset. Take a moment to think about how certain emotions, such as fear or worry, can control your thoughts. You have to find a way to keep your emotions out of the market. Experienced traders call the right mindset the winning mindset. The following are some key characteristics that will help you gain your winning attitude.

1. *You need to be self-disciplined.* You want to make sure that you take all the steps to ensure you are doing what you need to do to reach success. This means that you complete daily research to see how the forex market is doing, and you document all your currencies, trades, and any other information. Fortunately, most marketing

platforms keep your information in its history. However, it is always best that you find a way to keep the files on your computer so that you always have them. You follow any rules and guidelines that your mentor or yourself have set up.

2. *You are also able to keep your emotions in check.* This might mean that you follow certain strategies you set up for yourself, such as deep-breathing exercises. You don't allow yourself to give in to your excitement if a trade goes well or when you see your account balance. While you might smile and be proud of yourself, you don't allow the feeling to take over as you can become too confident. This can lead you to make mistakes, which can put you and your finances in jeopardy.

3. *You understand that mistakes are going to be made.* Instead of focusing on your mistakes and allowing them to control your future decisions, you learn from them. Many traders write down their mistakes in their trading journal or daily reports.

4. *You understand that the market is fluid and are able to adjust to the changes.* For instance, if a price notes that you need to make a change in your portfolio, then you make a change. Your portfolio is the place where you keep all the currencies that you can sell or trade.

5. *You understand your risk tolerance.* No matter what strategies you use to try to limit your risk, there is always a risk. If you aren't comfortable with a lot of risks, you will want to focus more on trades that are low risk.

Currency-Value Fluctuations

There are internal-market reasons and external reasons for a currency's value changes. Internally, one country's currency can increase while another currency you hold decreases. These fluctuations are often dependent on how many people are buying and selling the currency. For example, if the yen isn't strong, then more people will purchase the yen, which makes the value increase. This could show a decrease in the American dollar in comparison to the yen because traders are using the American dollar to purchase yen. In other words, the more people purchase currency, the stronger its value. The more people sell a currency, the lower its value.

External factors can be anything from politics to other events going on within the country. These are factors that traders cannot control but you should always be aware of. Because of this, many traders will spend at least half an hour every morning going through the news in order to get an idea of what the market is going to look like that day. Doing this will allow you to know if you should purchase a currency or trade one within your portfolio.

Broker Risk

While not every trader has a broker, it is important for a beginner to look into a broker. This person can help you learn about the market and give you advice on what moves to take. However, there are broker risks. In order to limit these risks, you want to ensure you can trust your broker. Do some research before you decide to take on a broker. The best way you can do this is by choosing a broker who is part of a government body as it is regulated. Government bodies have to follow guidelines and ethics.

How To Start

Whenever you start trading, you want to ensure you follow certain steps for success.

First, you always want to do your research. You want to learn as much as possible. This means you will read books, join forex trading forums, find a trusted broker, and anything else you feel is necessary. Once you feel like you know forex trading like the back of your hand, you will be able to move on.

Second, ensure you understand the language. Forex trading has its own language. Take your time to learn these terms, and if you have questions, find another trader to discuss your concerns with.

Third, you want to find your trusted broker. This person will help you make decisions and explain the world of investing to you. Take your time to find the best broker for you. Your broker will help you set up an account.

Fourth, take time to analyze the forex market. Learn about the charts and what they mean. Look back in the history of some currencies so you can gain a better understanding of trading. For example, charts can help you analyze the best time for trading and which currencies are best within the market and help you find the best currencies.

Fifth, if you are trading full-time, set up an office and your schedule. You want to find time to ensure you are self-disciplined enough that you won't struggle with distractions. Take the time to set a start date.

Sixth, once your day arrives, start trading. Make sure that you go through your morning routine, such as reading the paper and seeing how the currencies are doing. Notice any changes that occurred overnight. You also want to ensure you go through your daily schedule and close out your day with your evening routine. For example, check your stocks for the day, and discuss anything about your day in your journal.

How To Profit

Once you start trading, you will want to do what you can to limit your risks. While you will always have some risk, you can find a comfortable level of risk. Another way to profit is by diversifying your portfolio. This means that you will have different currencies and not focus on the same ones.

You also want to be patient. Forex trading is not a get-rich-quick scheme. It will take time to start seeing a profit. Don't give up, and don't fall into the wrong mindset. If you need any help, talk to your broker, a mentor, or someone in the forum. There are many experienced forex traders who are happy to help beginners.

Continue to communicate with your broker, mentor, and anyone on the forum. Even if you spend months researching, people will always be important when it comes to your success. Don't allow yourself to get into the mindset that you know everything. Continue to learn as much as possible. Take time to practice analyzing reports. You have to do whatever you need to so you feel comfortable as a trader.

Chapter 2 Elements Of Forex

Before you get started on your first trading in the forex market, take a moment to think about how you want to approach your trades. There is more to the forex market and currency trading than what is instantly obvious, and I believe the way you trade is one of the essential elements of your trading success.

Your success typically comes in the form of a trading plan. With your plan, you get to decide how, when, and why you would like to make a certain trade, establish rules, or manage expectations. It is sort of like your own trading signature that you use to make your decisions.

In this chapter, I will help you consider the focal points of trading as you outline your own method of trading currencies. Once we accomplish that, we can review the features of some of the most frequently used trading methods. Then we go through the process of developing your trading plan.

We will also focus on technical analysis, helping you understand how to read the market. Then we can focus on making sure that you do not miss out on opportunities as much as possible. Finally, we can evaluate the methods by which you can manage risks.

All the above steps help you slowly acclimate yourself to the forex market.

But first, what exactly is a trading style?

Your trading style dictates when you would like to make a specific trade, the frequency of your trades, and what you expect your profit margins to be on a particular day.

So how do you develop your own styles? By creating an effective plan.

Arm Yourself! Creating A Trading Plan

You need a systematized trading plan for yourself, or you won't succeed much in the markets. The distinction between making and losing money when dealing with currencies can be as simple as trading with a plan or trading without one. A trading plan is an ordered approach to implementing a trade tactic that you have established based on your market outlook and analysis.

There are three components that I believe you have to ponder upon for your trading plan:

Finalizing Size of the Position

How big a position will you adopt for your trade strategy? A position simply refers to a particular transaction you are going to take or you have already taken. When you choose your position size, you can effectively decide how much money you are willing to invest in each trade.

Where to Begin Your Position

At what point will you try to open your preferred position? What happens if you do not reach the level you aimed for during your entry?

Setting Stop-Loss and Take-Profit Levels

You have to decide where you would like to exit the position, both when you have a winning hand (take profit) and when you have a losing trade (stop-loss). Your exit strategy allows you to determine your plan for the next position whenever you decide to start it.

That is all there is to it; you just need three fundamental elements. However, you will be surprised to know how many traders (both beginners and veterans) end up opening positions without having prepared a thorough game plan. There are more points to consider when preparing your trading plan, but for now, I want to place emphasis on the point that trading without a systematized plan is like navigating in a dark cave with your blindfold on and with no draft of air to guide you. Where are you planning to go without a proper guide?

Also, it does not matter how well thought out your trading plan is; it is not going to be effective if you are not following it. You might say, "Well, isn't that obvious, Mr. Author?" Actually no. Numerous traders are excited about developing a plan only to toss it all aside when they become impulsive. They face an influx of emotions, which only tends to distract them and their well-crafted plans.

Sometimes, an unforeseen piece of information or news causes traders to let go of their trade plan midway without even considering what their actions are going to cause.

When someone abandons his or her plan, it is as good as never having created a trading plan at all.

Forming a trading plan and making sure that you adhere to it are the two main components of trading with currencies. If I had to narrow down and let you know which is the most important characteristic of a good trader, then it would not be his or her skills in using technical analysis, the experience accumulated, or even the tenaciousness—though they are all vital. It would be his or her discipline. You see, if you can practice discipline, then you can learn the other skills and requirements easily.

Traders who stick to a disciplined attitude are the ones who endure for years and make the most profits from their trades. It does not make them perfect—far from it. They are still capable of making numerous mistakes. However, it is their discipline that allows them to recover faster and get back into the trade, eventually netting them profits and recovering their losses.

Expect Your Expectations

When you are trading in currencies as a beginner, then you have a whole lot of expectations on your trade. This is understandable since new traders do not have a history they can rely on as a reference. They are still unfamiliar with price shifts and currency movements. They often think about how much they can make in a single trade.

That is not an easy question to answer and, quite frankly, not a question to think about when you are just starting out.

You have to understand this vital point—the forex market is not an ATM. You cannot simply deposit money into it and then withdraw that money whenever you feel like it (well, you can actually, but that does not mean you get back what you had invested). There are a multitude of traders speculating on the direction that various currency pairs are going to take; some of those traders are going to make the right speculation and earn a profit, and some of them are going to be wrong and not earn profits. In some case, traders might be right for a certain period before ending up on the wrong side of their prediction.

Ways to Trade

You need to understand that you have numerous ways to engage with your trade. Not all of them might be suited for you. What you need to do is practice with various techniques. After that, narrow down the trading style that best fits your requirement. Once you are able to do that, you can ensure that you are reading data before making any decision.

Short-Term Trading

There is a fundamental difference in the way we trade in currencies in the short term as opposed to other forms of securities. If you have ever been in the stock market, then you know that you cannot simply buy and sell a stock at a time of your convenience. This means that you cannot purchase a stock and then decide to sell it at the end of the day. But with the currency market, the situation is completely different. This is because you get to deal with a market that fluctuates in small increments quite frequently. When you are dealing with pips, you are dealing with an extremely small point change (imagine 0.0001 jump or dive in a currency).

This is why, in a short-term forex trading, you can strategize your sale in such a way that you do not have to keep your trades with you for longer than an hour. That could benefit those who do not have a lot of time to spend on their trades in a given day or those who prefer quick trades and small gains over time. However, the time factor is not the most appealing of all factors in short-term trading. The thing that really attracts traders to this style of trading is the small pip changes. Traders who indulge in short-term trading create profits by frequently opening and closing positions after seeing an increase in just a few pips, sometimes even as little as 1 or 2 pips.

An interbank market is a network where financial institutions interact with each other in order to trade in currencies. In their world, when someone (or an entity) deals with extremely short-term trades, where they are opening and closing positions quickly, then that particular trading is called as "jobbing" the market. Online currency traders, on the other hand, have another name for it—scalping. You can call it whatever you like, either jobbing or scalping, both terms can work. Traders who engage in this style of trading are considered to be some of the most attentive and focused traders. This is because they have to make quick-second decisions for their trade.

If you want to be a successful scalper, then do not stick to a particular position. You should not worry about the up and down movement of the currency. What you are focused on is the pips. That is what will get you the returns you seek. If the position you have chosen is not working for you, then make a quick exit. Look for volatility and liquidity of the currency as your prime factors.

Here are a few tips for short-term trading:

1. Make sure you are focusing on high liquid pairs, such as USD/JPY, EUR/USD, EUR/JPY,

EUR/GBP, and EUR/CHF. The pairs that are the most liquid have the smallest-sized trading spreads and fewer sudden price leaps.

2. And what exactly is a spread? Well, in the world of forex trading, you have to deal with two terms, "ask" and "bid." The price that is quoted for selling a particular currency pair is termed as "ask" while the price that is quoted to a trader for the purchase of a currency pair is called "bid." The difference between them is called a spread. So in this case, you do not want to have a big gap with the ASK and BID, or you might not make a lot of profits.

3. Trade with just one currency pair at a time. Dealing with multiple currencies means having to deal with the risks, trends, and quick fluctuations of those currencies. When you are dealing with the price movements of currencies that happen every second or minute, you do not want to be distracted easily by different pairs. You might not only end up making mistakes but also not make

a profit at all. Additionally, you also get to feel comfortable with the pair that you are dealing with.

4. Make sure you manage your risk and reward expectations. As each spread you receive will be different, you need to know that what you can earn from those spreads will be unique. Most major pairs have close to 2- to 5-pip spread, and you should be aiming to get a hold of 3 to 10 pips per trade in order to negate any losses that the market might suddenly have.

5. Do not trade around the time that data releases. When the market releases some data, then there is usually a gap in the prices. This happens because the data is being added into the systems, and you might notice after a little while. This level of unpredictability might not suit the short-term trade strategy that you have set up. When you deal with currencies, you might notice that the markets receive price adjustments almost 15 to 20 minutes before the release of any major date. This could

cause a sudden shift against your position that may not be solved before the data comes out.

Medium-Term Trading

In medium-term trading, you are holding a position for a period that extends from a few minutes to a few hours. Some people might extend that to more than just a few hours, but traders rarely hold the position for more than a day. Because of short periods involved in medium-term trading, you do not concern yourself with the length of time but the pips you are working with. And yes, this is quite similar to short-term trading as well.

However, short-term trading does not deal with the overall position of the market. Its main concern is the profit that it can make from small price fluctuations. On the other hand, medium-term trading wants to focus on getting the general direction of the trade correct and make a profit from major currency movements.

Here are some tips for when you are using medium-term trading:

1. Keep your eyes attached to the news. You are going to need it! This is because you need to have at least a basic idea on the direction in which a currency pair is likely to shift. This means that while you are performing minute changes, you are vaguely aware of the overall situation, making use of the knowledge to your advantage.

2. You need to rely on technical analysis. This is important because you should base your market expectations on chart readings, trend lines, support and resistance levels, and momentum studies. When you utilize technical analysis, you may be able to locate an opportunity somewhere on your charts, but by empowering yourself with global events, you might be able to make informed decisions. This, in turn, helps you open positions comfortably.

3. When you know about events, you become informed about factors such as central bank events, interest rates, unemployment rate, and more. These factors help you predict the

outcome of the position you are about to open, and they give some you ideas on when to make a closing.

Long-Term or Macroeconomic Trading

This form of trading is for those with deep pockets and plenty of moolah to spend. We are talking about hedge funds and multimillion-dollar (and even multi-billion) corporations. When traders and institutions deal with long-term strategies, they open positions for a period of weeks, sometimes even months. In some cases, the trade is held on to for years because the returns from those positions are incredibly massive. However, that does not mean long-term trading does not have its own set of flaws. For example, it has a high degree of probability of facing numerous short-term volatile situations.

Carry Trade Strategies

In a carry trade, you invest in currencies that generate high returns and then sell currencies that have a lower yield than the currency you bought. Traders can benefit from this strategy in a couple of ways:

By having a long position in a high-yielding currency and a short position in a low-yielding currency, you can earn the difference in the interest rates between the two currencies. This interest is commonly referred to as "carry." However, if you end up in the opposite position (when you have a long position in a low-yielding currency and a short position in a high-yielding currency), the rate of interest ends up working against you, and you end up in a loss that is termed as the "cost of carry." A carry trade, in short, is simply making use of the difference between currencies of two different yields.

Now one of the most important aspects to consider is that you should jump in on a trade when you hear or see news about central banks working on their interest rates. This is because more traders end up taking advantage of the margin between the two currencies to make a profit out of it.

Let us take an example to illustrate this point. Let us assume that a particular trader spots the fact that interest rates in Japan are currently set at 0.5%. In the United States, the interest rate is close to 5%. What does this mean? The trader is hoping to make a profit of 4.5%, which is the difference between the two rates. He will first borrow yen and change them to dollars. Next, he will search for securities to invest in that will pay him using the US rate. With that, he will be able to pay back what he borrowed and make a cool profit out of his transaction. Pretty neat, huh?

Of course, there is always a downside. In this case, you can chalk it out to market volatility. If the price of the yen improves, then the trader might end up getting lower profits. If the value keeps increasing, then the trader can effectively kiss his or her original plan goodbye. However, many traders take into account this risk and place their expected profits at a rate that is adjusted for any changes in the market. However, once again, you cannot always predict that the trader's plan will work. What if the market suddenly shifts even further?

Carry trades are best focused on when the market has low volatility. This is because you can expect the financial markets to remain stable and avoid massive shifts. Another thing to keep in mind is that you need to have a big-enough interest rate between the two currencies to make a significant amount of money. Ideally, I would recommend looking for at least an interest rate of 2%.

Chapter 3 Forex Trading
On A Budget

If you have just started in Forex trading, you must have been wondering whether you need to have a huge amount of money in order to start trading. So, is it possible for you to trade the Forex market with little money?

The fact is that you can trade with little money, but your profits will be limited. With a few tips though, you can successfully trade the markets without having to put down thousands of dollars on the line.

Educate Yourself

Before you can place your money on the line, you need to be educated about what to do before you jump in. Make sure you understand the basics of trading the Forex market and know whether your limited funds will give you profit.

Understand the risk management processes as well as other concepts before you put any money on the line. If you have put some money on the line, then you should withdraw part of it and put it in a course. It will give you concepts that you can use to turn your money regardless of how much you have.

Learning resources also introduce you to analysis techniques that give you an idea of what trade to place and when to do it.

Start Small

As a new trader, it is prudent that you start off with a small amount compared to putting all your money into the trade. Remember that you can't have the success you desire trading dollars when you cannot trade for pennies. To do this, you need to find the right broker that gives you a low limit trading account.

Patience is Key

Forex trading is all about having patience. When you start small, you might see it be frustrating and slow, but it keeps you disciplined. Make sure that you start small and grow your account step by step.

Profitable Forex investing takes time and patience. All those traders that you see making money on the market were novices on their first day, some were even worse than you. However, most of them started small and grew step by step to become the pro traders that they are right now.

Do It Regularly

As you refine the craft, make sure you make trading your habit. To do this, start investing regularly as you learn the ropes. Add funds to your account several times a week and you will see the account grow. The good thing is that you won't lose too much in any trade compared to putting up a lot of your money for trading.

How to Earn With Forex

There Are A Few Steps To Make Money With Forex. Let Us Look At What You Can Do.

Grow Your Skills

When You Have The Right Skill, You Will Make Money With Forex Trading. The Forex Market Is Dynamic, And You Have To Keep Up With The Changes. As You Trade, You Get More And More Knowledgeable About The Things That Happen In Forex Trading. Take Time To Learn New Techniques And Engage With Other Traders To Understand What They Do To Be Successful.

The best way to learn about Forex trading is to make sure you look at the various reasons the market is moving in a specific direction. For instance, you might look at the analysis methods that are used by top traders and why they use them. You also need to understand what triggers make the prices to move in a given direction as opposed to another.

Learn to Perform Analysis

The analysis is all about using charts and other visual tools to come up with a decision. Forex trading gives you two major types of tools to use – fundamental and technical analysis. Fundamental analysis focuses on events that will change the performance of a currency pair. On the other hand, technical analysis involves looking at price action and its effect on the market – including the trends, momentum, and reversal patterns.

We shall look at these analysis methods in details later, but at the moment, just know that you have a chance to make more profit when you perform the right analysis before placing a trade.

Work with the Right Broker

A Forex broker makes it possible for you to execute transactions. This is just one of the major functions – a broker handles various other tasks that are vital to trading.

Before you can choose a broker, make sure that you understand what they offer in terms of features and look at the reviews that are left by previous traders. If you come across fraud alerts or issues with the withdrawing of funds, then look for another broker.

So, making money on Forex is all about buying a currency pair at a low price, and then selling it off at a higher price to make profits. The profit, which represents your income, is the difference between the price you buy the price of buying and selling the currency pair. You pay the broker a commission from the trade called the spread.

If you believe that you don't have the capacity to place trades with your money, then you can use a feature given by the broker called the leverage. This is money that you follow from the broker to make your deposit higher.

Remember that the higher the deposit the more the risk.

Advantages of Trading Forex

When you get into forex trading, you enjoy various benefits that come with the trades that you place.

Low Commission

The commission is the money that the broker makes on each trade that you place. Usually, when you trade in a different place, the broker takes a percentage of the money that you deposit to the account.

However, many brokers don't attach any fees on the trade, meaning that you can enjoy high-profit margins when you trade Forex.

Trading Flexibility

Forex gives you a lot of flexibility for both traders and investors. You don't have a limit to the amount you place on trade each day, which allows both smalltime traders as well as seasoned investors to make money.

Additionally, you don't have too many rules and regulations when it comes to Forex trading. This means you have the flexibility to work 24 hours without any disruption.

The flexible working hours make it possible for those people working day jobs to have some time to trade as well.

You have Complete Control over Your Trades

One of the top advantages of trading Forex is that you have total control when you place a trade. You don't have to run a trade that you are not comfortable with.

It is all upon you to decide when and how to place a trade without any obligation. You also decide the level of risk that you can take in every trade.

Demo Accounts Ideal for Practicing

As a rookie in the business, you need all the guidance and information to make it in the market. For you, a demo account is all you need to achieve the skills necessary to give you the push you need.

The demo account is a simulation of the way the live trading system works, and it gives you the practice you need.

When you use the demo account, you don't face any risk and it gives you an idea of whether the market is ideal for you or not. You also get to test, improve, and organize the new skills that might be beneficial when you start live trading.

Total Transparency in the Information You Get

The Forex exchange is a huge market and it operates 24 hours across different countries in various time zones. However big the market is, you get all the information you need to place trades. You will get information about the current forecast as well as the rates.

The information is real-time meaning that you get the information when it is displayed. This information is ideal for analysis so that you make deductions to the trend of the market.

Low Cost of Investment

Compared to other investments in the markets, Forex trading comes with a low cost of investment. The low cost of investment is due to the direct involvement by dealers which results in covering of risks; this means it doesn't need so much brokerage.

High Leverage

Compared to other forms of investments, Forex gives you the highest level of leverage than other investing markets. Even though you place a smaller amount of capital into the business, you have the capacity to win or lose big in the deals.

Wide Currency Pairs

When you enter the Forex market, you can trade in many currency pairs to your own advantage. With so many options to pick from, you get to enter a spot trade or opt for future agreement contracts.

You can choose the pair according to the budget or the type of risk that the pair comes with.

High Liquidity

The Forex market has the biggest number of players compared to other markets.

This leads to high liquidity that brings to the fore big players that fill large orders of the trade. It eliminates the manipulation of price, thus this promotes efficient pricing models.

High Volatility

In Forex, you can easily switch from one currency to another if you find it more profitable.

Remember that there is a high risk associated with investing capital in such a market, but with volatility, you end up with higher profit especially when you switch to a different currency that promises a good return.

This, in turn, gives you a higher advantage and increases profit.

Works for 24 Hours Each Day

The trading program operates 24 hours each day in a week which means you will always have a chance to trade no matter the situation. You can get from your day job and then handle any trades that you want during the evening.

You can take up Forex trading as a day job and you can work within the normal hours or your own preferred time. The good news is that you can still access the various tools and information that helps you to run the trades.

High Confidence Levels

When you make a profit, you get stimulated to run more trades. This creates a lot of goodwill. You can also get into the trade more thus make more money than ever.

The Disadvantages

Lack of Transparency

When you work with a brokerage, you tend to lose the transparency that needs to come automatically.

Make sure you work with a broker that follows all the rules that are involved in Forex trading.

While the market might not work under any regulations, which is a good thing, it might be constrained to the rules of the broker.

Price Determination

The platform goes through the price determination process, which is very complex. The outcome is that the rates are influenced by a host of multiple factors and reasons.

For one, the global economy and politics are a huge influence in the rate of the currency and they end up creating uncertainty in the price of the exchanges.

You have to use your technical knowledge and other indicators to determine whether you are to face a loss or not.

Many Risk Factors

There are various risk factors that are involved in Forex Trading. For instance, there is high leverage that the results in high risks.

The uncertainty comes due to the price and the currency rate which, in turn, results in high profit or loss, so you have to be focused and knowledgeable about the market.

You are Fully Responsible for the Outcome

The Forex market allows you to interact with many investors that can help you run trades successfully. However, at the end of the day, you are fully responsible for the outcomes of the trades that you place.

This is the reason many newcomers end up quitting because of the losses that they suffer when entering the market with limited knowledge of the processes.

High Volatility

We have looked at high volatility under the advantages, but depending on how you experience it, this can turn out to be a disadvantage as well.

Changes in the economy usually turn out to be an issue on the process, thus it can be difficult for you as an investor to take a risk when investing the money.

When the changes are against you, it can lead to a huge loss to the investor especially when the market goes downhill.

Market Unpredictability

The market never shuts down; this means that you, as an investor, also have to be fully attentive, so that you don't miss out on any update. You have to stay updated at all times with the trends because these get updated each minute.

The market can change at any time, and thus you have to be conscious of what is happening in the market the whole day long. This means you have to be able to sit on the computer for hours waiting for the right trend.

Overconfidence

As time goes by, the trader experiences a set of winning trades that makes them overconfident. They fail to realize that they need to take caution with every trade, ending up with losing trades.

This overconfidence makes them lose their morale because they fail to realize that trading comes with losses as well.

The Need for Education

For you to enter the Forex trading market, you need to have enough knowledge of the subject. While you can learn on the job, it is advisable that you take a course or some classes to understand what it is all about.

Many people that have entered the market without any knowledge have had to contend with losses.

Many Scammers on the Loose

Another disadvantage of this trading method is that there are too many scammers ready to grab your loot. This is why you need to identify the best broker to work with that will not cheat you and that can guarantee you better returns.

Emotional Trading

Many traders end up trading emotionally, a factor that makes them lose more than they win. The biggest emotion in trading is fear, which is due to the uncertain trading environment that you are faced with.

Chapter 4 The Position Trading Strategy

This trading technique focuses on the bigger picture of the market (weekly or monthly charts). It eliminates market noise, such as monitoring and fluctuations. You don't have to monitor the charts constantly, and you execute fewer trades. You won't overtrade and feel the temptation to enter the market daily, and it will help you survive the market volatility.

It's easier to define trends with trading divergences. The position trading strategy enables you to detect hidden divergence opportunities. Hidden divergence patterns become more obvious with higher time frames.

You are selling a currency with a low interest rate and buying a currency with a high interest rate. You are generating a profit from a difference in interest rates between the two countries.

Identify support and resistance levels. You are trading moving averages on higher time frames due to fewer false signals. It takes some time, so it is safer but without you having to spend all day in front of a computer.

One of the most important pieces of information about position trading is resistance and support. Resistance is when the price is no longer rising. Support is when the price is no longer falling. When looking into the best strategy for you to use as a position trader, you will want to ensure you understand resistance and support. It's at certain prices when you will purchase or sell a position. If you don't understand support and resistance, you won't be able to trade at the right moment.

Is Position Trading For You?

If you are more into following the bigger picture of your currency's trend, position trading is something to look into. Position traders don't focus on minor details. Instead, they look at the trends in months and years. It is the opposite of day trading, which is when you purchase your trades and sell them in one day.

If you decide you don't want to spend a lot of time trading, you will want to look into position trading. Because you focus on the long run, you don't need to worry about the day-to-day parts of trading. For example, you won't need to read the newspaper every morning or have an evening routine. Instead, your routine will focus on the times you spend checking in on your currencies.

Position trading is right for you if you're patient and not too excited about trading, and you want an investment that builds over time. Another way to know if it's your fit is how well you listen to public opinion. As a position trader, you will focus more on your thoughts and strategy than on people who tell you the country is in a recession.

As a position trader, you are going to make under four trades a year. When you look at the patterns, you will focus more on a monthly or yearly pattern. While this is investing for the long term, you don't want to limit your details too much. You want to understand what your stock is doing on at least a week-to-week basis. Furthermore, you want to analyze the trading patterns yearly. How much have they changed? Have they increased or decreased over the years? Ask yourself questions to try to understand the pattern of the currency.

How To Apply Position Trading

When it comes to position trading, you need to understand the three elements to make it a success.

1. *Planned entry.* You don't want to jump in on a currency. You want to have a plan before you go into a trade as this will give you the right mindset. You will create this plan as you are analyzing the history of the currency. You will select the point when to trade in the currency, preferably when the price is at a lower point.

2. *Planned exit.* Whenever you trade, you want to make sure that you have a strategy in place just in case something goes wrong. You always want to do what you can to eliminate loss. This includes setting a low point before you sell. This means that if the price drops below your lowest point, you sell it immediately.

3. *Controlled risk.* One of the best ways to become successful as a trader is to eliminate risk. This will go with any trading strategy you use. However, strategies will present different risks. One risk with positions trading is you don't spend enough time on investing. While you don't need to get into the day-to-day details, you do want to pay

attention to price fluctuations. You also need to understand when to exit and when to have patience and wait for a low price to increase. Prices are always fluctuating in the market. Therefore, it's important not to jump to conclusions.

Another factor is you lock your capital in for a long time, such as six months to a year. Therefore, you want to ensure you will not need the money you invest in this period. This can create a risk if you don't plan. If you are putting a significant amount of money into the currency, you could find yourself needing the cash if you have an emergency. This can create a problem with loss when you sell.

Strategies to Use

1. *Breakout strategy.* When you use the breakout strategy, you will get involved in the trade during the early stages of the trend. You might make your move when the price is on the lower end, or you can choose the higher end.

2. *Range strategy.* When you use the range strategy, you will focus on purchasing

investments that are oversold or overbought. Most investors use this strategy when the market is highly unpredictable and fluctuating often.

3. *Short-term strategy.* Even though position trading is known as a long-term strategy, you can use it as a short-term strategy. What this means is, instead of holding on to your investment for months or a year, you plan to hold it for a few days or weeks. You might decide this is the best because of the trend or because you are trying out position trading. You might also use a short-term approach quickly if you made a mistake when purchasing the investment.

Pros And Cons Of Position Trading

Pros

1. Position trading is relatively easy for you to learn because it doesn't take up a lot of your time.

2. You can continue to learn about investing after you have made your first trade.

3. You can start to see a profit quickly compared to other types of trading.

4. Compared to other types of trading, your stress is lower.

5. You don't need to have a lot of capital in order to become successful.

6. You can predict the market trends easier through analysis because of this strategy's long-term nature.

Cons

1. You need to have a lot of patience.

2. You can struggle to receive regular benefits because of this strategy's long-term nature.

3. You can wait too long to make a trade, which means a higher loss. This often happens when traders want to wait for the price to increase.

4. Your money is tied up for months to a year or more.

5. If you don't understand when to trade, you can lose a lot of money. This can lead to

financial hardship and depression or other psychological strains.

Tips For Beginners

If you think positions trading might be your strategy, here are a few tips to help you get started.

Think Long-Term

You need to make sure you can completely invest the money. You need to think ahead for at least a year or two. This means to take a look at where you sit financially. Ask yourself questions to make sure you can afford this investment. Do you have enough money for an emergency? Do you have any backup financial plans in case something happens?

You also want to think long-term when it comes to trends. Start by taking a look at two years ago and then a year ago before you go monthly. You don't need to care about the minute-to-minute trend unless you want to. However, it is always wise to go into daily trends. This can be something that many beginners miss because they are too focused on long-term trends. Daily trends can help you analyze charts so you know what could happen in the near future.

Set Your Entry and Exit Strategies

This is often missed with beginners because they think they can mentally keep track. The fact is, you are more likely to let your emotions take control of your decisions as a beginner. By setting your entry and exit strategies, you are able to control your emotions. You just need to make sure you follow your plan of action.

Pay Attention, but Don't Stress over Minor Fluctuations

One of the benefits of position trading is you don't have to watch your currencies on a daily basis. However, you need to be aware that this can cause you problems. One factor about the market is that it can change in a flash. This means if you go a week without checking the price fluctuations of your investment, you can find yourself with a deep loss. Therefore, you want to be cautious about price fluctuations, but you don't want to stress over them.

Always remember that just because the price reduced, it doesn't mean it will continue to. It can rise in a heartbeat; however, it can also decline. You need to understand the trends in order to help yourself through price fluctuation. You also need to keep your emotions in check.

Chapter 5 Developing Your Trading Plan

Having a strong trading plan is an important part of successfully trading on the Forex market. Even the experts develop one, so it is important that as a beginner, you do too. In this chapter, you are going to learn about why you need a roadmap and how you can develop one.

What Is a Trading Plan?

Developing a trading plan allows you to define a goal and create a system for you to work towards that goal through your trades. Due to the volatility of the market, you cannot create a finite blueprint for your trading plan. However, you can create a general strategy and goals for you to work with. There are certain rules and elements to consider when you are developing your plan to ensure that you have one that is strong and will serve you for the best.

Who Needs One?

It is important that anyone who is doing trading on the Forex market, or anywhere else for that matter, to have a strong trading plan. This allows them the opportunity to reap in all of the benefits of having a trading plan from risk management to learning discipline in your trades. Even experts develop plans before entering the Forex market, so it is imperative that as a beginner, you also develop a plan.

Why Do You Need a Trading Plan?

There are a number of benefits to having a trading plan when you are getting involved in the Forex market. For one, it is great for you to minimize your risk due to your ability to have a plan for what you will do in certain scenarios. You can also use it to establish your exit strategies beforehand so that you know when you are going to exit if necessary. Having a plan also allows you to stay focused on your goal and make large strides towards that goal, so you can stay on par for your goals with your trading decisions. Another reason why having a plan is important is because it allows you to ensure that you are constantly evaluating your trades to ensure that your money is working well for you and that you are making strong decisions. If you find that your trades aren't having high enough yields or are too risky, you can reevaluate your plan and fix your strategy for a better outcome.

General Planning Rules

There are a few plans when you are preparing to trade on the market. There are no blueprints, though there are some considerations you need to think about when you are developing the plan. The following four "rules" are important when you are in the process of creating your trading plan, to ensure that you have the best results.

- Write down your goals all the time. If you make any changes, write that down as well. You will want to write down virtually every single part of your plan. This way, you can ensure that your thoughts are organized and your plan is solid. It also helps you stay focused on your goals and work towards them with every move you make.
- Make sure that in addition to writing out your plans, you record your progress as well. This allows you to see how your plan has worked, and to learn from previous trades that you have made as well so that you can continue to learn and make better decisions. This process will give you a better opportunity to improve your trading strategies and ensure that you recall which markets you have been exposed to.

- Aside from writing everything down, you must control your finances. It is important that you manage your money properly in order to ensure that you are staying on top of everything to prevent yourself from investing too much into the market. You want to make sure that you are managing your risk and exposure and staying on top of how much you are making and losing in the grand scheme of things.

The best way to keep track of everything is to have a trading journal that allows you to keep track of your plan and all of the moves you make. It also allows you to keep track of your finances to ensure that you are making wise decisions and not investing too much or losing too much in certain moves.

Creating Your Plan

Before you create a plan, you need to ask yourself some questions. You should write these questions down in your trading journal to ensure that you are focused on what your goal is and that your plan aligns with the answers you have for the following questions.

- Why do you want to trade with Forex?

- What is your opinion on risk?

- What is the amount of time you're willing to invest in trades?

- How much do you know about trading already?

Identifying the answers to these questions is the best way to discover what your goals are with trading and how you position yourself in the market on trades that you will make. You need to answer these questions before you start creating your plan, as they are the basis for the plans that you make.

Once you answer those four primary questions, there are more you will want to consider. The answer to these will be exactly what you need to know in order to create your specific plan and move forward with it. Your answers don't need to be deep and thoughtful, but they do need to be answered clearly.

- Where are you right now, financially? Have you had any involvement in the market yet? If so, what is your involvement?

- At this time, what type of trader are you? What are your thoughts on trading and risk?

- Based on your level of knowledge right now, how confident do you feel in trading?

- What is the amount of capital you have to start your trading with?

- What are your financial goals with your trading?

- How long do you want to be trading for in order to reach that goal?

What is the success going to look like?

Answering these questions gives you a firm guideline of where you want to go and what you want to do with your trading. If you go in saying "I want to make a lot of money" but never define what "a lot" is, you are not going to be able to identify when you get there. You will also not know how to identify if you have been losing too much money. The market is something that you enter for specific purposes, as that is what will assist you in making the money you desire. You don't necessarily need to have a purpose such as retirement or education funds, but having a goal of what you want and a timeframe of when you want to achieve it will significantly assist you in mastering it and making as much as you desire.

Chapter 6 Think Before You Trade

No one can tell you exactly what the market is going to do, because it is influenced by so many different factors. Some of these factors remain a mystery even to the most experienced Forex trader. When you are starting, t is best to look at six-month support and resistance levels. These levels occur when a group of buyers and sellers find a trade that they believe is overpriced or discounted. Together, these buyers then create action in the market that changes it.

Find Supply And Resistance Levels

In order to find the supply and resistance levels look at a chart that contains six months of daily trade between two currencies that you might be interested in buying or selling. While some experts recommend that you look at a five-year period that complicates matters and makes complicates your work. Looking at periods shorter than six months, does not give you enough data to base your buying and selling decisions on.

Easy Way To Find The Level

Lay the chart on the table in front of you and get a ruler. Lay the ruler on top of the chart and move it up and down until the lines on the chart touch the ruler the most often. Draw a straight line across the paper.

Watch The Market For Dips

Now, watch the market. When the market dips below your determined level, then consider buying. Do not worry about rather the market has hit its absolute bottom or not, as you will probably make money when you buy at this point. The reason that the market dips below the line is that more people are willing to sell their shares than there are people looking to buy the share.

Watch The Market For Rises

Additionally, watch for times that the market rises above your line. These are good times to sell your stock. Again, it is not necessary to wait for the market to raise to the absolute top because no one can tell you exactly when that will occur and you do not want to miss the opportunity. The reason that the market rises above the line is that there are more people wanting to buy the share than there are people looking to sell the share.

Eliminate Confusion

While many experts will try to confuse you by having you look at multiple trading strategies including moving average convergence-divergence (MACD), stochastics, and relative strength indicators, your charts will become so messy that it will be difficult to spot the trends. It will also become difficult for the brain that is trying to assimilate all the new information to make sense of the information.

Master The Basics

Once you master the basics of supply and resistance levels, then you can begin adding more complex trading strategies if you desire. Be forewarned, however, that these additional trading strategies often result in making less money.

Chapter 7 Trading Strategies

Forex Scalping Strategies

Making fast money with Forex is what we all desire. There are various scalping strategies in Forex however, most of those strategies may be difficult to follow or may just not work. Though, the fastest method of making money in trading is through scalping.

Scalping can be defined as a fast-paced style of trading which specializes in making fast profits on small price changes, often times, after entering a trade that became profitable. It is one of the most important trading strategies in Forex. It requires the trader to stick to a precise exit strategy and is often done on the lower time frames including M1, M2, and M15.

Traders get trading opportunities by searching for small price changes within the market. In scalping, it is important to have prompt execution as well as precise timing. Although this method of trading has some risks, it still yields some profit to some traders. Because of the need to capitalize quickly on opportunities that become available, a scalp trader is likened to a marathon runner.

You must always remember that a huge loss can nullify whatever little gains the trader has obtained through Forex scalping. Due to the fact that most scalpers are not patient enough to wait for other opportunities to become available for a trade, the profitable trade becomes a loss as the opportunities reduce. To an extent, scalping exploits leveraging which makes people stay away from it. Being too greedy or trading too big is not advisable in scalping as these are easy methods of losing lots of money.

Having the focus to place trades, the proper tools, as well as a low spread broker is necessary for the success of this strategy. The following are factors which help scalpers make decisions:

• Your daily trades should be based on the watch list of hot stocks you create.

• Buy breakouts and watch observe an immediate up move after entry.

• In the absence of a move up, sell immediately.

- To ensure high percentage accuracy, once you have a little profit, sell half and adjust exit to your entry point on the position remaining.

- Take 3 – 5 trades until you have achieved your daily target.

Liquidity is a vital part of scalping as traders get in and out of their trades at different times in a day. Additionally, it guarantees that the best prices are gotten by trades as they get in and out of trades.

To make a profit, scalpers keep up with the latest news and future events which will likely cause price movements. They also tend to observe the low and high prices of a currency pair during a trading session and estimate the direction over a short term. This, however, requires high concentration and immediate execution.

Setting profit target amount per trade is another means of making a profit, and it ought to be relative to how much the currency pair is. Scalpers are expected to have a win/loss ratio of more than 50% so as to make a profit.

Different Timeframes

Try to consider the timeframe before you begin trading. This could be as low as the 1M chart in which the candle is formed every minute, to monthly charts formed once in a month. Do not forget that unless you are trading with the range bars that are totally immune to the time factor, all candles last for a particular time period.

In terms of trading, whatever is less than the hourly time frame should be seen as a short term. Examples of short-term trading include scalp swings and scalping. Hourly timeframes and other time frames less than a daily timeframe are classified as medium-term and are best considered for intraday and intra-week swing trading.

Time frames considered as long-term are daily, weekly, and monthly charts. In these timeframes, trades are usually executed 4-5 times in a year and do not just happen regularly. Do not forget that if you lose focus and are distracted from your charts, a 1M chart trading strategy has a really high probability of overwhelming you.

Scalping Indicators In Forex

Due to the fact that there are many poor indicators, getting a good indicator could be difficult, here are some that can be used.

• Forex Scalping of Multiple Charts Strategy

• Ribbon Entry Forex Trading Strategy

• The Relative Strength and Weakness Exit Strategy

These strategies although may seem like those used on longer time frames, they can actually be modified for trading on small-time frames like a 2 minute or 5-minute chart. A range bound market with little interference from fundamental factors is usually the best when implementing any scalping strategy. Poor performance in scalping arises during times of trend movement as well as volatility.

Forex Scalping of Multiple Charts: One of the best to implement in forex scalping as well as one of my favorites is this strategy. A 15- minute time frame of your preferred chart should be pulled up in order to set this up. Ensure that there are no indicators on the chart and then set up 3 horizontal lines which you then use for a 45-90-minute trading session. The first line indicates the opening print while the remaining two are to show the low and high trading range.

There is a need to also set up this on a 2- minute time frame after monitoring the price action at the three levels. When the resistance and the scalp support line up on both timeframes, you'll get the highest profits.

Ribbon Entry Forex Strategy: Placing the simple moving average (SMA) 5-8-13 combination on a 2 minutes chart, is the major objective of this scalping strategy. This helps to ascertain what trades are to be sold or bought on counter swings in the small trends. It is easy to master this strategy or method as it only needs the 5-8-13 ribbon to be lined up. Where it will then, point to either lower or higher during solid trends. A diminished momentum is determined by penetration in the 13 bar SMA which then favors a reversal.

The ribbon will become flat at the swings and range-bound periods and the price may also pass the ribbon sometimes. The changeover would then be observed by the scalper when the ribbon turns both lower and higher.

The Relative Strength and Weakness Exit Strategy:
This simple method of scalping is about finding out
when the best time to cut losses and take profits in
short term scalping trades is. This is of great
importance. Using the 5-3-3 stochastic indicator as
well as ribbon signals and an SD Bollinger band works
well on markets like the indices.

The best method of ribbon trades works when
stochastic turn to become lower than the overbought
level, or higher than the oversold level. Ensure your
exit is timed correctly; observe the interaction with
the band at a particular price. The concrete bands
predict the trend, making it the best point to take
profit. Retracement in the market is something Forex
scalping strategies cannot afford to undergo.

As the stochastic indicator rolls over giving you a
signal to leave the trade, ensure you take time to exit
the trade. This exit signal could be the inability of the
price to penetrate the band.

A Simple Scalping Setup

Lagging and signal delays can make Forex scalping
extremely difficult. This sometimes makes it more

profitable to use a price action scalping system without indicators. You will know what to do from the price. Your best indicator and signal are the price. As long as you adhere to the risk management recommendations and rules, you should be able to get good profits using the following scalping system.

Even if you have not traded with Forex in the past, this scalping strategy is very easy to use for every trader and does not make use of difficult rules. This system does not make it necessary for a trader to follow essential Forex rules such; as ignore signals against a trend, do not trade against a trend, as the system itself confirms trend following.

Scalping is difficult for amateurs; ensure you practice with the system on your demo account for a month's trial before going live.

This could be the best Forex scalping strategy for new traders, and it is a trend following strategy. It also has the added advantage of being easy to apply on the 1-, 5-, and 15-minute chart trading.

Currency Pairs: USD/JPY, USD/CHF EUR/USD, AUD/USD, NZD/USD and GBP/USD

Time Frame: 1m to 15m

Indicators:

Stochastic (STO) (14, 3, 3) with levels 10 and 90

Bollinger bands (BB) (14 period) (green)

Buy position: The price first needs to broke down below the lower Bollinger Band. Now, wait till the candle closes in the Bollinger Band again. Stochastic should be crossing up 10 from below 10.

Sell position: The price first needs to be broken above the upper Bollinger Band. Then wait until the candle closes in the Bollinger Band again. The stochastic should be crossing down 90 from above 90.

Forex Risks To Be Wary Of

Most foreign exchange trades are made up of foreign exchange swaps, spot transactions, currency swaps, futures, and options. Because it is a leveraged product, the risks associated with forex trades are much and can lead to significant losses.

Losses related to forex trading might be larger than that expected at first as a result of all the risks associated with it. A small initial payment can lead to illiquid assets and a significant amount of losses, because of how leveraged trades are designed. Also, political issues, as well as time differences, could lead to serious consequences on countries' currencies and financial markets. Although the trading volume in the forex market is the highest, there are obvious risks which could cause significant losses.

Interest Rate Risks: Basic macroeconomics courses teach that interest rates affect a country's exchange rates. Increase in a country's interest rates will lead to a stronger currency because of the influx of investments in the country's assets, as it is believed that a stronger currency leads to higher returns. Contrarily, as the interest rates reduce, the currency becomes weak because investors start to take back their investments. The differences between currency values can lead to drastic changes in forex prices because of the nature of the interest rate and its indirect effect on exchange rates.

Leverage Risks: In order to gain access to significant trades in foreign currencies, a margin, which is a small initial investment, required by leverage in forex trading is needed. Small price fluctuations lead to margin call where the investor is expected to pay an additional margin. Aggressive use of leverage would lead to significant loss of investments and investors when the market conditions are volatile. The interest differences between currencies can lead to a dramatic change in forex prices.

Transaction Risks; These are risks associated with transactions. Transaction risks are referred to as the unstable exchange rate from the initial time a contract was made to the time it is finalized. In Forex trading, when contracts are made, it is very possible for the exchange rate to change before the contract is concluded. The trading hour for Forex is 24 hours. During this time, the same currency can be sold or bought at varying prices at different times. The higher the time interval between the beginning of a contract and its conclusion, the greater the transaction risks. Whenever there is a change in the exchange rate due to this time difference, the cost of the transaction becomes very high.

The Counterparty Risk; A counterparty risk is a risk of defaults caused by the supplier in any business. A counterparty refers to the brokers or suppliers of assets to investors. They are the companies that provide the services or valuables to others known as investors. In Forex, there are contracts known as spot contracts and forward contracts. Spot contracts deal with spot currencies, and in this trade, the risk may result from the brokers or market makers. There might be a breach of contract by the counterparty if the market conditions are not favorable.

Country Risk; When considering your options before making investments especially in currencies, make sure you consider the solidity and standard of the country issuing it. Exchange rates of developing countries or underdeveloped countries around the world depend on the currencies of other great countries like the United State dollar. Therefore, central banks must exercise efficient measures to maintain fixed exchange rates. Once the currency is devalued, it can affect Forex trade. Currency devaluation is as a result of recurring balance of a payment deficit, a condition where the rate at which a country imports goods and services is higher than the rate it exports.

Investments are not based on facts and investigation, but rather based on supposition. Therefore, once an investor feels the value of a currency will soon reduce, he removes his assets. This act, however, causes the value of the currency to reduce more. The investors that will still be trading the currency, will discover that their assets are not easily sold or exchanged. In Forex, currency crisis leads to assets not being sold, credit risk and further devaluation of the currency.

Chapter 8 Fundamental Analysis

In order to trade in the forex market successfully, one of the most important things you can learn is the most reliable way to spot a trade that is going to end up being reliably profitable from one that blows up in your face. This is where proper analysis comes in handy, whether technical or fundamental. Fundamental analysis is easier to learn, though it is more time consuming to use properly, while technical analysis can be more difficult to wrap your mind around but can be done quite quickly once you get the hang of it. While both will help you to find the information you are looking for, they go about doing so in different ways; fundamental analysis concerns itself with looking at the big picture while technical analysis focuses on the price of a given currency in the moment to the exclusion of all else.

This divide when it comes to information means that fundamental analysis will always be useful when it coms to determining currencies that are currently undervalued based on current market forces. The information that is crucial to fundamental analysis is generated by external sources which means there won't always be new information available at all times.

This chapter and the next are dedicated to fundamental and technical analysis, respectively.

Generally speaking, fundamental analysis allows you a likely glimpse at the future of the currency in question based on a variety of different variables such as publicized changes to the monetary policy that the countries you are interested in might affect. The idea here is that with enough information you can then find currency pairs that are currently undervalued because the market hasn't yet had the time to catch up with the changes that have been made. Fundamental analysis is always made up of the same set of steps which are described in detail below.

Start by determining the baseline: When it comes to considering the fundamental aspects of a pair of currencies, the first thing that you are going to want to do is to determine a baseline from which those currencies tend to return to time and again compared to the other commonly traded currency pairs. This will allow you to determine when it is time to make a move as you will be able to easily pinpoint changes to the pair that are important enough to warrant further consideration.

In order to accurately determine the baseline, the first thing you will need to do is to look into any relevant macroeconomic policies that are currently affecting your currency of choice. You will also want to look into the available historical data as past behavior is one of the best indicators of future evets. While this part of the process can certainly prove tedious, their important cannot be overstated.

After you have determined the historical precedent of the currency pair you are curious about, the next thing you will want to consider is the phase the currency is currently in and how likely it is going to remain in that phase for the foreseeable future. Every currency goes through phases on a regular basis as part of the natural market cycle.

The first phase is known as the boom phase which can be easily identified by its low volatility and high liquidity. The opposite of this phase is known as the bust phase wherein volatility is extremely high, and liquidity is extremely low. There are also pre and post versions of both phases that can be used to determine how much time the phase in question has before it is on its way out. Determining the right phase is a key part of knowing when you are on the right track regarding a particular trading pair.

In order to determine the current major or minor phase, the easiest thing to do is to start by checking the current rates of defaults along with banks loans as well as the accumulated reserve levels of the currencies in question. If numbers are relatively low them a boom phase is likely to be on its way, if not already in full swing. If the current numbers have already overstayed their welcome, then you can be fairly confident that a post-boom phase is likely to start at any time. Alternatively, if the numbers in question are higher than the baseline you have already established then you know that the currency in question is either due for a bust phase or is already experiencing it.

You can make money from either of the major phases as long as you are aware of them early on enough to turn a profit before things start to swing back in the opposite direction. Generally speaking, this means that the faster you can pinpoint what the next phase is going to be, the greater your dividends of any related trades will be.

Broaden your scope: After you have a general idea of the baseline for your favored currencies, as well as their current phases, the next thing you will need to do is look at the state of the global market as a whole to determine how it could possibly affect your trading pair. To ensure this part of the process is as effective as possible you are going to need to look beyond the obvious signs that everyone can see to find the indicators that you know will surely make waves as soon as they make it into the public consciousness.

One of the best places to start looking for this information is in the technology sector as emerging technologies can turn entire economies around in a relatively short period of time.

Technological indicators are often a great way to take advantage of a boom phase by getting in on the ground floor as, once it starts, it is likely to continue for as long as it takes for the technology to be fully integrated into the mainstream. Once it reaches the point of complete saturation then a bust phase is likely going to be on the horizon, and sooner rather than later. If you feel as though the countries responsible for the currencies in question are soon going to be in a post-boom or post-bust phase, then you are going to want to be very careful in any speculative market as the drop-off is sure to be coming and it is difficult to pinpoint exactly when.

If you know that a phase shift is coming, but you aren't quite sure when, then it is a good idea to focus on smaller leverage amounts than during other phases as they are more likely to pay off in the short-term. At the same time, you are also going to want to keep any eye out for long-term positions that are likely to pay out if a phase shift does occur. On the other hand, if the phase you are in currently is just starting out, you can make trades that have a higher potential for risk as the time concerns aren't going to be nearly serious enough to warrant the additional caution.

Look to global currency policy: While regional concerns are often going to be able to provide you with an insight into some long-reaching changes a given currency might experience in the near future, you are also going to want to broaden your search, even more, to include relevant global policies as well. While determining where you are going to start can be difficult at first, all you really need to do is to provide the same level of analysis that you used at the micro level on a macro basis instead. The best place to start with this sort of thing is going to be with the interest rates of the major players including the Federal Reserve, the European Central Bank, the Bank of Japan, the Bank of England and any other banks that may affect the currencies you are considering trading.

You will also need to consider any relevant legal mandates or policy biases that are currently in play to make sure that you aren't blindsided by these sorts of things when the times actually comes to stop doing research and actually make a move. While certainly time consuming, understanding every side of all the major issues will make it far easier to determine if certain currencies are flush with supply where the next emerging markets are likely to appear and what worldwide expectations are when it comes to future interest rate changes as well as market volatility.

Don't forget the past: Those who forget the past are doomed to repeat it and that goes double for forex traders. Once you have a solid grasp on the current events of the day, you are going to want to dig deeper and look for scenarios in the past that match what is currently going on today. This level of understanding will ultimately lead to a greater understanding of the current strength of your respective currencies while also giving you an opportunity to accurately determine the length of the current phase as well.

In order to ensure you are able to capitalize on your knowledge as effectively as possible, the ideal time to jump onto a new trade is going to be when one of the currency pairs is entering a post-boom phase while the other is entering the post-bust phase. This will ensure that the traditional credit channels are not exhausted completely, and you will thus have access to the maximum amount of allowable risk of any market state. This level of risk is going to start dropping as soon as the market conditions hit an ideal state and will continue until the situation with the currencies is reversed so getting in and making a profit when the time is right is crucial to your long-term success.

Don't forget volatility: Keeping the current level of volatility in mind is crucial when it comes to ensuring that the investments you are making are actually going to pay off in a reasonable period of time. Luckily, Luckily, it is relatively easy to determine the current level of volatility in a given market, all you need to do is to look to that country's stock market. The greater the level of stability the market in question is experiencing, the more confident those who are investing in it are going to remain when means the more stable the forex market is going to remain as well.

Additionally, it is important to keep in mind that, no matter what the current level of volatility may be, the market is never truly stable. As such, the best traders are those who prepare for the worst while at the same time hoping for the best. Generally speaking, the more robust a boom phase is, the lower the overall level of volatility is going to be.

Think outside the box on currency pairs: All of the information that you gather throughout the process should give you a decent idea regarding the current state of the currency pairs you are keeping tabs on. You should now have enough to be able to use this information to determine which pairs are going to be able to provide you with the most potential profit in not just the short-term but the long-term as well. Specifically, you are going to want to keep an eye out for pairs that have complimentary futures so that they will end up with the greatest gap between their two interest rates as possible.

Additionally, you are going to want to consider the gap between countries when it comes to overall output and unemployment rate. When looking into these differences you are also going to need to be aware of the fact that shortages can cause constraints to capacity or when the unemployment rate drops, both of which can lead to inflation as well. This, in turn, leads to an increase in interest rates which leads to a general cooling of the country's economy. As such, these factors are extremely important when it comes to determining the overall disparity between the interest rates of specific countries in the near future.

Furthermore, you are going to want to keep tabs on the amount of debt that the countries in question are dealing with, as well as their reputation of repayment on the global market. Specifically, you are going to want to look for a balanced capital to debt ratio as the healthier that this number is the stronger the national currency is going to be no matter what else is currently taking place. To determine this ratio, you will want to know how much capital each country currently has on hand as well as their position when it comes to other nations and their level of reserves and foreign investment.

Understand their relative trade strength: If you find a currency that is currently in the middle of a boom phase, the overall strength that its fundamentals show will determine how likely those who are holding it in various currency pairs are to hold or sell. The same also goes for currencies that boast an overly strong or overly weak interest rate when compared to other, similar currencies. What this means is that when a given currency is in the earliest part of the boom phase you will be able to easily find a strong market for its related currency pairs which combine agreeable fundamentals and strong interest rates. While all of these factors are important, as a general rule a strong interest rate will always trump subpar fundamentals.

Watch out for market sentiment

While determining specifics in undervalued currencies is useful most of the time, sometimes the market simply doesn't behave in the way that it realistically should. In these cases, it is the market sentiment that has hijacked the price of the currency in question and learning how to stay on the lookout for its influence is guaranteed to save you from some seriously unprofitable trades in the long run.

Like many things in the forex market, this is easier said than done, however, which is why it is best to take the following suggestions related to reading market sentiment to heart if you ever hope to get a clear idea of how strong the momentum regarding a given currency truly is.

Choose the right trend: Each and every move that a currency makes is ultimately based on a trend that started building hours, if not days before. As such, if you spend time trading with either the 15 or 60-minute chart then you may find yourself accidentally moving forward based on part of a larger trend that is ultimately going to end up moving in the opposite direction. As such, in order to avoid such mistakes, you are going to want to start by identifying the trend in the daily chart and then working inward from there until you reach your target chart. This will allow you to more easily determine the breadth of a given chart and allow you to avoid trading based on anterior movement as well.

Find the right price movement: On the topic of price movement, depending on the pair you are trading in, you will likely come across profits that you might not otherwise bank by simply getting a feel for the way your favored currency pairs move on a regular basis. Getting a feel for price movement means understanding the speed at which the pair typically moves, in both directions, to ensure that you know the most effective time to strike.

When the movement is clearly headed in an upwards direction with a quickness, only to slowly descend after the fact, time and again, then you can expect other traders to be steadily buying into the pair without taking the time to do all the relevant research. This, in turn, means you can expect the overall sentiment of the market to be bullish which means you can respond appropriately.

Similar information can also be determined based on the way the market responds when new relevant information, both positive and negative, comes to light. As an example, if there was just a round of positive economic news out of the United Kingdom but the positive change in the GBP and USD pair doesn't seem all that enthusiastic, then you can safely determine that the market is moving in a bearish direction when it comes to GBP/USD.

Watch your indicators of volume: While there are a wide variety of different indicators that measure volume, there are no better means for doing so than the Commitment of Traders Report which is released each and every Friday. This report clearly outlines the net of all the trades made, both long and short, for the week, for both commercial and private traders. This is a great place to start if you aren't sure what currencies to favor as this will show where most of the interest was for the proceeding week.

As previously noted, it is best to always trade on the trend which means that if there are more net longs overall you are going to want to buy and if there are more net shorts overall then you are going to want to sell. When this is not the case is if the buy positions are already at extreme levels then you will want to sell or at least wait until things move in the other direction because there can be no more increase if everyone who is going to buy has already bought. Eventually, you will see a reversal in this case which means that if this is the case then you are better off trading in the medium term instead.

Look more closely at international trends: When you are first getting your start in the forex market you are likely going to be surprised at just how interconnected the world as a whole really is. While some of these connections are going to be obvious, other will certainly catch you off guard the first time you encounter them which means you will want to pay attention to the way news affects various currency pairs, even if you are not actually trading in them at the moment as you never know when that information might be useful again at a later date.

Chapter 9 Trading Journals

This chapter will teach you how to create a trading journal. Read this material carefully: trading journals can help you become a successful forex trader.

The Importance of Trading Journals

According to experienced traders, discipline is more important than accuracy. It would be almost impossible to determine all the crucial indicators every time. But with self-discipline, you'll know the "when", "what", and "how" of your trading strategies easily.

Recording your thoughts and transactions in a journal is one of the best ways to develop self-discipline. In fact, most people in the investing world keep a journal of some sort. They use the journal to record their initial capital, entry points, and intended exit points. Often, they also list down the rationale of their investing/trading decisions. That means they can review their previous choices and make the necessary adjustments.

Important Note: Trading journals can help you learn from your mistakes and avoid unnecessary risks.

Setting Up Your Trading Journal

Creating a trading journal consists of three steps:

First Step: Generating a Currency Checklist

Your journal should begin with a printable spreadsheet. You'll fill out and print this spreadsheet on a daily basis. The checklist will help you in "understanding" the market and identifying potential trades.

Make sure that your checklist has all of the available currency pairs. Save these pairs in the leftmost column of the spreadsheet. Then, label the next three columns as "Current", "Low", and "High", respectively. Add the indicators on the right side of the file. If you want to keep things simple, you may focus on the four primary currency pairs, namely: GBP/USD, USD/CHF, EUR/USD, and USD/JPY. You may add more currencies once you gain more trading experience.

The checklist might appear to be complex and lengthy, but you should be able to fill it out in just twenty minutes. Remember that the goal of the checklist is to present the trends and trading ranges present in the currency market. Acquiring these pieces of information is a huge step towards huge profits from forex. Without a detailed idea about the market, you will blindly trade currencies. You will pick assets based on breakouts and prevailing trends. Unfortunately, this undisciplined approach often leads to huge losses.

Important Note: Market trends can give you excellent profit potential. If a pair is on an uptrend, you should buy it during retracements. If the trend is downward, however, you should sell during a rally.

The initial column of your spreadsheet's indicator group must be labeled as "ADX (14) > 25". ADX (i.e. Average Directional Index) is one of the most popular tools for evaluating trends. A trend exists if the value of the index is higher than 25. In general, high index values indicate strong trends.

The second column relies on "Bollinger bands". Strong trends usually hit one of the said bands. The third, fourth, and fifth columns, on the other hand, will hold the long-term SMAs (i.e. simple moving averages). If the numbers go below or above the averages, the market might be on a trend. You can verify the trend by checking crossovers (if any) that are in the trend's direction.

The group's first column will contain the Average Directional Index. This time, however, you'll look for an ADX that is lower than 25. These index values indicate weak trends. The remaining columns will contain the RSI (i.e. Relative Strength Index), traditional oscillators, and stochastic. You should conduct range trading when you have a weak ADX, high technical resistance, and oversold/overbought levels of stochastic and RSI.

Important Note: The resulting sheet can be of great help in your forex transactions. However, they are not guaranteed to work all the time. The goal of this spreadsheet is to open your eyes to the current status of the currency market.

Second Step: Identifying Potential Trades

The next part of your journal displays the trades you can make for the current trading day. Use the spreadsheet you created earlier to complete this part. Here is a basic example:

December 18, 2016

Buy USD/JPY - .8999 break (high of the previous day)

Stop at 8800 (30-day SMA).

First Target - 0.9000 (based on Fibonacci retracement)

Second Target - 0.9200 (upper Bollinger)

Third Target - Lowest point of the past ten trading days

This approach gives you clear courses of action once your desired entry price level appears. You will know the best action to take, as well as the ideal spots for your limits and stops. Keep yourself updated regarding the market conditions while working on this part of your journal.

Third Step: Listing Down the Current and/or Completed Trades

This part helps you in enforcing self-discipline. It also aids in turning your mistakes into learning opportunities. Whenever a trading day ends, take the time to review the results of your transactions. Why did you profit from a deal? What made you choose the wrong currency pair?

The main goal of this part is to determine trends and mistakes. It is likely that you are making mistakes. However, you won't know which of your actions and/or plans are faulty if you won't analyze them in detail. That means recording your transactions can help you understand your thoughts and behaviors as a forex trader. The entries in this part should look like this:

December 5, 2016

Transaction: Short 5 lots of GBP/USD @ 1.2000

Stop: 1.2500 (current all-time high)

Current Target: 1.1500

Result: The transaction got completed on the next trading day. I exited the position @ 1.300.

Comments: I thought the price will drop soon, so I didn't exit at my predetermined stopping point.

Lesson: Stick to your trading plan.

According to forex experts, an excellent trade is a trade whose fundamental and technical results match.

Consequently, you shouldn't submit orders based on technical or fundamental analysis alone.

Choosing the Market Indicators

After setting up your journal, you should choose the market indicators to include in your analysis. Many forex traders fail because they consider their preferred indicators as foolproof. For example, some traders perform trades based solely on the levels of stochastic. But this strategy can result to huge losses when the currency market starts to trend. You should learn how to adapt to the changes in the market if you want to survive in the world of forex.

As a trader, you should always consider the environmental factors of the market. Prepare a list of factors so you can easily determine whether the market is range-bound or trending. Expert forex traders will tell you that selecting trade parameters plays an important role in forex.

The selection of parameters is important in every market. However, it is of the most importance in the forex market. That's because about 80% of all forex transactions are speculative. It is not surprising for currencies to stay in a specific trading environment over the long-term. In addition, the forex market is compatible with technical analysis (mainly because of the former's size).

Forex experts divide market environments into two types: trending and range trading. And defining the current market environment is the initial step of an effective trade.

Important Note: In Forex-related analyses, the shortest period of time that you can use is 24 hours. Use this timeframe even if you are making five-minute transactions.

Step 1: Profiling the Environment

Forex traders use various methods in determining the trading environment. There are many people who use visuals. But it would be best if you'll set specific rules in guiding your transactions. Here are some of the most popular rules today:

- Ranges

- ADX < 20 - The ADX is an excellent indicator of a trend's strength. Indices that are lower than 20 suggest weak trends. As you probably know, weak trends often occur in range-bound markets. If the ADX is on a downtrend, the environment will likely stay in its current condition for some time.

- Decreasing Volatility - There is a wide range of techniques that you can use in analyzing volatility. The simplest approach, however, involves comparing the short-term and long-term volatility of the market. If the short-term volatility falls after surpassing the highest point of the long-term volatility, the range trading situation is likely to reverse.

- Volatility heightens if one or more currency pairs experience fast movements. It lowers when the trading activities are quiet and the ranges aren't wide. You can use Bollinger bands to track the volatility of the market. Narrow bands indicate small ranges and low volatility. Wide bands, on the other hand, reflect wide ranges and highly volatile trading environments.

- Risk Reversals - Risk reversals consist of two options (i.e. a "put" option and a "call" option) on a currency. Their sensitivity and expiration are the same as that of the spot rate. Theoretically speaking, the volatility of the put and call options must be similar. But these options show different levels of volatility in the real world.

- You can obtain crucial data through risk reversals. In fact, many traders use these reversals to evaluate existing positions.

- Trends

- ADX > 20 - During a trending market, you should search for a rising ADX that is higher than 25. If the AFX is higher than 25 but is downward sloping, it might be a sign that the trend will disappear soon.

- Momentum and Trend Direction - Aside from using ADX, you should also check the market's momentum indicators. Your goal is to find a momentum that matches the trend's overall direction. During an uptrend, for instance, traders will search for upward RSI, moving averages, MACD (i.e. moving average convergence/divergence), and stochastic.

During a down trend, traders will want the said indicators to start a downward trend. If your moving averages show a perfect alignment, the momentum has considerable strength. Here are some examples of perfect alignment:

- During an uptrend - 10-day moving average > 20-day moving average > 50-day moving average, with the 100- and 200-day moving average under the short-term moving averages.

- During a downtrend - The long-term moving averages are above the short-term moving averages.

- Options - When the market is trending, you should look for reversals that favor puts or calls.

Step 2 - Identify the Time Horizon

Profiling the trading environment is not enough; you should also specify the timeframe of your intended trade. Here are some indicators and guidelines that traders use. Note that your trades don't have to meet all of the guidelines below. However, excellent trades tend to meet most of these guidelines.

- Range Trading - Intraday

- The Rules

- *Identify entry points using hourly charts.*

- *Confirm the existence of range trades through daily charts.*

- *To find entry points within a range, you may use oscillators.*

- *Search for RSIs or stochastic that reach extreme levels. These indicate reversals in the oscillators.*

- *Trades are strong when currency values maintain support levels. You have to use moving averages and the Fibonacci retracement technique for this.*

- The Indicators

  o RSI

  o MACD

- Options

- Stochastic

- Bollinger bands

- Fibonacci retracement

- Range Trading - Medium-Term

- The Rules

- *Focus on daily charts.*

- *You have two choices:*

  - Look for upcoming opportunities - Search for volatile markets, where long-term volatility levels are considerably lower than short-term ones.

  - Play in current ranges - Identify active ranges using Bollinger bands.

- *Search for one or more reversals in the market oscillators (e.g. stochastic).*

- *Check the price action - the price should fall at important resistance points and rise on important support points. You can use the traditional indicators for this task.*

- *Make sure that the ADX is lower than 25. A falling ADX is great, but not mandatory.*

- The Indicators

- *RSI*

- *MACD*

- *Options*

- *Stochastic*

- *Bollinger bands*

- *Fibonacci retracement*

- Trend Trading - Medium-Term

- The Rules

- *Find trends using daily charts. Check weekly charts to prove the existence of trends.*

- *Analyze the market's characteristics. What parameters are satisfied?*

- *Go for retracement/breakout situations on moving averages or Fibonacci levels.*

- *The trade shouldn't have any significant resistance levels in front of it.*

- *Check your trade using candlestick patterns.*

- *Enter the market during significant lows or highs.*

- *It would be best if you'll wait for the contraction of volatilities before entering the market.*

- *The fundamental characteristics of the currency pairs (e.g. growth) should be positive.*

- The Indicators

- *RSI*

- *Elliott waves*

- *Fibonacci retracement*

- *ADX*

- *Parabolic SAR (i.e. Stop and Reversal)*

- *Ichimoku Clouds*

- Breakout Trading - Medium-Term

- The Rules

- *Concentrate on daily charts.*

- *Search for contractions in the short-term volatility levels. The contraction point should be way much lower than the long-term volatility levels.*

- *Confirm breaks using pivot points.*

- *The moving averages should favor the trade.*

- The Indicators

- *Fibonacci Levels*

- *Moving Averages*

- *Bollinger Bands*

Managing Risks

The concept of risk management is easy to understand. However, many traders fail to consider it when choosing, buying, holding, and selling currencies. There are countless situations where profitable positions became losing ones, and excellent strategies became horrible financial blunders. Your IQ and your knowledge about the market don't guarantee success in the forex market. If you pay little attention to risk management, your trades will likely lead to losses.

In a nutshell, risk management consists of defining the risks you can shoulder and the profits you want to get. Without these pieces of information, chances are you will exit the market prematurely or remain in losing market positions. It is not uncommon for forex traders to have more profitable positions than losing ones, but end up with huge losses instead of profits.

The following guidelines will help you in managing risks:

- Stop-Loss Orders - These orders assist you in specifying maximum losses. By setting a stop-loss order, you can prevent horrible positions from ruining the profitability of your entire portfolio. A trailing stop is particularly useful in securing your earnings. Successful traders usually adjust their stops whenever their assets increase in value.

Meanwhile, some traders close a segment of their existing positions.

- Treat new transactions as if they are independent ones, regardless of whether your positions are winning or not. This approach is excellent if you want to ride a trend or gain more profitable positions. When adding to an existing position, analyze the currency as if it is not in your portfolio yet. If the favorable trend continues, you may close a segment of your position while adjusting your stops. This task requires you to consider the rewards you want to get and the risks you can shoulder.

- How to Use Stop-Loss Orders - Because money management is important in successful forex trading, you should always implement stop-loss orders in your positions. Keep in mind that these orders specify the highest amount of loss that you'll experience. If the value of the currency hits your stopping point, your position will close quickly and automatically. Thus, utilizing stop-loss orders can greatly reduce the risks involved in your trades.

- Placing a Stop-Loss Order on Your Trades - Traders implement stop-loss orders in two ways:

- Parabolic SAR - You'll find this indicator in most forex charting computer programs. In a nutshell, Parabolic SAR shows the best position for the stop-loss order as a dot.

- Two-Day Low Approach - With this approach, you will place the order 10 pips lower than the pair's two-day low. For instance, if the pair's current value is 1.1300 and its two-day low was 1.1280, you should place the stop at 1.1270.

- Risk-Reward Ratios - You must specify the risk-reward ratio of all your trades. Basically, this ratio states that amount you can lose, and the amount you want to earn. Your ratios should be 1:2 or better. Setting these ratios before entering the market can help you avoid financial losses.

The Psychological Aspects of Currency Trading

Choosing the right indicators and monitoring the trading environment can certainly help you in your trading adventures. However, you cannot underestimate the effects of your psychological outlook on your trades. By having the appropriate psychological outlook, you can boost your chances of succeeding in the forex market.

Controlling Your Emotions

Do not allow your emotions to affect your trading decisions. The most successful traders display emotional detachment: they don't build emotional connections with the assets they acquire. They consider objectivity as an important part of their toolbox. Unskilled traders, on the other hand, make huge mistakes because they base their trades on their emotions. They switch to another plan after experiencing some losses, or become reckless after getting some profits.

Taking a Break

If you are experiencing consecutive losses, you should avoid trading to stop greed and/or fear from influencing your decisions.

You will face unprofitable transactions over the course of your trading career. Thus, you should be prepared to cope with financial losses. Traders, even the best ones, experience losing streaks. To succeed, however, you should display tenacity and concentration while going through such rough times.

Stop trading when you are on a losing streak. In most cases, forgetting about the market for several days is an effective solution to your dilemma. Sticking to your trading routine in an unfavorable market condition can lead to huge losses. And these losses can destroy your self-confidence and psychological condition. Accept your mistakes. It would be impossible to profit from all of your transactions. You will make mistakes; and your ultimate goal is to keep the damaging effects of your errors at a manageable level.

Here are some rules that you should remember:

- Do not go against the trend.

- Determine the expectations in the market.

- Define the risk-reward ratio of your trades.

- Allow your returns to increase.

- Minimize your losses.

- Secure sufficient capital.

- If you have a losing position, don't add to it.

- Record your thoughts and actions using a journal.

- Assign maximum losses or profit retracements.

- Make sure that your positions have logical sizes.

Chapter 10 Engulfing Pattern Trading With 3ms Principles

Engulfing pattern is one of my favorite trading setups. Identifying good engulfing bars can help you yield big potential profits. Yet, there are also a lot of false signals in the market. Let's refer to the below example.

As can be seen, the market had formed a strong resistance level at 1.5091 (the red horizontal line) before the engulfing pattern appeared (see the first two arrows). The market failed to break the resistance level twice, which clearly indicates how strong the resistance is. You can see the resistance remains unbreakable two more times (the third and fourth arrow) before becoming a very strong support later (notice the fifth arrow).

The engulfing pattern in the picture did NOT appear on a resistance level, meaning that its chances to attract seller pressure is not so high. Hence, it failed to work as a reversal signal. In these cases, it is advisable not to enter any trades. You are not stacking the odds in your favor when the candlesticks have not reached key support and resistance level.

Principle 1: Do not trade any candlestick pattern if it is not present on a key support or resistance level.

Let's take a look at another example when an engulfing pattern that does not meet all entry criteria may bring unexpected losses to traders.

In this case, a daily engulfing pattern was present at a strong resistance area, which meets the first condition of a turnaround. However, it failed to start a reversal of the trend. We are going to look at a smaller time frame to see the reason behind its failure to initiating a downtrend.

In the 4-hour chart, things are much clearer. First, please be noted that the engulfing pattern on the daily time frame is the totally highlighted area in yellow in the picture.

From the 4-hour chart, it is obvious that the market was creating a strong upward trend from A to H. Afterwards, the H1 low was formed during the process. From H1, the market failed to create a higher high than H, signaling that the bulls are taking a rest. Yet, we still do not have any confirmation about a downtrend. Remember a minimum condition for a downtrend to form is the creation of at least two lower highs and one lower low. In this example, if we see H as the first high and H1 as the first low in a downtrend, then we are lacking one lower low and one lower high.

Once again, let's take a look at the yellow area which illustrates the bearish engulfing pattern on the daily chart. You can see how the engulfing candlestick and even a few following candles constantly failed to break the X line - a horizontal line drawn from H1. This indicates that the market structure still remained unchanged, i.e the uptrend still prevailed at least until the close of the daily engulfing pattern. In other words, the selling pressure was not strong enough to win against the bulls' force. When we observe the 4-hour chart, it is obvious that the above-mentioned engulfing candlestick did not carry in it any evidence of a reversal in connection with market structure. Put differently, it also failed to meet the third condition of a reversal.

If you are not careful in analyzing this candlestick pattern, you may feel something of a betray when a considered profitable pattern failed to work. However, once you know that it failed to meet two out of three needed criteria for a reliable function, you will be relaxed watching the candlesticks to move without putting yourself in dangers. In a "probability market", we should be prudent.

Trading any reversal after successfully confirming all three conditions would greatly increase the chances of stacking the odds in your favor. Below is another example of a bullish engulfing pattern present at a key support level failing to start a reversal.

On the daily time frame, things might be ideal for a reversal to the upside...

However, if you had entered a buy entry right after the highlighted bar, you would have encountered a loss. Let's see what happened on the 4-hour chart below.

Notice that the daily bullish engulfing pattern is comprised of a few 4-hour candlesticks which are in the yellow box.

Still basing on the above method of analyzing the market, we all see the engulfing bar was located in a key support zone, which satisfies the first criterion of a reversal.

As can be seen, the market was in a clear downtrend from A to F, forming lower highs and lower lows. Then, the bullish engulfing bar tried to break the dominant trend by preventing the market from forming a lower low. Unfortunately, it failed to close above E – the newest lower high at that time. Such failure indicated that no change in the market structure was made, thus any ideas of buying the currency pair should be removed. You can see how the market continued its strong downtrend and form a lower low at H. An uptrend had not been formed till several 4-hour candlesticks later. Once again, the second and third criteria of a reversal were not satisfied. Trading right after the bullish engulfing bar would put you in great dangers.

Principle 2: Do not join a reversal trade until the overall market trend/structure has been successfully broken/ changed.

Let's see when and how we could join the market in this situation.

Still on the downtrend, the market continued to make a lower high at I. The problem with the downtrend initiated when the market failed to create a lower low at J. This tells us that, upon touching a strong support zone, the sellers were encountering a strong opposing force from the bulls. They then lost the battle at J, pushing prices higher. Should you be in a position like this, be prepared for a confirmed buy signal.

The market's effort to touch a key support level at J could also be seen as a retest before a strong upward trend. Trading on retests has always been my indispensable principle in every trade.

On analyzing any market structure, for example from a downtrend to an uptrend, the break of the newest high plays a very important part on whether we should enter a trade or not. In this case, notice how the prices strongly broke the X1 level from J, meaning that the nearest/ newest high during a downtrend was broken. And if you were patient enough, such break served to form a higher high at K. There we have it. Notice that after the market created another low at L, it were now having two higher lows (J and L) and one higher high (K), which meets the minimum conditions of an uptrend. A change in the market structure was confirmed by L, which is also the ideal entry price in this case. And here is the interesting point.

Here are the two core reasons I would place an order at L for a high chance of winning.

- Always trade on a retest. Do not be seduced by the market to enter a buy order when the market is present by a very long bull bar or enter a sell order in case of a long bear bar. As I mentioned in previous part, let's connect the price with a ball and you will get the explanation. Imagine how a ball quickly bounces back after strongly hitting the floor. And this is how prices work. Prices need a strong base for any strong advance or drop. Before a rally or plummet, just look for a correction of the overall trend. Technically speaking, it is when buyers and sellers are recharging energy for an imminent powerful move.

- When a support level is broken, it is likely to turn into a resistance level, and vice versa. Let's see how the X2 line played as a strong resistance area in case of E and G highs. After being broken, it played as a support area and prices tended to make retests upon the X2 level. Do not join any trade without a retest. What is the worst outcome of this rule? Missing a trade, that's it.

In fact, there is no need to worry if you know there are unlimited opportunities ahead.

And most importantly, my capital is safely protected by trading this way.

On coming back to the daily time frame, the break of X1 line was clearly illustrated by the second engulfing bar. A strong upward trend was followed by that candlestick.

Let's take a look at another example regarding the GBP/CAD currency pair, and see why the engulfing bar failed to forecast a reversal in the market.

On the daily time frame, an engulfing bar appeared at a key resistance area. However, it failed to trigger a strong enough selling force to pull the price to the below right away. Put differently, if you had placed a sell trade right after the engulfing pattern, your order would have hit the stop loss level. With the same way of explanation as in the previous examples, let's see what happened in the 4-hour chart time frame.

From the 4-hour chart, an uptrend had been prevailing before the bearish engulfing pattern appeared (the daily engulfing pattern is comprised of a few 4-hour candlesticks in the yellow box). It is clear that the engulfing pattern only served to create a new higher low during the overall uptrend. Hence, no reliable bearish signal was present at that moment, and it was best to stay on the sideline.

On looking further in the chart, let's see how the market continued to make a higher high and a higher low at H and I respectively. Yet, the failure to create another higher high at J released the first signal for a downward move.

Now, we have I as the newest/nearest low during the uptrend. From this, I draw a horizontal line, making the X1 line as in the picture. Notice that from J, the market tried two more times to push prices higher but it failed, again and again, forming a top at K. This was when the sellers gathered and battled with the bulls' force which was becoming weaker and weaker. The sellers then won the battle and pulled prices below the X1 line, breaking the nearest low in the uptrend. A new low was formed at L and this was when you should be prepared for a sell signal.

If you still remember a simple characteristic of a downtrend – the creation of at least two lower highs and one lower low – then you will see the importance of M's appearance. It was when the downtrend was confirmed and we had two lower highs (K and M) and one lower low (L). M was what we need to look for an entry price. In fact, it was better if M could touch the X1 line as a retest of the new resistance. Yet, in the picture, the bears seemed so powerful that they prevented the bulls from reaching the level. You can see how strong the downtrend was after the formation of M as the second lower high.

Now, let's stop for a minute for the clarification of MARKET STRUCTURE.

While we can easily identify support/resistance zones on the chart, a correct identification of a change in *market structure* is not a simple task at all. In the above examples, I just identify an uptrend or a downtrend based on one basic characteristic. In fact, it is an effective way of explaining the malfunctions of candlestick patterns. Yet, a reliable confirmation of a market structure's break should be based on specific components, which will, in turn, help to determine appropriate entry and stop levels.

As market structure is a concept that has been mentioned in a trading material for the first time here, let me break it down into smaller criteria for you to grasp and best apply in your trading.

Market Structure – Uptrend To Downtrend

To begin with, a reliable confirmation of a change from an uptrend to a downtrend must include:

- Firstly, the market fails to create a higher high. This (not any other criterion) should be the very first evidence on signaling the tiredness of buyers on pushing the price higher.
- Prices break the last low in the initial uptrend.
- The market successfully creates two lower highs in the new downtrend, and the second high must not be higher than the last low in the previous uptrend.

To avoid any obscurity, let's take a look at an ideal market structure's change from an uptrend to a downtrend:

From the example, we can see:

Firstly, the market fails to create a higher high than A. In fact, C could be at a same or lower price than A. It would be preferred if C is located lower than A.

Secondly, prices break the X line, which is drawn from the last low in the uptrend (B), creating a lower low at D.

Last but not least, the market successfully creates two lower highs at C and E, in which E is not higher than B.

Now, let's come up with a popular false pattern that you should watch out for:

In this example, the third criterion is not satisfied. Although the market forms two lower lows than A (at C and E), the second lower high (E) is higher than the last low during the uptrend (B). This may pave the way for another retest at F before an advance. In these cases, it is advisable to stay on the sideline and watch for other reliable market signals.

Market Structure - Downtrend To Uptrend

Similarly, for a reliable change from a downtrend to an uptrend to be confirmed, three following criteria must be met:

- Firstly, the market fails to create a lower low. This (not any other criterion) should be the very first evidence on signaling a tiredness of sellers on dragging the price lower.

- Prices break the last high during the initial downtrend.
- The market successfully creates two higher lows in the new uptrend, and the second low must not be lower than the last high of the previous downtrend.

Although these three signals are opposite to ones when we consider a change from an uptrend to a downtrend, they are all based on the same principle. Thus, for a quick reference, let me call these three above bullet points "*3MS principles*". Later, when I mention about "3MS principles", just understand that I am referring to three conditions for a market structure's change, either from up to down or vice versa.

Now, let's see how an ideal market structure's change from a downtrend to an uptrend looks like:

From the picture:

Firstly, the market fails to create a lower low than A. In fact, C could be at a same or higher price than A.

It would be ideal if C is located a little bit higher than A as in the picture.

Secondly, prices break the last high during the previous downtrend (B), forming a higher high at D.

Last but not least, the market successfully creates two higher lows at C and E, in which E is not lower than B.

Similar to the previous examples, you should be careful when the 3MS principles are not fully satisfied, especially the last criterion. Let's take a look at the below picture:

In this example, problems arise. Although the market forms two higher lows than A (at C and E), the second higher low (E) is lower than the last high during the uptrend (B). This may pave the way for another retest at F before a plummet. In these cases, it is better not enter any trade and to wait for more market signals.

For me, I always trade when there are all three 3M principles present in the chart. This is not to refute a fact that sometimes, we just need two or even one out of the three pieces of evidence for a successful trade. Yet, as I always state, we should be prudent in the Forex market. The more signals we gain for our trades, the better we are at stacking the odds in our favor. I will illustrate this point later in this book.

Coming back to market analysis, I often suggest that the more factors you collect in proving your setups, the more chances of success you will have. In many cases, you can analyze market structure in connection with a trend line, which is, in my opinion, a very powerful method for determining potential market movements.

Let's come up with another example regarding USD/CAD pair.

In this example, we have two daily bearish engulfing patterns not far away from each other. However, just one of them works.

It is ideal you combine with a trend line to see how strong the bearish signal was regarding the second engulfing pattern. Let's take a look at the 4-hour chart time frame, where I often use to determine entry points.

Here it is. Please be noted that the two yellow boxes indicate two daily engulfing bars. First, by using market structure analysis, you can easily explain the first one's failure to drag prices to the below price area, as well as how the second one provided an apparent evidence of selling force dominance.

While the two engulfing patterns are locating at a key resistance area, their voices on telling about market structure's change are different. On applying 3MS principles, it is clear that the first engulfing bar failed to meet all three criteria of a reliable change. Put differently, at the time of the first bar's presence, all three characteristics of the 3MS principles were not met, which accounts for its failure to work that time.

On analyzing market structure's change in the second engulfing bar, we can see it *strongly broke the last low* during the uptrend (D) and then *formed two lower highs* (A and B) in which the second low (B) was located at a lower level than the last low in the uptrend (D). The highest peak during the prior uptrend played as the highest top during the following downtrend. The 3MS principles are fully completed (though the *failure to create a higher high* (forming a top at A) came later than expected).

Moreover, you could see how the second engulfing pattern (the second yellow box) was obviously present during the break of X1 line. This means that the bar itself carried one component of the market structure's break.

All of these account for the reason behind this bar's function on market reversal's angle.

Moreover, by drawing an upward trend line, it is even clearer the first engulfing pattern failed to break the trend line on the 4-hour chart. Conversely, the second engulfing pattern indicated a much stronger selling pressure, breaking the trend line and pulling the price to the below area.

In short, the market structure clearly tells us the correlation between bulls and bears, which side is stronger. Ignoring this may mislead you and result in unexpected losses. In the Forex market, nothing is 100% certain. Hence, the more criteria you have gained through technical analysis, the higher chance you stand on winning trades. This is how you put the odds in your favor.

Chapter 11 Psychology Of Forex Trading

Psychology and trading, most people might think that these factors don't relate to one another. Well, it very well does. As I mentioned earlier, most trading mistakes occur because the traders don't understand the importance of trading psychology. However, most traders don't trade successfully, mainly because of emotional problems. Especially, naïve traders don't handle emotions well, so they don't remain in the market for long. But, it is not something good which is why educating naïve traders is important. Even before they enter the market, it is important to spend the time to learn the market. However, the most common issue with trading is fear. But, fear is commonly seen when the trader moves into the live trading account. But, initially, the temptation is often found in naïve traders. When they enter the market, they enter with the thought of trading as much as possible to make money. Hence, this thought will not let them achieve what they actually should achieve. Therefore, when a trader is tempted to trade, he or she may trade even without analyzing or anticipating the trades.

However, as mentioned fear can also create a lot of issues in a trader's journey. Many traders give up trading completely because of fear. But, the fight or flight reaction is a human thing, that is commonly seen in traders. But actually, this reaction cannot be changed that easily, but of course, traders can handle this reaction wisely. If you study trading psychology, things will become simpler when trading the Forex market. Anyway, when you fear to trade, it will impact your trading behaviors negatively. Most of the time, you will look for a safer method to trade and, perhaps, it is not possible to find safer trading methods in the Forex market.

As you already know, the Forex market involves a lot of risks, so as traders, you must learn to handle them carefully. For example, when you enter into a trade, your instincts point out the chances of losing and you will eventually exit from the trade, and it might have been a profitable trade. So see, your mind has a direct connection to the way you trade.

Even if you have a defined plan, you can still steer away from trading because the power of psychology is immense. You might even become anxious and consider short-term positions because you are afraid to enter into long-term positions even if they seem profitable. Well, yes, fear, greed, and all the other emotions can cause a lot of problems to your trading journey. Hence, you must understand trading psychology. If you do, you will be able to assist those emotions wisely and handle trading successfully. Normally, if you overcome fear, it will be beneficial to your trading journey as well as life.

Typically, traders don't fear the market when they are preparing to enter into a trade, but when the market opens, their emotions play the role. As humans, you can never get rid of emotions because it is a part of humankind. But, you can always learn the methods to control your emotions when excitement is a dangerous emotion when trading the Forex market. When you are excited, you might make mistakes when entering a trade or anticipating market movements. Thus, when you are trading, you have to try to keep your emotions neutral.

Most traders succumb to accept that they are making trading mistakes that are related to psychology. But normally, when people can't accept, denial is the first reaction. Over time, they tend to accept the truth. Just like that, even the naïve traders will learn to accept the truth. However, Forex trading is not only about trading system and strategies. You must accept that mindset is an important part of Forex trading. The way you anticipate the Forex market has a lot to do with trading. Also, only if you understand the trades will you be able to enter into it. Thus, a trader's mindset has a lot to do with trading.

If you look at certain websites that advertise robotic trading systems, you might find trading psychology as an absurd thing. But, remember, those trading systems will not provide benefits as they portray. Nothing is as best as trading manually. You must use your knowledge and skills to trade the market; only then will you be able to trade successfully. Also, those websites are doing their duty to market their product, and if you rely on them and purchase it, you might have to pay them for using their product. Hence, when you come across something like this, make sure to think logically. As a beginner, you must try to settle for a simple yet effective strategy, so that you will be able to trade peacefully.

Anyway, why do you think most naïve traders struggle to make money? You might have seen many people who fail in trading the Forex market. Well, there are many reasons why traders fail, but the major reason is the ones who enter the Forex market don't really know the market. A higher percentage of traders enter into the Forex market by believing the fabricated ads. And it makes them set unrealistic goals. Eventually, they struggle to meet those unrealistic goals and end up quitting trading. But the worst part is that there are traders who quit their day job after they enter the Forex market. Well, it is not a wise move because they must test to check whether trading works for them. Or some other traders believe trading is easy money and no matter how many times I repeat it, some people still believe it is possible. These thoughts create tension and stress, so eventually, the trader becomes emotionally unstable. Thus, when traders trade with an emotionally unstable mindset, they lose money.

So, how can a trader develop a trading mindset? If you want to develop a trading mindset, you need to do your part. It is important to put the required effort to accomplish what you are looking for. Well, you can't build a trading mindset that quickly because you have to learn and accept the Forex market as it is. If you try to deny facts about the Forex market, you will not be able to create a trading mindset.

You must start developing your trading mindset by handling the risks in trading. First of all, understand that risk management isn't for one trade, preferably it is applicable for all the trades that you enter into. You must make sure to calculate the risk for each trade before you enter into it. When you are managing risks, certain emotions might try to confuse you, but you must not let it happen. Once you start handling your emotions wisely, you will be able to manage trades also. However, the simplest way to control emotion when managing risks is to risk ONLY the amount that you can lose. You must create a mindset that enters into a trade while knowing the probability of losing trade. If you follow this, you will be able to remain in the trading world for a long time. But, it takes practice and patience to create a trading mindset that accepts losses. Also, you must master your trading edge. No matter what trading strategy you are using, you must know it completely to trade successfully.

And, remember, overtrading will never create profits. Instead, overtrading will blow all your hard-earned money. You must trade only when you actually see a profit signal. Don't try to trade just because you feel like trading. Or don't try to guess trade because that doesn't work in Forex trading. If you overtrade, it can be challenging to stop, and you'll become an emotional trader.

If you want to build a trading mindset, you must have an organized mindset. So, basically, when you have an organized mindset, you will think about the trading plan, journal, and much more. You must accept the fact that Forex trading is a business. Hence, don't try to gamble in the market. When you are making trading decisions, you must remain calm and steady; only then will you be able to think clearly.

But then, after you build a trading mindset, you must not let emotions play their role. However, the most common emotions that you must avoid are:

Euphoria

You might argue that euphoria is good, yes, it is good. But when it is related to the Forex market, it becomes dangerous. For example, if a trader wins a few profitable traders, he or she might become confident when trading the next trade. Well, it is good to feel confident when entering the next trade, but feeling overly confident is not a good thing. When traders become overly confident, they don't watch or study the market as they did before. The consecutive profitable trades should not get into your mind and increase the level of confidence. When trading Forex if you are overconfident, you will not be able to accept the loss if the trade doesn't react the way you wanted. Hence, it is better to remain calm even if you make profits continuously.

Fear

Most traders who enter the market with no knowledge about trading tend to fear the market. Also, some traders might fear because they cannot effectively trade using any specific strategy. However, usually, when a trader continuously experiences losses, he or she may tend to fear to trade. Perhaps, it is understandable because losing hard-earned money isn't easy. But, you can avoid the mistake of risking more than the amount that you are comfortable with. Most naïve traders don't follow this rule even if we keep repeating it. If fear persists, you will not be able to trade better trades or become successful. It has the power to keep you away from good trades as well. Hence, try to overcome fear by limiting the amount you risk in trading. For the naïve traders, start your journey on a demo account without directly entering the live account. If you do so, you'll be able to learn to control emotions.

Greed

You might have heard that people say only bulls and bears make money, but pigs get slaughtered. If you don't understand what it means, it means greed. If you are greedy, you will not be able to make money in the market. Instead, you will be kicked out of the market. Mostly, traders become greedy when they don't have self-discipline. Most traders make quick decisions when the market shows profitable trade signals, but it is not recommended. Instead, you must be calm and collected. Take some time to understand the market, focus on the risk ratio, set a plan, and then enter into the trade. Also, remember, if you are risking more than what you are ready to lose, it apparently shows your level of greed to make money. Thus, you must overcome greed if you don't want to lose your account.

Revenge

This is one of the funny behaviors of traders because what is the point in revenging the market? For the Forex market, you are just one amongst the millions, and it doesn't make sense. However, if you are trying to revenge trade just because you lost a few trades, remember, this might lead to further losses. When you are emotional, you will not be able to make wise decisions. Hence, you must wait for some time until your mind is stable and ready to trade.

So, when learning the psychology of trading, you might find it exciting. But, success can decide when you take these things into practice. You don't have to try these tips and ideas on the live account, instead use the demo account. The Forex market is one of the best markets because it has provided solutions for almost all the issues. So, as traders, if you solve your personal trading issues, you will be able to become a successful trader. But how to succeed in trading?

Chapter 12 Tips For Success

Keep the risk in mind

Before you go ahead and make the decision to ultimately pull the trigger on any potential currency trade you are currently considering, the first thing you are going to want to go ahead and make sure that you know how likely you are to get your money back as well as actually turn a profit. This is why it is always so important to analyze the data that you gather as there is no other way of determining the mood the market is in which means essentially going into a trade just to gamble, and there are better ways to gamble than through the forex market. Additionally, you will want to know when to go ahead and cut your losses and having a clear idea of the overall level of risk will make this easier to determine as well.

With a clear idea of what sort of risk is going to be required for the trade in question, you will then have more tools at your disposal when it comes time to actually mitigate the risk that you have found, or at least to decrease it as much as possible. Ensuring that the odds of actually turning a profit are in your favor means setting a tight stop loss and not letting your emotions get in the way in the heat of the moment. The point that you start a trade and the point that you set your stop loss at can be considered the maximum amount of risk you are accepting for a given trade.

It is important to always determine the acceptable amount of risk you can handle before you actually make the trade, when your emotions are of a nominal concern. If you wait to set a stop loss until after the trade is already in progress, then you run the risk of letting your emotions cloud your better judgement and losing profits in the process. If you feel the need to change your stop loss coming on then you are going to want to take a moment and consider exactly what it is you are thinking about doing and if it is something that you would consider if you were just getting in at that moment. With a few moment's consideration, your answer should be clear.

To keep your emotions from getting the better of you, prior to going into each trade you are going to want to keep in mind the point that you will always get out when you are happy with your profits, no matter what. When it comes to maximizing your profits, a stopping point is just as important as a good stop loss point. You may be tempted to stay in as long as possible in an effort to squeeze the most profit out of a good trade as possible, but this will lose you more than it will make you in the long run, guaranteed. Instead, the right choice is to cash out half of your holdings and then pick a new point further up so that you protect your profits while also maximizing them.

Finally, regardless of how much of a sure thing a specific trade may appear to be, you need to get in the habit of never investing more than you can afford to lose in a single trade. This means that if you start with $5,000 that you can invest in the forex market then you never want any single trade to cost you more than $100. This is what is known as the 2 percent rule and it is crucial to remaining financially solvent while investing in forex, especially when you are just starting out. While you will likely come up against moments where you want nothing more than to buck this trend, especially when you are riding high on a quality pair, sticking with it is what separates successful forex traders from amateurs. If you can't afford to lose it, don't put it in the pot, it is as simple as that.

Trade with the right mindset

If you ever hope to stick around the market long enough to think of yourself as an expert trader, there are several skills you are going to need to become very adept at using. First and foremost, this means always trading with a cool head, no matter what. When you are trading, your goal should be to be as emotionless and robotic as possible. The only thing that matters when you are trading is the numbers and if you worry about anything else while doing so, you are doing it wrong. Trading in the forex market successfully often means having the ability to make split second decisions, something that just can't be done if you let your emotions get in the way.

Understanding the fact that your emotions are only getting in the way and acting on that fact are two extremely different things. The first emotion that you are going to need to focus on banishing is anger. It can be easy to get angry when a trade that appears as though it is going to be a sure thing suddenly turns sideways, but a more effective use of that time is to instead immediately do what is required to minimize the losses, rather than standing there yelling at them. Aside from anger, the most common emotion that you are likely to come across is going to be fear. It can be easy to become afraid, especially if you broke the 2 percent rule and invested too heavily in a single pair; that doesn't mean it is productive, however, and indeed it can be even more dangerous than anger as it can be paralyzing as well. To prevent this from happening you will need to train yourself to push the emotion aside and act on the facts if you ever hope to find real success in the forex market.

Chapter 13 FAQs On Forex Trading

It is obvious that you will have a few questions pop up when you take up a new topic. In this chapter, we will look at some of the most common questions that get asked on the topic of forex trading and answer them to help you understand it better.

Is The Forex Trade Lucrative?

Yes. Forex trading is a lucrative business. You will have the chance to make a lot of money if you understand how exactly to play. We looked at the basic concepts and strategies that you need to employ when you choose the currencies to trade in. Once you choose the best pair, you can easily make a lot of money from it. You have to remain alert and attentive, and that will help you in a big way. You can make thousands of dollars a year by indulging in forex trading.

Should I Be Commerce Literate For It?

No. You don't necessarily have to be commerce literate for it. You also don't have to have any relevant experience in the stock market in order to invest in forex trading. You will be able to start from scratch and make it big in the world of currency investments.

The currency market welcomes everyone with open arms and does not really discriminate. It will not know who is a beginner and who is an expert and will treat everyone the same way. So don't think of your lack of knowledge or experience as a drawback to trade in the stock market.

What About Bid/ Ask, Spread, Etc.?

Bid/ask and spread are all terminologies that you should acquaint yourself with before you start investing. These are common terms that are used across all stock market trades and are not unique to just forex trade. Once you understand what these terms stand for you can easily start trading in forex. You can go through a glossary of all these terms and understand each carefully.

How Much Money Should I Invest?

That is completely up to you. When you open an account to trade in forex, the company might ask you to deposit a certain sum. This sum can be $100 or $250 depending on the company. You don't have to use up all of the amount to invest and can allow some of it to remain back in the account. You might have to maintain a certain minimum amount which cannot be used or invested and will make for a buffer in case you are unable to pay for any of the investments that you have already made. There are people who use as less as $10 to make thousands of dollars of profit.

Can I Trade On My Own?

Yes. You can independently trade in the forex market. You don't have to rely on others to do it for you. It follows a very simple process where you type in the name of the currencies and also type in the amount. Once it is approved, you will be given your currency. You then hold it until you wish to sell it again. You can continue with this process for as long as you like. There is no limit on how much you can buy and sell. If at the very beginning you find it tough to indulge in this process then you can take the help of an expert to get started with it.

Can I Trade Over The Phone?

Yes. You can trade over the phone. You need to call your broker and ask him to buy you the certain currencies. You can also have the currency buying software installed on your phone and use it to buy and sell your currencies. It is really simple and will help you trade in currencies on the go.

Why Do The Currency Prices Fluctuate?

There are many factors that contribute towards the fluctuation in the currency prices. There are economic and political causes that affect the prices and cause it to change. There are also other geographic and business-related causes that can cause the currency prices to vary. There is just no telling what will end up influencing the prices of the currencies and will entirely depend on the current events.

Can I Have My Account Funded?

Yes. You can have your account funded by someone else. They will have to directly add the money to your account in order for you to invest it. But you have to show evidence that they have willfully added in the money into your account for you to use in forex. There is no limit on the amount that can be transferred to your account.

Can I Withdraw All Profits?

Yes. You can withdraw the entire amount that you get as profit from your forex trade. But you might have to leave behind a certain amount that is seen as the minimum balance that needs to be maintained. You have to leave that much behind and ensure that you don't invite any unnecessary fines. Some companies might not even have this minimum balance scheme, and you can easily withdraw all the money at once.

Will I Get Possession Of The Foreign Currencies?

Yes and no. It depends on the time that you wish to hold the currency. If the time exceeds the 5-day limit, then you might have to take possession of the currency. If you are indulging in intra-day trading, then you will not have to take physical possession of it.

These form the different FAQs that get asked on the topic and hope you had yours answered successfully.

Conclusion

Forex trading is not for everyone. You should never trade what you cannot afford to lose. In addition, you should be committed to keeping your emotions out of your trading decisions while making smart decisions based on facts.

If Forex trading is for you, then it is important to set realistic expectations. Even the very best traders like Warren Buffet only increased their portfolio by 20 percent a year while most hedge fund managers are thrilled to grow their portfolios by 10 percent a year.

There are many approaches to Forex trading. Your personality, your available time and your ability to read market indicators all play important factors in determining the best approach for you. Regardless of your approach, however, it is important to think before you trade as statistics show that the best way to lose money in Forex trading is to trade too often.

DAY TRADING FOR BEGINNERS

THE FUNDAMENTAL BIBLE OF MARKETS. HOW TO FIND THE RIGHT MINDSET TO MAKE MONEY WITH THE BEST STRATEGIES RELATED TO INVESTING IN FOREX, FUTURES & OPTIONS TO MAKE A LIVING

Description

With the millions of people who exchange dollars in the online trading market, any investor should understand that there is a huge potential worth taking advantage of in trading. One important question that new traders should ask themselves is whether trading the right activity for them.

Before you engage in trading, you should have the right reasons why you need to trade. In this case, it could be that you want to grow your capital and open a thriving business. Also, you might be willing to trade for the benefit of gaining experience out of it. Depending on the reasons that you have in mind, they should motivate you in trading. This means that you will end up trading without any regrets if things fail to work out as planned.

You will need a sober mind to succeed in day trading. Unfortunately, there are common mental errors which could affect how well you perform in your trading activity. For instance, if you lack confidence in your plan, how do you expect to stick to it? You have to believe that your plan will lead you to make profits that you anticipate. This mentality will develop a positive attitude about the whole trading activity.

Therefore, you will have all the reasons to be disciplined and stick to your plans no matter the circumstances.

Most importantly, you should always remember that there is a lot to learn from day trading. It doesn't matter whether you succeed or fail in day trading; once you begin trading, there are important real-life lessons that you can take home. You will be in a better position to make more informed decisions.

This book gives a comprehensive guide on the following:

- What is day trading?
- Dos and Don'ts of Day Trading
- Personalizing Your Day Trading Plans
- Finding and Picking Stocks and Trading Strategies
- Demand and Supply and Market Types
- Developing Your Day Trading Strategy
- Trading Psychology
- Support or Resistance Trading
- Fibonacci Trading Strategy
- Finding Entry and Exit Points
- Portfolio Diversification
- Managing Risk in Trading ... AND MORE!!!

Introduction

While there will obviously be some differences when day trading in different markets, there are always going to be a number of steps that are the same. First, you will need to locate an underling asset that you are interested in trading based on your research which should be based on either fundamental or technical analysis. Second, you will need to decide if it aligns with your personal trading plan as just because a trade is potential profitable doesn't mean it is going to be the right choice for you, right now. From there, assuming you are still interested in making the trade, you can then take a position that you believe will soon be profitable based on the current state of the market. Finally, you will do the same thing around 100 times a day.

Pros and cons of day trading

While the above description might make it sound as though day trade is relatively straightforward, the fact of the matter is that it is an extremely complex process requiring the successful use of a variety of tools and skills that not everyone will be able to follow through on reliably. As such, this list of pros and cons should make it easier for you to determine if this type of trading is one that you are interested pursuing in the long-term in search of your ultimate financial goals.

Pros: The biggest pro when it comes to day trading is the potential for gain when everything goes according to plan. The average successful day trader tends to buy a large number of shares at a time to ensure that they stand to make a serious profit from even an extremely small amount of movement. Additionally, they have the potential to work for themselves, only trading when they feel the urge or when the market is in a place that is too good to pass up.

Another major benefit to day trading for certain types of traders is the amount of excitement they can expect to see on a daily basis. As they only ever trade in the absolute shortest timeframes, the average day trader sees far more action than most other types of traders would in the same amount of time. What's more, day trading provides those who are up to the challenge with the opportunity to face off with many of the best traders in the world, dozens, if not hundreds of times each day. If you are the sort of thrill seeker who is sure to appreciate a good spike of adrenaline then day trading might be for you.

Another benefit to day trading is that you can teach yourself as easily as you can pay someone else to teach you what to do, making it one of the few ways you can get a job in the financial sector with a formal education. As long as you are willing and able to put in the time and dedicated enough to see it through to the end, then there is no reason you can't acquire the skills you need on your own and then hone them through countless hours of practice.

Cons: The biggest downside to day trading has to do with the wide variety of costs associated with being able to do so successfully. As they are dealing with very small amounts of movement, day traders need a sizeable amount of trading capital just to get off the ground. An amount of around $20,000 should be enough to let you get started in a truly productive fashion. Beyond that, the number of daily trades being made means that the costs paid in commission are going to be far higher than with most other types of trading.

Not only that but due to the high number of shares that come along with the average trade in this field, the potential for loss if a trade turns against you can be quite significant as well. In fact, statistically speaking, day trading is the most difficult type of securities trading to make a profit from in any sort of reliable fashion. In fact, a majority of new day traders experience mostly losses for at least the first month, and only about 30 percent move on from that state to be able to reliably turn a profit.

What's more, the monetary issues aren't the only barriers to entry either, and one of the biggest is the fact that the average amateur day trader is generally competing against professional organizations with a cadre of traders at their disposal and pockets that are extremely deep. As such, if you want to hope to chance of entering the market successfully then you will need to be prepared for what you are up against. Finally, many brokerages will simply not let you day trade in any way shape or form until you have already proven that you are capable of trading in a competent fashion on a more manageable scale to start.

In addition to these issues, the fact that the average day trader is self-employed means that it will simply not be the right choice for those who don't have the internal fortitude to put in the required work without having a boss standing over your shoulder ensuring that they are doing all that is needed for them to be successful. What's more, the average day trader has to fend for themselves when it comes to things like health insurance, a steady retirement plan or even a steady paycheck.

Chapter 1 What is day trading?

The stock market is a vast place and there are millions of trades that take place all over the world, within a single day. There are both buyers and sellers in the market and they will all have the same motive in mind; to increase their wealth potential.

Of all these trades, not everything will be of the same nature. Some will be long-term investments and some short. Long-term investments refer to those that are held for a long period of time. They are preferred by those who are not in a hurry to make money. Short-term investments on the other hand are those that are liquidated within a short period of time. They are not meant to be held for a long time, as the owners will be interested in disposing them off early.

Short-term investments can be of many types based on the time that they are held. Some can be held for a month, some for a week and some will be disposed off on the same day. This book will focus on the last option.

Better known as Intraday trading, day trading is one of the most preferred ways to trade in the stock market. Preferred mostly by those willing to part with their investment within a single day and realize a profit, or loss, from.

Intraday traders are interested in realizing a profit by capitalizing on the difference in the rates of these securities as opposed to long-term investors who will be in it for the Dividends.

Intraday trading has the capacity to help you attain a big leverage, as the rate of return on your investments can be quite high. However, it can also go the other way and cause you to lose out on a lot of money owing to poor investments. It is up to you to make the right choices and invest your money wisely.

Chapter 2 Dos and Don'ts of Day Trading

Dos of day trading

Risk capital

You have to understand that the stock market is a very volatile place and anything can happen within a matter of a few seconds. You have to be prepared for anything that it throws at you. In order to prepare for it, you have to make use of risk capital. Risk capital refers to money that you are willing to risk. You have to convince yourself that even if you lose the money that you have invested then it will not be a big deal for you. For that, you have to make use of your own money and not borrow from anyone, as you will start feeling guilty about investing it. Decide on a set number and invest it.

Research

You have to conduct a thorough research on the market before investing in it. Don't think you will learn as you go. That is only possible if you at least know the basics. You have to remain interested in gathering information that is crucial for your investments and it will only come about if you put in some hard work towards it. Nobody is asking you to stay up and go through thick texts books. All you have to do is go through books and websites and gather enough information to help you get started on the right foot.

Diversification

You have to stress on diversification in your portfolio. You don't want all the money to go into the same place. Think of it as a way to increase your stock's potential. You have to choose different sectors and diverse stocks to invest in. you should also choose one of the different types of investments as they all contribute towards attaining a different result. Diversification is mostly seen, as a tool to cut down on risk and it is best that you not invest any more than 5% in any one of the securities.

Stop loss

You have to understand the importance of a stop loss mechanism. A stop loss technique is used to safeguard an investment. Now say for example you invest $100 and buy shares priced at $5 each. You have to place a stop loss at around $4 in order to stop it from going down any further. Now you will wonder as to why you have to place the stop loss and undergo one, well, by doing so, you will actually be saving your money to a large extent. You won't have to worry about the value slipping further down and can carry on with your trade.

Take a loss

It is fine to take a loss from time to time. Don't think of it as a big hurdle. You will have the chance the convert the loss into a profit. You have to remain confident and invested. You can take a loss on a bad investment that was anyway not going your way. You can also take a loss on an investment that you think is a long hold and will not work for you in the short term. Taking a few losses is the only way in which you can learn to trade well in the market.

These form the different dos of the stock market that will help you with your intraday trades.

Don'ts of day trading

No planning

Do not make the mistake of going about investing in the market without a plan in tow. You have to plan out the different things that you will do in the market and go about it the right way. This plan should include how much you will invest in the market, where you will invest, how you will go about it etc. No planning will translate to getting lost in the stock market, which is not a good sign for any investor.

Over rely on broker

You must never over rely on a broker. You have to make your own decisions and know what to do and when. The broker will not know whether an investment is good for you. He will only be bothered about his profits. If he is suggesting something, then you should do your own research before investing in the stock. The same extends to emails that you might receive through certain sources. These emails are spams and meant to dupe you. So, don't make the mistake of trusting everything that you read.

Message boards

You have to not care about message boards. These will be available on the Internet and are mostly meant to help people gather information. But there will be pumpers and bashers present there. Pumpers will force people to buy a stock just to increase its value and bashers will force people to sell all their stocks just because they want the value to go down. Both these types are risky, as they will abandon the investors just as soon as their motive is fulfilled. So you have to be quite carful with it.

Calculate wrong

Some people make the mistake of calculating wrong. They will not be adept at math and will end up with wrong figures. This is a potential danger to all those looking to increase their wealth potential. If you are not god at calculating, then download n app that will do it for you or carry a calculator around to do the correct calculations. The motive is to make the right calculations and increase your wealth potential.

Copy strategies

Do not make the mistake of copying someone else's strategies. You have to come up with something that is your own and not borrowed from someone else. If you end up borrowing, then you will not be able to attain the desired results. You have to sit with your broker and come up with a custom strategy that you can employ and win big.

These form the different don'ts of the stock market that will help you keep troubles at bay.

Chapter 3 Personalizing Your Day Trading Plans

While we have discussed some of the trading strategies that I found to work best for me, there's still a chance that they may not be the best ones for you, though they're good places to start. As you become more experienced with day trading, you'll probably have to tweak these strategies or revamp them, depending on your day trading results.

Regardless, the best day trading plans are those that are most suited to your personality and your goals. In this chapter, let's take a look at some of the important things you'll need to consider when personalizing your day trading strategies or plans.

Your Strengths and Weaknesses

To optimize your day trading plans' chances of helping you accomplish your goals, it must be one that you can actually use. By this, I mean your day trading strategy should be one that's commensurate to your current level of trading or investing experience. That's why if you remember, I encouraged you to practice on your chosen trading platform's simulator first before day trading for real.

Remember that day trading is a very fast-paced activity and as such, it requires very quick decision making. And you can only make wise and quick trading decisions if you have enough experience and skill.

If you're not the type of person who can easily make quick decisions under pressure, then go for simpler day trading plans like moving averages, which allow longer decision-making periods and provide clearer entry and exit points. If you're very comfortable with making such decisions and have already gained enough experience and skills through practice, you can use the more advanced strategies.

Your Non-Trading, Personal Circumstances

Creating a generally successful trading plan, you'll also need to factor things outside of day trading that may affect your ability to execute such plans effectively. These may be personal circumstances or situations such as lack of fast internet connection, working a day job, or going through personal challenges. I'm not saying that you should only adopt strategies or plans that will not be affected by such circumstances. I'm just saying that you must take into consideration these things so that you can anticipate challenges they may face and proactively develop solutions to address them, should they arise.

Your Risk Appetite

Your maximum position size and maximum trading amount, both of which are crucial components of any day trading plan, must not be above and beyond your personal risk appetite or tolerance. If you take positions or trade amounts that are greater than what you're comfortable risking, your chances of trading based on strong emotions like fear or anxiety will be very, very high. It's because your trading more than what you feel you're capable of losing without any major impact on your personal finances.

So, how do you estimate your personal risk tolerance or appetite? One way is to get five percent of your maximum trading capital or equity and make this your single position-taking limit if you have no clear idea of your risk appetite just yet.

Another way to determine your risk appetite is to determine how much time can you really devote to day trading on a daily basis. The less time you can devote to day trading daily, the higher your risk appetite should be because less time means fewer opportunities to monitor and time your day trades optimally.

Another way to determine risk appetite is to ask yourself: How much money can I lose comfortably? Not that you're day trading to make money but the truth is, you'll expose yourself to risk of losing trades, too. Even the best veteran day traders still have losing trades, but the difference is that their total day trading profits are much greater than their day trading losses.

Chapter 4 Finding and Picking Stocks and Trading Strategies

In this chapter, we get down to the actual work of day trading. We will cover how to read the market by discussing the types of charts used by day traders and how to read them. We'll also discuss strategies for picking stocks and what to look for in stocks for day trading. Finally, we'll cover the most common trading strategies and how to execute them.

Reading the Market

We've already discussed charts and charting software in passing. Now you need to know how to read the charts your software or your broker provide to you. There's three basic types of charts you're likely to look at when you're reading the market: line charts, bar charts, and "candlestick" charts.

Line Charts: line charts are the simplest type of chart you are likely to use while day trading. A line chart tracks only the closing prices for your selected time interval and will display as a jagged line from left to right. This is the type of chart you are probably most familiar with outside of the world of trading, and it provides the least information of the common chart types. However, many traders still use line charts for certain trading strategies. Since a line chart is less cluttered, it can make inflection points in the market more obvious to the eye and can be useful for drawing lines to identify ranges or trends.

Bar Charts: bar charts, also known as OHLC bar charts or HLC bar charts, include information on the open (O), high (H), low (L), and close (C) price of an asset over a given time interval. The chart will appear as a series of horizontal lines following the same sort of jagged line you would see in a simple line chart, with a small line jutting from each side at the open and close. There's a lot of information in these charts, so it may take quite a bit of practice to get used to reading them.

Open: the open on a bar chart is the opening price for the time interval and shows on the chart as a small line sticking out of the left side of the bar.

High: the high price during the interval is indicated by the top of the bar.

Low: the low price for the interval is indicated by the bottom the bar.

Close: the closing price for the interval shows as a small line sticking out of the right side of the bar.

Direction: you can tell the direction of the market during the interval by comparing the positions of the opening and closing prices for the interval. If the open is higher, the market is moving down. If the close is higher, the market is moving up.

Candlestick Charts: candlestick charts contain the same information as bar charts but presented in a different fashion that many traders find easier to read. At a glance, the candlestick chart will look similar to a bar chart, but more colorful. Each time interval will display as a colored bar (the "body" of the candle), red or green, with a line (the "tail") extending some distance above and below the body of the candlestick. Here's how the information is represented:

High: the high price for the interval is indicated by the top of the tail above the candle.

Low: the low price for the interval is indicated by the bottom of the tail below the candle.

Open: the opening price for the interval is indicated by the bottom of the body of the candle.

Close: the closing price for the interval is indicated by the top of the body of the candle.

Direction: the direction of the market is indicated by the color of the body of the candle - red if the market is moving down, green if the market is moving up.

Chart Parameters: when generating a chart, you will need to pick the interval that will be represented by each point in your chart. The interval could be based on time, "tick", volume, or price range.

A chart generated by time is the most intuitive, and will generate a new bar, candle, or point based purely on the passage of time - even if very few or even no transactions occurred during the interval. This is the most useful way to generate a chart if you are looking to see how a stock or asset performs in real time.

A chart generated by "tick" uses an interval based on a set number of transactions. For example, if you generate a 200-tick chart, the graph will produce a new point every time 200 transactions occur. This can be useful for comparing trends between stocks with different levels of activity.

A chart generated by volume will generate intervals based on a set number of shares exchanged.

You will also need to define the scope of the chart. Depending on your strategy, you may want to look at a chart for the entire trading day, or a chart that covers the last minute.

Trend lines: most trading software allows you to draw your own trend lines on charts or will have options for displaying trends such as the simple moving average automatically. While you can get a lot of information just from your chart without trends, most of the decisions you will make in executing your trading strategy will come from looking at trend lines.

Picking Stocks

Now that you know the basics of reading the market and looking for trends, you're ready to learn about how to pick stocks for day trading. The type of stock you will be looking for depends on a lot of different factors, and you may be looking for different types of stocks to fit different trading plans and different trading strategies. We'll cover this topic in three parts: (1) things you should look for every stock you plan to trade while day trading; (2) some broad-based picking strategies for different trading plans; and (3) the distinct characteristics of stocks that are suitable for specific day-trading strategies.

(1) Things to Look for in Every Stock You Plan to Day-Trade: while what you're looking for will be different depending on what strategy you're planning to execute, there are a couple things you should always be looking for when picking stocks.

The first is volume: you should always look for stocks that have a high level of daily activity. If you buy into a stock with insufficient volume, you can easily find yourself stuck - the asset price won't move enough for you to take profit and you'll lose out on other trading opportunities until you can move out of your position. Typically, you should be looking for a stock that has an average daily volume of at least 1 million shares.

The second is volatility: you are looking for stocks that will move enough in a typical day for you to make a profitable trade. Set your stock filter to look for stocks with an average day range above 5% over the last 50 days. It's important to remember that volatility is not necessarily the massive up or down swings that can follow breaking news - it can also be the regular and constant turbulence that exists in all exchange traded markets.

(2) Broad Strategies for Picking Stocks: you need a broad strategy for picking stocks beyond simply looking for the desirable characteristics discussed in this chapter. How you go about researching and picking stocks depends on how much time you have available to trade and how much research you are willing to do.

If you don't have much time to trade, you may wish to specialize. That is, pick one or two stocks, or a single industry sector (such as healthcare), and only trade in those stocks or that sector. This lets you become an expert in those stocks: you know how they usually behave, where the opportunities will be, and what news events will cause swings and how. This means that you don't have to spend a lot of time sifting through charts or learning the basic facts about new companies - you already know what's likely to happen. A popular way to execute this strategy is to target an ETF, such as the S&P 500 SPDR (Ticker symbol SPY). Specializing like this works well with a range-trading or "trade the news" strategy.

If you're looking for a little bit more flexibility, you might choose to pick a set of stocks to trade each week. Each weekend, run a stock screener to identify a set of 2-4 stocks that have good volume and volatility for your trading strategy. After you have picked your stocks for the week, trade those stocks, and only those stocks following your trading plan. If you've achieved good results, you could choose to remain on the same set of securities for multiple weeks in a row. This strategy is suitable for a trader who has a little more time to dedicate to day trading but isn't prepared to trade full time.

If you're looking to pursue a full-time career as a day trader, you might choose to run a stock screener every single day. This is probably what you want to be doing if you are pursuing a momentum strategy - as you will be trying to identify stocks that have a strong current trend, instead of trying to capitalize on small movements caused by underlying volatility. Obviously, this strategy is very time consuming, and may require additional tools to execute effectively.

(3) Distinct Characteristics Suitable for Specific Strategies: depending on your strategy, you may be looking for more specific factors than simple volume and volatility.

If you are looking to trade on a momentum strategy, you should look at stocks that are close to 52-week highs and lows. Stocks that have reached extreme price points are more likely to be volatile or to be close to an inflection point that can afford a big trading opportunity.

You may also want to keep an eye out for stocks that have a gap against the trend. That is, if you look at your chart of the stock's current price, you'll see that there is a space (a "gap") between the price and the trend-line. This is a good way to identify stocks that have been overbought or oversold, or where the stock price has failed to adjust to breaking news. The moment when the gap closes is the moment when you have an opportunity to make a profitable trade.

Finally, you can set up a scanner to identify specific situations where there is an opportunity to trade based on a specific pattern in the market. One example of this is a method commonly referred to as "sniper" trading, which was originally implemented on the FOREX market.

An Overview of Common Day Trading Strategies

By sticking to your strategy, you maintain a stable level of risk and can reliably make your expected earnings goals. Here's a quick overview of some of the most common strategies for setting entry points and price targets.

Scalping: Scalping is one of the most common strategies for day trading, and with good reason - it's incredibly simple. When you are using a scalping strategy, your target price is essentially whatever price is high enough to make your trade profitable over commission. It's as easy as that: pick your asset, pick your entry point, and sell as soon as it's profitable for you. As always, make sure you have set a stop-loss if you have misjudged the buy and bought into a downward trend.

Fading: In many ways, a fading strategy is the opposite of scalping. When you are scalping, you are looking to profit on an upward trend - while fading, you are looking to profit on a downward trend. Scalping is absurdly simple, while fading requires a fairly high degree of sophistication to be really successful. Here's a basic overview: a trader who is using a fade strategy looks for a stock that has risen very quickly. Having identified a potential trade, the trader shorts the stock. The price target is a predicted low inflection point where buyers begin to step in after profit-takers exit.

This probably seems counter intuitive to a trader starting out, since it requires you to bet a stock that has been on an upward tear is going to fall in the same day. So, here's a quick explanation of the reasoning behind a fade strategy: (1) a stock that has risen very quickly is probably overbought - the price has been driven higher than demand can justify; (2) early buyers are probably ready to start profit taking - you can expect that traders who bought into the trend early are ready to unload stock, dropping the price; and (3) existing buyers may be scared out of purchasing at the current, inflated price - creating an opportunity to short the stock at a point below the peak, but above where the upward trend started.

Fading is a risky strategy, since it requires you to identify a very specific situation - but, as always, higher risk can yield higher rewards than a low-risk strategy like scalping. You may wish to consider a fading strategy after you have gotten comfortable reading the market if you can afford the additional risk.

Momentum Trading: generally speaking, momentum trading is a simple sounding strategy that can get complicated fast. When you are using a momentum strategy, you are looking to identify an existing market trend that you expect to continue for some time. While trading using a momentum strategy, use your tools to look for a consistent upward or downward trend - but not, for example, the sort of extreme upward trend you would be looking for under a pure fading strategy.

If you have identified an upward trend, under a momentum strategy, you buy in while the stock is rising, much like under a scalping strategy. Unlike scalping, however, you aren't looking to sell at the minimum point where you can make a profit. Instead, you're aiming to set your price target at the inflection point where the price will begin to fall. This can be done either by monitoring the current prices and charts and selling as soon as you observe momentum shifting, or by setting a price target at a point where you are making a reasonable profit.

If you have identified a downward trend, you can also short under a momentum strategy. Like a normal fade strategy, you are looking to set your price target at a low inflection point where seller volume will decrease, and buyers will begin to re-enter the asset.

Trading the News: trading the news is a specific form of momentum trading that tries to identify an upward or downward trend before it even begins. If you are looking to execute on this strategy, you will be monitoring news headlines for events that will have an effect on a specific stock, a specific business sector, or even the market as a whole. Your goal is to correctly identify a market trend at the point it begins based on that news. This can allow you to increase your profit margin compared to a normal momentum strategy where you are simply buying into an existing trend.

There are regularly occurring, scheduled events that can be helpful to watch out for when trying to execute a news-based strategy. One example would be a publicly traded corporation's quarterly earnings calls. By listening in on an investor earning call, you can try to ascertain whether a company has done better or worse than it was expected to by market analysts. Depending on earnings performance, this can help you identify an upward or downward trend and set your positions early. Another example would be Federal Reserve meetings - the chairman's comments on the market or interest rates can put the entire market into an upward or downward trend on a dime.

Of course, everyone who is trading - especially the large, institutional investors - keeps an eye on scheduled events like this. This means it's hard to get a jump on the news - and big investors will get trades to go through faster than yours ever can. The real opportunities for profit come from unexpected events, or events whose market consequences aren't immediately obvious. If you think you're smarter than the market, maybe you can identify a rise or fall before it happens by taking in all the news you can find. However, betting on uncertain news or nascent trends is risky, and keep that in mind before you take action on an unusual news item.

Range Trading / Daily Pivots: All of the strategies we've discussed so far are somewhat dependent on market conditions where you can discern clear up or down trends in a given asset. However, you can still make money in a very stable market with the strategy of range trading, by taking advantage of the natural, low level volatility that exists in the market - the "noise" or "turbulence" that is always present. Here's a three-step summary of how to execute a range-based strategy:

(1) Identify the daily range of an asset. Your goal in a range strategy is to identify the daily high and low points of the target asset that are caused by natural market volatility, identifying the points of support and resistance that cause price inflection. The easiest way to do this is to pull up a longer-term chart, such as the 4-hour simple moving average, and draw a horizontal line across matching peaks and troughs. The peaks should exist at the point of resistance, where the asset is overbought and demand cannot sustain a higher price. The troughs should exist at points of support - where the asset is under bought and the supply is insufficient to meet demand at a lower price.

(2) Time your entry so you are buying into the asset when it is priced in the support zone. This is what you expect to be the market low for the day.

(3) Manage your risk. Even though this strategy is looking to take advantage of the predictable volatility in a stable market, you still need to appropriately manage your risk by setting a stop-loss in case you

have misjudged the low and set your price target at the expected zone of resistance.

We'll be taking a closer look at one range strategy, commonly referred to as the "day sniper" strategy in

Chapter 5 Demand and Supply and Market Types

The theory of demand and supply is quite interesting and will help you make the right type of investments.

As you know, every stock has its own demand and supply chain, which determines its value. This demand and supply is subject to market volatility and can be a bit hard to predict.

However, understanding the topic will help you predict stock trends to a large extent.

Demand

The demand refers to how many people are interested in buying the stock. As you know, all stocks and financial securities have a certain demand, which is brought about through people's want. If a certain group of people want a particular stock, then its demand will rise. The important thing here is to know what stock has how much demand. You can assess the same by going through news articles and conducting a small research on the market conditions. If you think there is strong demand for a particular stock, then you can consider buying it.

There are various factors that affect the demand of a stock and some are as follows:

Company profile

The name of the company will play a part in determining its demand. Big companies such as Microsoft and apple will have a high demand for their stocks at all times. However, these can be hit by inflation when their values might drop down. On the other hand, there can be some companies whose stock prices will not drop owing to the consistent demand for their goods. For example, Coca-Cola's stock price might not fall in summer despite inflation, as people will buy them at any cost. So, the profile of a company will play a big role in determining its demand.

News

When favorable news breaks about a company, the demand for its stocks rises. If news about a company's merger breaks out, then people will flock to buy its shares. On the other hand, it is also possible for bad news to affect a stock's price positively. So, any news about stocks might help it value rise in the market.

Tastes/ preferences

People's tastes and preferences vary from season to season and might have a significant impact on the demand for a product. Some will prefer to buy certain stocks only during the summer and some during the winter, some during spring etc. These tastes and preferences are hard to predict but can be analyzed through regular research of the markets.

Investor budget

An investor's budget also has a role to play in the overall demand for a commodity. If the investors have a sizeable amount at their disposal then they are sure to create a market and demand for a particular stock. For example, if a high-end investor picks an upcoming company and invests in bulk, then he will immediately create a demand for the company's stock. So, it will help you understand the amount that particular investors have at their disposal.

Future anticipation

In anticipation of a future event, some investors invest in a particular stock in bulk. This will raise the demand for the stock and make it valuable. This generally happens with undervalued stocks and as soon as somebody does the right calculations, others flock to buy the same.

Despite knowing that reasons such as these can affect the prices of stocks, it is still pretty tough to say for sure, how the demand for a stock will fluctuate.

Supply

The supply of a stock is also decided by the investors. Supply refers to having enough to distribute it to whoever is interested in investing. If there are many people wanting the stock but only limited supply then its value will rise. How high it will rise will depend on how many are in need of it and how many sellers are willing to sell.

Supply of stocks is a very important subject to consider while making stock market investments. You will have the chance to look at the number of buyers and sellers for a particular stock when you create a watch list for yourself. If you see that there are more suppliers and only a few buyers, then the stock's value will drop. On the other hand, if there are more buyers and fewer suppliers, then the value of the stock will rise.

You have to sell stock when there are more buyers, and buy stock when there are more sellers, in order to profit from your investments.

Price of stock

The price of a stock will affect its supply. If the price of a particular stock is too high, then demand for it will be low thereby increasing the supply. On the other hand, if the price is low enough for many people to afford, then its supply will be low and its price will rise. So, it is important to understand the price factor variation in order to predict the supply chain of a particular stock.

Price of other stocks

As you know, there will be many stocks floating in the market belonging to various categories. If the price of a particular stock in a particular category changes, then it will impact the price of other stocks in the same category as well! So, it is important to understand how the price of a particular stock will impact the price of another stock.

Government control

The government has control over many stocks and that can significantly impact its prices. The government has limited, nonetheless, powers to affect both the demand and supply of a stock. So, you might have to read up on news about any such policies against certain companies that might affect its stock's supply.

These form some of the factors that can affect the supply of a stock.

Bullish market

A bullish market is better known as an investor's market. The bullish market is quite ideal as the prices of stocks will be on a steady rise. This makes it a lucrative opportunity for investors to invest money in the market.

The term bullish comes from the word bull. Just like how the bull raises its horns in the air to attack its prey, the market lifts up the stocks and flings them in the air. The bullish market is every investor's dream market.

But remember, even if a bullish market exists, it does not guarantee that each and every stock will remain bullish. Some stocks are not affected by the overall market conditions and will follow a course that they have etched for themselves.

Bearish market

A bearish market is the opposite of a bullish market. A bearish market is one where all the prices of stocks are falling. So, it is better known as a seller's market as people will prefer to sell the stocks out of fear of losing out on money.

The bearish market is dreaded by most investors, as it would be risky to make any investment at such a time. However, contrarians will be eager to buy stocks at such points in time.

The term bearish comes from the word bear. Just like how a bear swoops down to attack its prey, the market swoops down on the stocks.

Bullish bar reversal

The bullish bar reversal is one where the days lowest is lower than the previous day's low and the current price is higher than the previous day's high. As soon as this happens, the situation is called a bullish bar reversal. This type is ideal for a stock, as its price pattern will begin to reverse, which means that it will start getting better for the stock. Investors rejoice when such a pattern occurs.

Bearish bar reversal

Bearish bar reversal is the opposite of the bullish bar reversal. Such a situation arises when today's current price is lower than yesterday's closing price. This means that the price of the stock is on a downward trend. This can be because of many reasons and it is best to wait this period out rather than making hasty decisions.

Chapter 6 Developing Your Day Trading Strategy

For new traders, it would be good news to hear that there are many day trading strategies that one can adopt. You can choose to read books such as this or take courses which would train you on the best strategies which you could adopt. Regardless, it is important to understand that trading can be a DIY career. Most successful traders develop strategies which work for them. As such, building your own strategy should always be part of your consideration. In line with this, you shouldn't be convinced that building your own strategy is a challenging task. In fact, once you get down to business, you will notice that it is pretty straightforward. This chapter will take you through the basics of developing your own day trading strategy. Important steps that will be discussed in detail include the process of selecting a market, defining your entry and exit points, evaluating your strategy and ways to enhance your trading strategy.

Market Selection

With the advent of online trading, this has made it possible to have a wide array of financial instruments that traders can depend on. In this case, individuals can trade on other financial instruments besides stocks, futures, and options. Recently, there have been other trading options including the Foreign Exchange Market (forex), Single Stock Futures (SSF) and Exchange Traded Funds (ETFs).

It is worth pointing out that the existing financial securities have been improved to include electronic contracts of notable commodities such as natural gas, gold, silver, grains, and crude oil. These futures are getting popular each day amongst day traders. It is for this reason that pit-traded commodities have been overtaken by the high volume of mini and electronic contracts.

Essentially, the internet has made it possible to trade on anything. Take, for instance, real estates, it is possible to enter this industry without actually owning any properties. This is made possible through Real Estate Investment Trusts (REITs). To understand how you can select an appropriate market to trade, it is imperative to learn about the different markets individually. There are several markets which you could trade in. However, we'll focus on the most popular including stocks, futures, forex and stock options. These markets will be scrutinized based on capital requirements, leverage, liquidity, and volatility.

Capital Requirements

Of course, one of the main considerations that most traders would bear in mind is the amount of capital that they require to initiate their trading activity. Therefore, it is worth examining the markets based on the amount of capital that you would require to begin day trading. Often, experienced traders will recommend the idea of starting small and growing gradually. This gives a novice trader ample time to learn and master the art of day trading.

Leverage

Another essential factor to mull over is leverage. After understanding how to trade on different markets, a trader could always make the best out of the little capital they are using to trade. In this case, leveraged markets give them the opportunity of maximizing their profits by simply using a small amount of capital. Consequently, the advantage gained in using leverage is that a small account can be developed quickly.

Liquidity

Understanding markets based on liquidity is essential. Focusing on liquid markets warrants that traders circumvent the common market issues of slippage and manipulation. Undeniably, any trader would want to make sure that they receive accurate fills for their orders.

Volatility

Without volatility, it would be impossible to make money from different markets. Therefore, markets have to be moving for people to make money. In relation to this, understanding the most volatile market guarantees that a trader puts their money in viable markets.

By now you must be curious to know how markets vary. The following paragraphs will discuss basic information about the different markets you could turn to out there. Undeniably, knowledge is power. Hence, knowing what to expect from these markets is important for any trader.

Trading in Stocks

The thought of trading in stocks scares away many investors. Individuals who have never traded are terrified by the fact that one can easily lose money with wrong decisions. The reality is, stock trading is a risky activity. However, when approached with the right market knowledge, it is an efficient way of building your net worth.

So, what is a stock? A stock is a share. It is also termed as equity. Basically, it is a financial instrument which amounts to ownership in a particular company. When an individual purchases a stock or shares, it means that they own a portion or fraction of the company. For instance, say a trader own 10,000 shares in a company with 100,000 shares. This would mean that the individual has 10% ownership of the stakes. The buyer of such shares is identified as a shareholder. Therefore, the more shares one owns, the larger the proportion of the company which they own. Every time the value of the company shares rise, your share value will also rise. Similarly, if the value falls, your share value also declines. When a company makes a profit, the shareholders are also bestowed with the profits in the form of dividends.

Preferred stock and common stock are the two main types of stocks you should be aware of. The difference that lies between these stocks is that with common stocks, it carries voting rights. This means that a shareholder has an influence in company meetings. Hence, they can have a say in company meetings where the board of directors is elected. On the other hand, preferred shares lack voting rights. However, they are identified as "preferred" shares or stocks because of their preference over common stocks. In the event that a company goes through liquidation, shareholders with preferred shares will be preferred to receive assets or dividends.

Far from the information provided about the varying kinds of stock, a day trader doesn't necessarily have to understand the difference. Remember, you are only a day trader. Thus, you will only buy shares for a short period before selling them within the same day.

Basing on the factors pointed out above, the stock market could be evaluated as follows.

Capital Requirements

According to the Pattern Day Trading Rule, the minimum brokerage balance you are required to maintain for you to trade in stocks is at least $25,000. Without a doubt, this is a lot of money to start with. Surprisingly, there are tons of traders who began with a lower amount than that. To understand how this rule applies, you need to know what it means to be a pattern day trader. This is the type of trader whereby they execute more than four traders within five business days in their margin accounts.

Leverage

There are two ways of trading in stocks. You could either choose to trade using a margin account or a cash account. With the margin account, it gives a trader the opportunity of buying their stocks on margin. Conversely, with cash accounts, you only buy the stocks for the amount of money present in your account. In other words, you will be trading with a leverage ratio of 1:1.

The notion of trading on margin implies that you will be seeking for funds from your broker. This means that you will be able to buy more stocks far beyond what you can normally afford. To use a margin account, a trader will be required to have at least $2,000 as their starting capital. However, some brokers will demand more. Once your margin account is open, you can get a loan amounting to 50% of the buying price of the stock.

In a real-life example, say you make an initial deposit of $10,000 to your margin account. Since you deposited about 50% of the buying price, it means you are worth twice as much, i.e., $20,000. In other words, your buying power is worth twice what you deposited. Therefore, when you buy stocks worth $5,000, your buying power will reduce to $15,000. Your leverage ratio is therefore 1:2. Traders with a good trading relationship with their brokers could have this ratio increased to even 1:8.

Liquidity

With regards to liquidity, you can be certain that trading in stocks is not a bad idea. There are over 10,000 stocks present in the U.S. stocks exchanges. Most of these stocks are traded on a daily basis. Dealing with these stocks guarantees that you evade the common issues of slippage or manipulation.

Volatility

A trader shouldn't worry about the volatility of the stocks market as they often go through cycles of high and low. This is not a bad thing as a trader simply needs to study when the markets are rising and be wary of instances when markets seem to fall.

Basing on these factors, it would be true to argue that stocks have got good volatility and liquidity. The only issue with stocks is that they have a high capital requirement.

Trading in Forex

Most traders would argue that trading in forex is quite complicated. However, it's not. Just like any other form of trading, you have to stick to the basic rules. In this case, you need to buy when the market is rising and ensure you sell when the market is dropping. Basically, trading in forex involves the process of trading in currencies. In simpler terms, a trader exchanges currency for others based on certain agreed rates. If you have traveled to foreign countries and exchanged your currency against their local currencies, then you should understand how trading in forex works.

At first, it could seem confusing to choose the best currencies, but a trader should simply go for major currencies. Some of the frequently traded currencies include the U.S. dollar, Japanese Yen, European Union Euro, Australian dollar, Canadian dollar, and Swiss franc. An important thing you ought to understand about forex trading is that you need to trade in pairs. This means that when you are buying one currency, you should do this while simultaneously selling another. If you do some digging, you will notice that currencies are quoted in pairs, i.e. USD/JPY or EUR/USD. Below is an image showing how currencies are quoted in pairs.

Source: "What is a Currency Pair? | ALL Forex Infos."

Often, the most traded forex products include:

- USD/JPY

- EUR/USD

- GBP/USD

An important thing to keep in mind with regards to forex trading is that the market is highly volatile. This means that a trader could easily lose a lot of money within a single day. Before venturing into this market, a trader should take time to understand this market in detail.

The forex market could be evaluated as follows.

Capital Requirements

With the number of brokers over the internet, it is relatively easy to begin forex trading. The best part is that different brokers will require varying amounts of capital from you. Hence, you could settle for the best depending on how much you can afford. You can trade in forex with just $1,000 as your starting capital.

Leverage

Typically, leverage in the forex market stands at 1:100. This implies that if you have $2,000 in your trading account, you can trade $200,000. The ratio varies depending on the forex trader you deal with. There are traders who offer leverage of 1:200.

Liquidity

Liquidity is not an issue in the world of forex trading. The only problem is that a trader doesn't have access to real-time volume data simply because the market is decentralized.

Volatility

Considering the fact that there is high leverage in forex trading, it implies that little movement in the market could earn one huge profit. The market's volatility is quite impressive but not as volatile as the stock market.

Basing on these factors, trading in forex is a smart move. A trader can begin trading with as little as $1,000. Also, with the high leverage present in this market, it is easy to earn huge returns with the right moves.

Trading in Futures

Today, most traders prefer to trade in futures due to its associated advantages. Trading in futures is quite flexible and diverse. The good news is that a trader can employ almost any methodology to trade. Some traders shy away from this form of trading due to their limited knowledge about futures. Also, others are discouraged from trading in futures because they think that it is difficult. Well, to some extent, this is true. Comparing trading in futures to trading in stocks, the former is very risky.

There are different forms of futures contracts including currencies, energies, interest rates, metals, food sector futures, and agricultural futures. The best futures contracts you will find in the market are briefly discussed in the following lines.

S&P 500 E-mini

Most traders will fancy the idea of trading in the S&P 500 E-mini because of its high liquidity aspect. It also appeals to most investors because of its low day trading margins. You can conveniently trade in S&P 500 E-mini around the clock not to mention that you will also benefit from its technical analysis aspect. Essentially, the S&P 500 E-mini is a friendly contract since you can easily predict its price patterns.

10 Year T-Notes

10 Year T-Notes is also ranked as one of the best contracts to trade in. Considering its sweet maturity aspect, most traders would not hesitate to trade in this futures contract. There are low margin requirements that a trader will have to meet when trading in 10 Year T-Notes.

Crude Oil

Crude oil also stands as one of the most popular commodities in futures trading. It is an exciting market because of its high daily trading volume of about 800k. Its high volatility also makes the market highly lucrative.

Gold

This is yet another notable futures contract. It might be expensive to trade in gold; however, it is a great hedging choice more so in poor market conditions.

Capital Requirements

The amount of money required to begin trading in futures will vary. Some brokers will require a trader to have about $5,000. However, there are those who would require only $2,000. It is vital for a trader to choose the best broker who is flexible enough to allow them to trade with the little capital they have.

Leverage

Leverage will also vary depending on the type of futures you trade in. The contract value will also have an impact on the amount of leverage that you will have.

Liquidity

Just like leverage, the liquidity aspects of futures will also depend on the futures you are trading. Accordingly, it is important for any trader to regularly check the respective volumes of contracts before trading on them.

Volatility

Futures are volatile. The advantage gained by using high leverage ensures that a trader makes good profit with little price changes in the market.

Keeping the above factors into consideration, futures are a good market to trade. A trader can easily day trade with as little as $2,000. The high leverage ratio will also guarantee that huge profits can be earned.

Trading in Stock Options

Trading in stock options is almost similar to trading in futures. Here, a trader also buys stocks at a pre-established price and later sells when prices rise.

Capital Requirements

Stock options trading also affected by the Pattern Day Trading Rule. This means that your minimum capital requirements will be $25,000. If you engage in more than four trades in a particular week, then you should have about $30,000 in your trading account.

Leverage

Since there are many options to choose from, leverage will vary. The exciting aspect of stock options is that they have high leverage amounts.

Liquidity

With regards to liquidity, stock options are not that liquid. A keen eye on this market reveals that a few options are traded on a regular basis. The low volume of trades is affected by the many options that traders can choose from. Fortunately, stock options are rarely manipulated by the market. Their values are not influenced by supply and demand.

Volatility

Stock options are highly volatile.

From the look of things, stock options have similar pros and cons like trading in stocks. Most new traders will shy away from this form of day trading due to its high capital demands. Its high volatility could be scary to most investors as it makes the market to be unpredictable. This makes this form of trading to be very risky. Therefore, it is not recommended for new traders.

Selecting a Trading Timeframe

Obviously, day trading will require you to choose a timeframe which is less than a day. It is worth noting that the time frame you choose will have an impact on the profit you make. For instance, if you choose a time frame which is less than 60 minutes, the chances are that your profits will be lower. If you trade using a larger time frame, it will increase your chances of getting more profits.

With smaller time frames, you get smaller profits. Nonetheless, the advantage here is that you lower your risks too. This means that if you are new to trading, smaller time frames would be a smart choice. There are pros and cons of short and long-term frames. You simply need to make a choice based on your financial goals. The best way to make your selection is by experimenting with varying timeframes. If your strategy doesn't work with a small timeframe, you could switch to a larger timeframe.

Defining Your Entry Trigger

Besides knowing the right market to trade in, you also need to know when to enter the market. Candlestick and bar patterns are ideal triggers to use. The following image shows you how the triggers will look like.

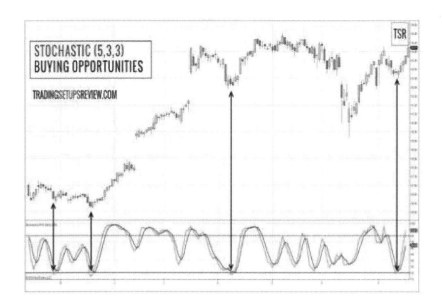

Source: "10 Steps To Creating Your First Trading Strategy."

Knowing Your Exit Trigger

Certainly, with day trading, anything can go wrong. There are times when markets will quickly drop which could affect your returns. Knowing when to exit is therefore important. Essentially, exiting is not just about selling when things don't go your way. You also need to exit when things are going as you expected. This ensures that you make the best out of your investment. You should always set your feelings aside as the market will not always be on your side. Know when to stop at the right times.

Define Your Risk

After knowing when to enter and exit the market, you need to know how much risk you can stomach. The best way of doing this is by position sizing. Position sizing helps you to know the amount of money you are ready to risk. If you double your position size, it means that you will also double your risk. Always ensure that you decide your position size wisely.

Know Your Trading Rules

At the beginning of your trading activity, you will notice that the trading rules you use are simple. In fact, you can memorize some of these rules. Regardless, it is recommended that you write your rules down. This is a practical method which guarantees you maintain discipline throughout your trading activity.

Constantly Improve Your Trading Strategy

Your trading strategy will not always bring you profits. This is normal since your strategy is not static. As you continue trading, you will gain knowledge and experience. Therefore, you need to find a way of also improving your trading strategy. When doing this, you should, however, adjust the strategy gradually and not drastically.

In a nutshell, having a trading strategy is vital for the success of your trading business. You should strive to use a trading strategy which you are comfortable with. With regards to choosing the right market to trade, also ensure that you make your choice based on your financial goals. Don't just pick a market because most people are trading there. Your decision should be based solely on what you think works for you.

Chapter 7 Trading Psychology

Throughout this book, we have discussed how psychological factors affect investors' behavior. Often, investors may choose to act in a cautious manner, while other times investors may choose to go in headfirst.

Also, psychology tends to wreak havoc on the average investor. This is especially true when investors are new to trading and get sucked in by the trends in markets. For instance, new investors may be driven to the siren's song of a "hot" stock. This can lead to a poor decision, in which the stock may rapidly drop in value, leaving the investor with heavy losses.

Other times, investors may be sucked in by a bubble.

A bubble is nothing more than an artificially-inflated price for an asset.

Thus, bubbles form when investors lose sight of the true value of an asset and get taken in by the actions of other investors. Since some investors decide to keep driving the price of an asset up higher and higher, they may end up doing more harm than good to the average investor. The average investor may then become drawn in by the potential of higher gain.

The problem with bubbles is that if the underlying asset is not really as hot is it might seem, then the price of that asset may come crashing back down to Earth. As we saw earlier, asset prices tend to revert back to their trend, unless they meet new resistance levels.

However, determining whether or not an asset has found a new resistance level is hard to predict and is often related to observing its 2-day, 10-day, and 50-day trends. When observing the trend of the price of an asset, it becomes easier to see where the asset's price is headed. As such, an investor may see a downward trend and may figure that a spike in its price is not justified.

On the other hand, the price of an asset may be trending upward, and the dip in its price is just an outlier. So, an investor may choose to do what is known as "buying on the dip". In this case, the investor is banking on the asset's price returning to its mean and therefore a higher price.

In these examples, bubbles are fueled by irrational expectations, which eventually lead to disappointment and potential losses.

Think of real estate markets.

Some cities in North America are in "housing bubbles"—that is, prices getting higher and higher. People are willing to pay more and more to get into a specific area. Those who cannot afford to get into that area are forced to watch from the sidelines.

The problem with housing bubbles is that markets turn on a dime and can leave homeowners with large mortgages while the value of their properties is slashed. This makes it virtually impossible to sell the property, as the sale price may not even cover the remaining amount of the mortgage. This leaves folks stuck with paying for an overpriced home in hopes of the market turning once again.

So, this is why a recurring theme is this book is about doing research and understanding the dynamics of each market.

The Fear of Missing Out

Investors also may run into a phenomenon known as the "fear of missing out". This concept refers to the fact that some folks are so concerned about missing out on opportunities that they choose to "get in on the ground floor" of an investment which may not be going anywhere.

This is especially true with IPOs.

Some investors may miss out on an IPO and regret having missed out. So, they vow to catch the next great IPO. Sure enough, an opportunity pops up. The investor, often without doing their due diligence, decides to go head first into the IPO. They sink considerable amounts of funds into the IPO.

Unfortunately, the IPO was hyped up too much, and investors are lukewarm about it. The IPO gains some traction but then fizzles out. The investor is then disappointed, because they didn't make the amount of money they had hoped to make.

In the best of cases, they might end up making less than expected on the IPO. In the worst of cases, they may end up losing money on the deal. Had the investor been rational, they may have sunk less into the deal or perhaps avoided it altogether.

This is why managing expectations, especially when the fear of losing out is prevalent, is of the utmost importance. Those investors who do not take care with managing their expectations may be tempted to try to hit a home run on a single pitch. While it is possible to hit a home run, it may not be as easy as one might think. Thus, investors need to keep a level head, especially when the market is red hot.

Herd Mentality

One other concept which has been presented earlier in this book is "herd mentality". This is when investors rush into an investment or asset class because everyone else is doing so.

You often hear this with gold and silver. You hear calls of so-called experts claiming the end of the world is near, and you must load up on gold and silver, in order to protect your wealth from Armageddon.

So, investors heed the warnings and go head first into gold and silver without actually studying the valuation mechanism for this asset class. As the price goes up, individual investors become worried that they will miss the boat. They are willing to pay ever-increasing prices.

As the herd begins to gobble up more gold and more silver, others join in, as they fear the worst is yet to come. In the end, the world does not end, and the price of precious metals falls. Investors are left with stockpiles of gold and silver, which fall below the price they originally paid. While this doesn't mean that the metals are worthless, investors will feel cheated and disappointed, because the funds allocated to the purchase of these metals could have been better invested elsewhere.

This example underscores the problem with following the crowd. So, when you see folks running in one direction, always ask yourself what it is they are running from. If you can figure why they are running, it might even be a better investment for you to go where they are running from than to follow the crowd.

Chapter 8 Support or Resistance Trading

Horizontal trade or resistance trade is the preferred negotiation style. The market knows no diagonals. It is reminiscent of the price level – the logic reason of horizontal support or resistance levels. However, the diagonal trend lines are deceiving and open to subjectivity – a reason to not use it as it can lead to bias, fraud, and illusions. Diagonal trend lines are the most unreliable implements. It traces false lines that can affect prices, movement, slope, and implication. For example, having an attempt to buy can make you draw a trend line a little more abruptly.

Support is a level of price where the purchase is solid enough to reverse a bearish trend. When a bearish trend finds resistance, it runs like a top marathon that reaches the finish line and then continuously moving away from it. The resistance level is denoted by a horizontal line in a diagram that connects more than two lines.

Resistance is a level of price where the sale is tough enough to reverse an up-trend. An uptrend that acquires support is like a person who accidentally bumped by a moving car when he crosses the street then eventually stopped and collapsed. The supported is denoted by a horizontal line on a diagram that connects more than two upper parts.

A slight support or resistance will cause the trends to continue while reversing through strong support or resistance. The traders tend to buy support while others sell against the resistance turning its value into rewarding foresight.

Summary of the Support or Resistance Trading

1. Each morning, when you create your daily watch list, look immediately at the day cards on your watch list and find the support or resistance area.

2. Control the price action in these areas in a 5-minute chart. If an indecisive candle is formed in this area, this is the level confirmation, and you enter the operation. Generally, to minimize the risk, you should buy closely as possible. The stop is your pause and should be done no more than 5 minutes under the support or resistance levels.

3. Advances are to expect on the next support or resistance levels.

4. Don't close your trade not unless it already reached its profit aim or extends another support or resistance levels.

5. Selling positions are commonly happening close the profit aim or support or resistance levels. Then, you set your stop to reach the entry or breakeven point.

6. Closing your shares nearby to the middle position of cash level when there are no evident of support or resistance levels.

Develop Your Strategy

You must still find your place in the market. You may be a 1-minute or a 5-minute trader; you may be a 60-minute trader. Some may be daily or weekly traders (swing traders). There's a place in the market for everyone. Consider what you are learning in this book as pieces of a puzzle that together make up the bigger picture of trading. You're going to acquire some pieces here; you're going to pick up pieces on your own from your reading and research, and, overall, you will create a puzzle that will develop into your unique trading strategy. This book will help you develop a strategy that is going to work for you, your personality, your account size and your risk tolerance.

The key is that you master a strategy. Once you have a strategy in the market, you can become a trader without breaking your bank account. This is more than sitting on a chair. Remember that the more time spent looking at your chart, the further you will learn. It is a kind of job where you survive until you can do it. You can start throwing later, but first, you must master only one strategy. It can be the exchange of VWAP, it can be a bullish indicator momentum strategy, it can be a reversal strategy, or it can create its own strategy. Reduce the options, convert this area of strength into a viable strategy and use that strategy to survive until you can develop others.

It is absolutely crucial for each trader to act on a strategy. Plan an exchange and change the plan. You have to act a strategy. If you exchange real money, you must have a written strategy and historical data to verify that it is worth trading with real money. You cannot change your plan if you have already entered the operation and have an open position.

The truth about traders is that they fail. They lose money, and a large percentage of those traders are not getting the education that you are receiving from this book. They're going to be using live trading strategies that are not even hammered out, they will be haphazardly trading a little of this and a little of that until their account is gone, and then they will wonder what happened.

You don't want to live trade a new strategy until you've proven that it's worth investing in. You may practice three months on a simulator, and then trade small size with real money for one month, and then go back to the simulator to work on your mistakes or practice new strategies for another three months. There is no shame in going back to a simulator at any stage of your day trading career. Even experienced and professional traders, when they want to develop a new strategy, test it out on a live simulator first.

Your focus, while reading this book and practicing in simulated accounts, should be to develop a strategy worth trading, and it's my pleasure to assist you with that process. Remember, the market is always going to be there. You don't need to rush this. A day trading career is a marathon and not a sprint. It's not about making $50,000 by the end of next week. It's about developing a set of skills that will last a lifetime.

Successful Trading Guide and Money Management

The philosophy in the business is that you only have to master a few solid configurations to be consistently profitable. In fact, a simple trading method, which consists of a few minimal configurations, confusion and stress helps reduce and allows you to focus more on the psychological aspect of the negotiation, which really distinguishes the winners from the losers.

Now that you have learned the basics of some business strategies let's take a closer look at the actual planning and negotiation process. Now understand the configuration you want to act, but as a beginner trader, you will have a difficult time in advance to plan a trade and start. It is very common to have a good set-up, but then go into a trade at the wrong time or let the money go and at the same time make money from others. I think the solution is to develop a process for your trade. Plan an exchange and change a plan.

Trading process:

- Routine morning activities

- Create an observation list

- Consolidate a negotiation plan

- Start the trade accordingly

- Implementation and execution of plans

- Diary and reflection

You must remember that what makes an operation profitable is the correct execution of all the steps in the previous process. Write your reasons for entering and leaving each operation. Everyone can read this book or dozens of other books, but few people have the discipline to function properly. You may have a good configuration, but choose an incorrect action to trade. An action manipulated by computers and institutional traders. You may find an appropriate action to negotiate but negotiate at the wrong time. A bad entry will ruin your plan, and eventually, you will lose your money. You can find a good stock for trade and enter a trade properly, but if you do not get the right one, it will become an unprofitable trade, a loss of decisions. All the steps of the process are important.

Think about something important that you often do in your life and then think about how you can do better.

Now think about how you are doing right now. This is a great mind process for traders. When making an exchange, you must make sure you focus on the right things, before you start and negotiate. Forming a system for this proper process will eliminate majority of the emotional dependencies that traders encounter when they try to get in and manage an operation.

Final Rule

Profitable trade should not encompass any emotional aspect. If you are a sensitive trader, you will lose your money.

Training and practice give you an overview of what is involved in the action, how you act and how you can grow and develop your skills. Once you have a perspective of what matters, you can continue to identify the specific processes on which you should focus. The key to success is the exact knowledge of their processes. You often learn them the hard way, losing money.

Sticking to your negotiation plan and the discipline inherent in your negotiation methodology have caused a snowball effect positive habits in your life in general, and these habits have contributed to more commercial success.

Yes, snowball effect of positive habits. Day trading requires practice, routine, and development of positive habits. If you make a conscious effort in day trading, you will become an effective and successful trader in time.

For example, start your negotiation actions by following the same routine when you wake up in the sunrise. You always do a race in the morning before the negotiation session begins. For example, you live in Vancouver, Canada, and the market opens at 6:30, your time. You wake up every morning at 5 o'clock. You go from 5 to 5:45 p. M. (Usually between 7 and 10 kilometers (or 4 to 6 miles)). You come home, you shower and at 6 o'clock you begin to develop your plan.

If your body was not active before operating, you would make bad decisions. There are scientific studies that show that aerobic exercise has a positive effect on the decision-making process. People who regularly participate in aerobic exercise (e.g., at least 30 minutes) have higher values for neuropsychological functions and performance tests of cognitive functions, such as attention control, inhibition control, flexibility cognitive, working memory update and the speed of processing capacity and the measurement of information.

In day trading, it is not enough to be better than the average. You have to surpass the crowd to win in the daily trade. Regrettably, most of the people who were attracted to day trading are the impulsive, plungers, and selfish ones – those who think that the world should provide them more than what they have.

This reality does not mean to say you have to be like or act like them. Note that in order to win, you need to develop self-discipline. Your mindset and behavior are far different from the losers. Analyze yourself, disregard the deceptions, and change your old negative ways. I understand that in a way it is difficult, however, if you want to succeed in day trading, you need to work hard for it. You need not only to learn how day trading works but to improve your behavior and personality too. A successful trader is smart, motivated, and focused.

Now let's go back to the negotiation: as already mentioned, trade cannot be considered a hobby. You have to take the trade seriously· So you get up at 5 in the morning, you walk for 30 to 45 minutes, you shower, you dress, and you eat porridge for breakfast before you start your trading session at 6 in the morning.

. You are awake, alert and motivated when you sit down and start building your watch list. This morning, the routine of your mental preparation has tremendously helped you get to the market. So, whatever you do, the morning starts in a similar way to paying invaluable dividends. Waking up and washing your face with water 15 minutes in advance will give you little time to prepare for the opening of the market. Sitting on the computer in pajamas or underwear does not make you attack the market.

Your follow-up list comes from a standard analysis that you use every morning. You will be less likely to get mixed up to other stuff because you are sure that the stock of this scanner has the best chance of operating. Review each action, in the same way, using a checklist to see if it really is marketable to you. Your watch list will be created at 6:15 a.m. and will not add anything after that time since there will not be enough time to review new stocks and plan an operation. So you can see the tickers on our watch list 15 minutes before the opening. This really takes you to another step in your process.

In the 15 minutes prior to opening, you will see the tickers on your watch list and develop trading plans for them based on the price action you see. This is the most difficult part and requires experience, knowledge, and education. Many traders fail in this step.

When the bell rings at 6:30 a.m., your plans are recorded in the notebooks because it can be so easily missed out each of the open ticker you saw.

What is your next move if it is set on the long one? How about your next move if it turns out the opposite? What are your assumptions on the actions you made? How feasible are profit aims? What part should you establish your stop? Does your profit frame good enough to negotiate? If you ask these questions when planning your exchange, you have a clear advantage, because then you can continue and follow a battle plan. If it's close to your face, you can easily emphasize it, and that will eliminate the fear you felt when the bell rang. All you do in the opening is find your signal and activate the exchange.

Upon checking your watch list, you saw that Sarepta Therapeutics Inc (NASDAQ: SRPT) had a 15% difference. They knew that interest in buying shares was low. Who would dare to buy if shares fell overnight by 15%? In fact, most investors are trying to go out and sell before it goes down as if there is something really bad about the company. They could not find support or resistance in the vicinity, so opt for VWAP and choose a short VWAP operation.

Once the stock is configured, an entry is signaled and activated; you will enter without questioning (well, that is the plan). Sometimes you can appreciate yourself, but not too often. You have set my profit objectives in your trading plan, as well as the technical level at which you will be going to your stops, so after entering, concentrate only on my brands and your reservation benefit.

There are some who say that the hardest part of negotiating is knowing when to leave. It can be very difficult to stop trading too soon if you do not have an established plan. If you have a plan in advance and you meet it, you are more likely to make your payroll work and reduce your losses quickly, rather than the opposite. This is also useful to keep your emotions in check during the trade.

Once the exchange is over, you will think about how well your plan worked and how well you have done what you wrote. Most of your exchanges will be considered at night when you review and recap your operations from that day. You should ask yourself: "Which part did I do well?", "Are there any mistakes I have done?" And "Should I have sold myself before?" These are utterly crucial questions for the buildup of your trade.

Be noted that there is fact that even if you have obtained good profits, that still does not mean that you are an excellent trader.

Being a good trader is able to determine the importance of both sides of the table.

First write or take a video summary of the trade and everything that comes to mind at your school, then combine it with other previous lessons and use them all as a reference for the future. Some lessons are more difficult compared to others, but rest assured that it will only improve over time. You just need some time to absorb all the knowledge and details, and then implement them

Why is this trade process important? This process is important because it describes how things are prepared for an operation and then keep the focus for execution. It helps filter social, emotional noise and gives you a better sight for a more rewarding victory.

As long you keep focus and implement on the right processes, you may be on the right path to trading success.

Chapter 9 Fibonacci Trading Strategy

Fibonacci numbers start with 0 and 1 and then increase exponentially from there by adding the 2 previous numbers together to get the next number in the sequence. As such it starts off with 0, 1, 2, 3, 5 and so on and so forth. The difference between these numbers is known as the Fibonacci ratio which includes .236, .382, .5 and so on and so forth. Finding these ratios in the pairs you are considering allows you to determine naturally occurring entry and exit points.

Using the Fibonacci sequence to perform a retracement gives you the ability to determine how much an asset moved in price initially. It uses multiple horizontal lines to point out resistance or support at either 23.6, 38.2, 50, 61.8 or 100 percent. When used properly they make it easier to identify the spots transactions should be started, what prices to target and what stop losses to set.

This doesn't mean that you should apply the Fibonacci retracements blindly as doing so can lead to failure as easily as it can success. It is important to avoid choosing inconsistent reference points which can easily lead to mistakes as well as misanalysis, for example, mistaking the wick for the body of a candle. Retracements using the Fibonacci sequence should always be applied wick-to-wick which in turn leads to a clearly defined and actionable resistance level.

Likewise, it is important to always keep the big picture in mind and keep an eye on trends that are of the longer variety as well. Failing to keep the broad perspective in mind makes short-term trades more likely to fail as it makes it harder to project the correct momentum and direction any potential opportunities might be moving in. Keeping the larger trends in mind will help you pick more reliable trades while also preventing you from accidentally trading against a specific trend.

Don't forget, Fibonacci retracements are likely to indicate quality trades, but they will never be able to do so in a complete vacuum. It is best to start with a retracement and then apply other tools including stochastic oscillators or MACD. Moving ahead without confirmation will leave you with little except positive thoughts and wishes that the outcome goes the way you want. Remember, there is no one indicator that is strong enough to warrant moving forward on a trade without double checking the validity of the data.

The other limitation of a Fibonacci retracement is that it doesn't work reliably over shorter time frames as there is simply too much interference from standard market volatility which will result in false apparent levels of support as well as resistance. What's more, the addition of whipsaws and spikes can make it difficult to utilize stops effectively which can result in tight and narrow confluences.

While a singular Fibonacci retracement can be meaningful on its own from time to time, two or more Fibonacci retracements or extensions that show the same thing are almost always going to lead to viable results. The concept of overlapping Fibonacci retracements is one that most traders discover on their own over time. It commonly includes the use of other types of retracements or extensions with the purpose of determining a variety of signals including support and resistance levels as well as relevant pivot points.

As such, a group of overlapping retracements is a significant improvement as two strong Fibonacci levels are all that are required in order to determine a reliable trade in many cases. Specifically, the presence of a pair of Fibonacci levels at a point of known resistance or support is almost always enough to yield viable results. The simplicity of this strategy is one of its greatest strengths and many traders use it to the exclusion of all else when trading in the forex market.

Using this strategy: When it comes to utilizing this strategy correctly, you can use any chart that you like as long as it contains either a run down or a run up of a given currency price in addition to multiple retracements. From there, you will need to begin adding Fibonacci lines to the chart. If you draw these Fibonacci lines on a powerful down trend, then you will be able to start from the high point on the chart before moving toward the lowest swing point. If you are following an uptrend, then the reverse is going to be true. Once this is done you will need to find the confluence points that comes from any Fibonacci level including 38 percent, 50 percent, 62 percent and 79 percent.

Fibonacci extensions: To use Fibonacci extensions with this strategy, the basics are going to be more or less the same. You are simply going to choose the chart of your choice before adding in the Fibonacci lines with the Fibonacci extensions enabled as well. A particularly useful time to utilize this strategy is when the market is ranging between the support and resistance levels. It doesn't matter if the actual range is long or short, it will eventually break because the market cannot stay in an indecisive position forever.

The best way to determine the direction that a ranging market is going to break in is by first determining the range on the timeframe you are considering before then determining the low and the high based on that range. If the Fibonacci levels indicate that the price is going to break above the range, then the uptrend is likely going to form and if it breaks below the range then a downtrend is likely to form. While this will allow you to more accurately determine the next major movement that is likely to occur, it is still important to wait for that instance to actually come to pass before you move to take advantage of it.

On the other hand, you may instead want to wait for the range to break out once, before getting in on the second wave. This is frequently a good idea as a vast majority of traders spend time waiting for the initial break, regardless of how far away it may be in the moment. What's more, when this does occur, the price moves a great deal in a very short period of time, causing most of these traders to close out which drops the price, which a third round of traders is then happy to take advantage of.

These first three waves typically happen quite quickly before a much larger fourth wave of traders swoops in after they finally get on board with what is actually happening. As such, the most profitable time to get in is during the third wave as you avoid paying a premium while still expecting a fair amount of the profits you would see if you managed to get in any earlier.

In order to take advantage of this movement, you are going to want to determine the initial range breakout before waiting for the price to start moving against it.

You will then want to wait some more and have the price return to moving in the breakout direction once again. Once this occurs you are going to want to take the proper position and set the target to the low support line with a stop above the 0.0 level.

At this point, you will need to wait for the price to break past the lowest support line as if this does not occur then you are going to want to close out your position and try your luck again the next time the price starts following the trade in question. If the price does ultimately break through the lower support line, then you are going to wait for it to retest the broken support so that you can confidently close out your position before waiting for the price to once more come into alignment with the trend. Once it breaks past the support line but fails to crest above it, then you are going to want to take the relevant position based on the trend and set a level of 161.80 as the new target.

Assuming the trend breaks at this point and presents itself in such a way that it appears as though it is strong enough to continue to 423.60 then you will want to ensure you have the proper position and set this as your target while putting the stop loss slightly above 261.80.

Mistakes to avoid

While Fibonacci levels can provide a great deal of insight into the trading process, it can also lead to serious issues and massive losses if used incorrectly. As such, you are going to want to be aware of the following commonly made mistake sin order to ensure that your strategy works out according to plan.

Avoid mixing reference points: In order to correctly fit your retracements to the relevant price action, you are always going to want to keep steady reference points. This means that if you are using a low trend as a reference past the close of a session or in the body of a candle, then your ideal high price should always be visible in the candle at the top of the trend. Mistake and misanalysis can make it easy to accidentally skew these reference points by moving from the wick to the body of the candle hurting your potential for profit in the process. Luckily, consistently holding on to your reference points will also make it easier for you to determine accurate support and resistance levels at the moment.

Avoid ignoring long-term trends: If you get in the habit of dealing with short term charts then it can be easy to lose focus on the big picture. This narrowing of your perspective can ultimately result in misguided short-term trades if you aren't careful. Keeping a close eye on long-term trends, even if you don't plan on actively trading them can help you determine if the short-term trends you have found are all that they appear cracked up to be. Even better, this level of perception will allow you to potentially act on trends that have a great deal of momentum turning a solid 50 pip profit into one that is 400 pips or more.

Chapter 10 Finding Entry and Exit Points

We've talked quite a bit about support and resistance levels and now it's time to turn a little more attention to them. Understanding these twin concepts and how they predict market behavior is crucial to knowing when to get in and out of the market. In this chapter, we'll get further into what these forces do and how to spot them.

The chart above is a good example of support. Look at the two low points, or "bottoms," on the chart. These are points where the price tends to rebound. Once you've calculated a support level, you can expect the price to "bounce" off of it.

Proactive Calculations

Using pivot point calculations, whether your own or from a technical analysis source you trust, is usually the starting point for finding support and resistance levels. Pivot point levels are called "proactive" support or resistance, as opposed to "reactive." What this means is that it is predictive of future behavior, rather than describing current behavior. Remember that no prediction is perfect, and the calculation methods may be proven incorrect. There is a margin of error expected in calculating resistance and support, but if the price continues its motion through the pivot calculation point, that means that a new top or bottom is being found. When this happens, the previous point frequently remains a point of resistance or support, but to a lesser degree. Proactive support and resistance calculations are not set in stone. Rather than reading them as gospel, treat them as guidelines. They'll give you information about where to set your stops, where you should keep a close watch on your assets, and how to calculate your potential reward/risk ratios. Get comfortable with this math because you'll be using it every day.

Reactive Support

An example of reactive support is the candlestick pattern known as "tweezers."

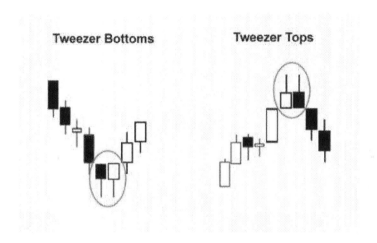

As you can see, they show a reversal in momentum that has already happened. When this stock history shows this pattern repeatedly at a certain price point, this is undoubtedly a marker of resistance or support at that level.

Trendlines

Over time, you may see that support and resistance levels change in a predictable pattern over time. We'll use support as an example, but it works exactly the same way for resistance levels. Let's say that the price of stock XYZ has bounced back up at $80 per share, then $75 per share, then $70 per share. If you were to draw a line through these support levels, you would see that the line trends upward, meaning that support is rising. If your pivot calculation gave you a likely support level at $65 for this stock on this day, you could be very confident in that calculation because it was supported by the trendline. If your pivot calculation was coming to $80 though, you might place slightly less faith in the calculation because it contradicts your trendline.

Round Numbers

An interesting psychological fact about support and resistance levels is how neatly they seem to place themselves at prices ending with "50" and "00." This is entirely due to the fact that people like round numbers and respect them more than other numbers when deciding whether to buy or sell stocks. Practically, this means that if there is a support or resistance at round number, it is much less likely that the price will punch through that level and break out of the prediction.

Chapter 11 Portfolio Diversification

Day traders generally execute trades in the course of a single trading day while investors buy and hold stocks for days, weeks, months, and sometimes even a couple of years. In between these two extremes are other forms of trading. These include swing trading and position trading, among others.

Swing trading is where a trader buys an interest in a commodity or stock and holds the position for a couple of days before disposing of it. Position trading, on the other hand, is where a trader buys a stake in a commodity or stock for a number of weeks or even several months. While all these trades carry a certain element of risk, day trading carries the biggest risk.

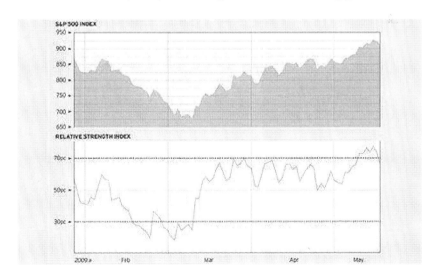

A trader with the necessary skills and access to all the important resources is bound to succeed and will encounter a steep learning curve. Professional day traders work full time, whether working for themselves or for large institutions. They often set a schedule which they always adhere to. It is never wise to be a part-time day trader, a hobby trader, or a gambler. To succeed, you have to trade on a full-time basis and be as disciplined as possible.

Introduction to Diversification

Diversification is considered an effective risk management technique. It is widely used by both traders and investors. The gist behind this approach is that investing funds in just single security is extremely risky as the entire trade could potentially go up in smoke or incur significant losses.

An ideal portfolio of securities is expected to fetch a much higher return compared to a no-diversified portfolio. This is true even when compared to the returns of lower risk investments like bonds. Generally, diversification is advisable not only because it yields better returns but also because it offers protection against losses.

Diversification Basics

Traders and investors put their funds in securities at the securities markets. One of the dangers of investing in the markets is that traders are likely to hold onto only one or two stocks at a time. This is risky because if a trade was to fail, then the trader could experience a catastrophe. However, with diversification, the risk is spread out so that regardless of what happens to some stocks, the trader still stands to be profitable.

At the core of diversification is the challenge posed by unsystematic risks. When some stocks or investments perform better than others, these risks are neutralized. Therefore, for a perfectly balanced portfolio, a trader should ensure that they only deal with assets that are non-correlated. This means that the assets respond in opposite ways or differently to market forces.

The ideal portfolio should contain between 25 and 30 different securities. This is the perfect way of ensuring that the risk levels are drastically reduced and the only expected outcomes are profitability.

In summary, diversification is a popular strategy that is used by both traders and investors. It makes use of a wide variety of securities in order to improve yield and mitigate against inherent and potential risks.

It is advisable to invest or trade in a variety of assets and not all from one class. For instance, a properly diversified portfolio should include assets such as currencies, options, stocks, bonds, and so on. This approach will increase the chances of profitability and minimize risks and exposure. Diversification is even better if assets are acquired across geographical regions as well.

Best Diversification Approach

Diversification focuses on asset allocation. It consists of a plan that endeavors to allocate funds or assets appropriately across a variety of investments. When an investor diversifies his or her portfolio, then there is some level of risk that has to be accepted. However, it is also advisable to devise an exit strategy so that the investor is able to let go of the asset and recoup their funds. This becomes necessary when a specific asset class is not yielding any worthwhile returns compared to others.

If an investor is able to create an aptly diversified portfolio, their investment will be adequately covered.

An adequately diversified portfolio also allows room for growth. Appropriate asset allocation is highly recommended as it allows investors a chance to leverage risk and manage any possible portfolio volatility because different assets have varying reactions to adverse market conditions.

Investor opinions on diversifications

Different investors have varying opinions regarding the type of investment scenarios they consider being ideal. Numerous investors believe that a properly diversified portfolio will likely bring in a double-digit return despite prevailing market conditions. They also agree that in the worst case situation will be simply a general decrease in the value of the different assets. Yet with all this information out there, very few investors are actually able to achieve portfolio diversification.

So why are investors unable to simply diversify their portfolios appropriately? The answers are varied and diverse. The challenges encountered by investors in diversification include weighting imbalance, hidden correlation, underlying devaluation, and false returns, among others. While these challenges sound rather technical, they can easily be solved. The solution is also rather simple. By hacking these challenges, an investor will then be able to benefit from an aptly diversified platform.

The Process of Asset Class Allocation

There are different ways of allocating investments to assets. According to studies, most investors, including professional investors, portfolio managers, and seasoned traders actually rarely beat the indexes within their preferred asset class. It is also important to note that there is a visible correlation between the performance of an underlying asset class and the returns that an investor receives. In general, professional investors tend to perform more or less the same as an index within the same class asset.

Investment returns from a diversified portfolio can generally be expected to closely imitate the related asset class. Therefore, asset class choice is considered an extremely crucial aspect of an investment. In fact, it is the single more crucial aspect for the success of a particular asset class. Other factors, such as individual asset selection and market timing, only contribute about 6% of the variance in investment outcomes.

Wide Diversifications between Various Asset Classes Diversification to numerous investors simply implies spreading their funds through a wide variety of stocks in different sectors such as health care, financial, energy, as well as medium caps, small, and large-cap companies. This is the opinion of your average investor. However, a closer look at this approach reveals that investors are simply putting their money in different sectors of stocks class. These asset classes can very easily fall and rise when the markets do.

A reliably diversified portfolio is one where the investor or even the manager is watchful and alert because of the hidden correlation that exists between different asset classes. This correlation can easily change with time, and there are several reasons for this. One reason is international markets. Many investors often choose to diversify their portfolios with international stocks.

However, there is also a noticeable correlation across the different global financial markets. This correlation is clearly visible not just across European markets but also emerging markets from around the world. There is also a clear correlation between equities and fixed income markets, which are generally the hallmarks of diversification.

This correlation is actually a challenge and is probably a result of the relationship between structured financing and investment banking. Another factor that contributes to this correlation is the rapid growth and popularity of hedge funds. Take the case where a large international organization such as a hedge fund suffers losses in a particular asset class.

Should this happen, then the firm may have to dispose of some assets across the different asset classes. This will have a multiplier effect as numerous other investments, and other investors will, therefore, be affected even though they had diversified their portfolios appropriately. This is a challenge that affects numerous investors who are probably unaware of its existence. They are also probably unaware of how it should be rectified or avoided.

Realignment of Asset Classes

One of the best approaches to solving the correlation challenge is to focus on class realignment. Basically, asset allocation should not be considered as a static process. Asset class imbalance is a phenomenon that occurs when the securities markets develop, and different asset classes exhibit varied performance.

After a while, investors should assess their investments then diversify out of underperforming assets and instead shift this investment to other asset classes that are performing well and are profitable in the long term. Even then, it is advisable to be vigilant so that no one single asset class is over-weighted as other standard risks are still inherent. Also, a prolonged bullish market can result in overweighting one of the different asset classes which could be ready for a correction. There are a couple of approaches that an investor can focus on, and these are discussed below.

Diversification and the Relative Value

Investors sometimes find asset returns to be misleading, including veteran investors. As such, it is advisable to interpret asset returns in relation to the specific asset class performance. The interpretation should also take into consideration the risks that this asset class is exposed to and even the underlying currency.

When diversifying investments, it is important to think about diversifying into asset classes that come with different risk profiles. These should also be held in a variety of currencies. You should not expect to enjoy the same outcomes when investing in government bonds and technology stocks. However, it is recommended to endeavor to understand how each suits the larger investment objective.

Using such an approach, it will be possible to benefit more from a small gain from an asset within a market where the currency is increasing in value. This is as compared to a large gain from an asset within a market where the currency is in decline. As such, huge gains can translate into losses when the gains are reverted back to the stronger currency. This is the reason why it is advisable to ensure that proper research and evaluation of different asset classes are conducted.

Currencies should be considered

Currency considerations are crucial when selecting asset classes to diversify in. take the Swiss franc for instance. It is one of the world's most stable currencies and has been that way since the 1940s. Because of this reason, this particular currency can be safely and reliably used to measure the performance of other currencies.

However, private investors sometimes take too long choosing and trading stocks. Such activities are both overwhelming and time-consuming. This is why, in such instances, it is advisable to approach this differently and focus more on the asset class. With this kind of approach, it is possible to be even more profitable. Proper asset allocation is crucial to successful investing. It enables investors to mitigate any investment risks as well as portfolio volatility. The reason is that different asset classes have different reactions to all the different market conditions.

Constructing a well-thought out and aptly diversified portfolio, it is possible to have a stable and profitable portfolio that even outperforms the index of assets. Investors also have the opportunity to leverage against any potential risks because of different reactions by the different market conditions.

An Example

An investor has a total of $100,000 to invest. The best approach is to put the funds in a diversified portfolio, but the challenge is properly or adequately balancing the portfolio. The first step is to check out market conditions and then conduct an assessment of possible returns versus any likely risks. As such, the investor can choose to invest in very secure investments that are likely to produce long-term income.

Such an investment can include between 10 and 12 stocks that are highly diversified. These are generally stocks from different sectors, industries, and countries. This kind of diversification helps to leverage against any possible risks and also ensures the portfolio is thoroughly mixed.

Portfolio Diversification Approach

Disciplined Investing is a Must

Everyone is in agreement that diversification is basically the right approach. However, as an investor, there is a need to be disciplined even as you invest and diversify your investments. Investing is an art form. Put your money in equities but not all your money. Instead, think of yourself as a mutual fund manager then come up with a list of companies to invest in. You can also invest in funds and trusts like REITs or real estate investment trusts and exchange-traded funds. It is also advisable to go beyond local borders and invest globally. This way, you spread your risk around and stand chances of enjoying much better returns.

Consider Investing in Bonds and Index Funds

Apart from investing in stocks across numerous sectors, a trader may also want to invest your funds in certain fixed-income or index funds. When you invest in securities that closely keep an eye on a major index is highly recommended as you will be able to monitor progress and known when to make adjustments and so on. Such funds charge very low fees, and you will be able to easily track your investments.

Portfolio Building is a Continuous Process

Try to always grow your investments. If you receive some cash from somewhere, you can consider investing part or the entire amount into your investment portfolio. Also, keep adding regular amounts to your portfolio. You can, for instance, add about $500 each month to this portfolio to grow it at a much faster pace.

Learn the Best Exit Times

Sometimes we tend to get comfortable with the purchase-and-hold approach. This is true, especially when our investments are on autopilot. Yet a smart investor you need to keep looking out for events and special moments. Always remain abreast of events and be ready to act depending on the nature of the event. This way, you will be prepared for the moment when you have to cut your losses and exit your trades.

Watch Out for Commissions

As a trader, you need to remember that there are commissions to be paid as well as fees and charges. These charges can add up over time and become a significant amount. Therefore, keep a lookout for the charges and ensure that they are always maintained at manageable levels. In general, investing should be informative, fun, rewarding, and educational.

However, you need to be disciplined as a trader in order to be profitable in the long term and possibly outperform some of the major indices. Apart from the buy-and-hold strategy, you should diversify your portfolio, keep growing your portfolio, and learn to read the signs and know when the time is right to exit a trade. This way, your trading ventures will become extremely fruitful in the long run.

Diversification Summary

Diversification can easily be summed up using a single phrase. Never put all your eggs in one basket. This is as simple as it gets. However, the statement does not explain exactly how to go about diversification.

The idea behind portfolio diversification is simple. A trader needs to diversify into a whole group of securities, and these should be from different asset classes. It would be wrong for a portfolio to contain only stocks from one company only. Should anything happen to that company, then the investor or even trader stands to suffer huge losses, and such losses can end the investment or trade dreams of a trader.

When an investment is split into two or more different companies and asset classes, then the potential risk facing a certain product is drastically reduced. Apart from investing in more than one company, it is also a great idea to put funds in other securities such as bonds, futures, and currencies.

Traders need to develop an asset allocation strategy. Such a strategy should mostly focus on investment in stocks and bonds. Asset allocation is closely related to diversification because when done properly, asset allocation leads to a sustainably diversified portfolio.

There are other additions that can secure a portfolio and improve its diversification. These include mutual funds that consist of varied securities. A mutual fund is generally a diversified investment so diversifying into a fund helps in further diversification of a portfolio.

It is advisable to learn how to arrive at a desirable risk to reward ratio. Such a ratio can help determine the best way to diversify funds. A risk-reward ratio provides the opportunity to enjoy a particular rate of return for those willing to assume a small level of risk. Therefore, those willing to take on higher risk levels are more likely to benefit more compared to those assuming lower levels of risk.

There are some who prefer lower risk levels because perhaps of their limited resources or perhaps they prefer minimal complications. Such investors simply mirror a single and balanced fund. Others choose to simply invest in the fund. However, this can be viewed as simplistic by others who may wish for a more diversified approach.

In conclusion, diversification is key for sustainable investment, especially in the long run. It is not just more profitable but provides a risk management element into the entire investment portfolio process. Finding a suitable balance in the choice of assets provides a great approach to apt diversification.

Reducing Day Trading Risks

Risk Management

With any trade, risk management is an essential component despite the fact that it is often overlooked. It is crucial that day; traders learn about risk management if they are to successfully trade and remain profitable in the long term. The good news is that there are some simple strategies that can be adopted to ensure that trades are protected and risks management appropriately.

Basically, risk management is one of the most important aspects of the life of any serious day trader. The reason is that a trader can actually see 90% of their trades make money, but the 10% losing money may result in a net loss if there is no proper risk management. Therefore, it is important to plan all trades carefully and to take measures to protect all trades against any losses.

Trades should be Planned Appropriately

It is a well-known fact that a good strategy will win the war rather than the battle. A good day trader needs to plan and come up with a winning strategy as the first step. A lot of traders often live by the mantra, "Plan the trade and trade the plan." This is also very similar to war planning because those who plan properly are likely to win.

Take Profit and Stop Loss Points

Traders need to come up with two very important points. These points represent two major keys that enable traders to plan ahead or in advance. A good day trader ideally knows their entry point as well as their exit points. These important points will guide the trades and will indicate at what point the trader should buy stocks and at what point the stocks should be sold off.

When a trader determines the price they wish to pay for a stock and the price they wish to sell, then it is possible to find out the likelihood of the stock performing as desired. If this can be measured and confirmed, then the trader should enter and execute the trade.

Also, traders who enter a trade without making these kinds of determinations are likely to suffer loss and will in effect cease trading and instead gamble with his resources. Whenever traders start to make losses, they believe that they can always recover their money if they invest more. This is often a lack of discipline, and the trader is likely to lose even more money.

A stop-loss is defined as the actual price where a trader will choose to sell a stock and incur a loss on the particular trade. This is a situation that happens when trades do not proceed according to the trader's plans. These points are ideally designed in order to limit losses before they get out of hand. It is always tempting for a trader who is losing money to hang in there in the hope that the losing trend will end and profitability will resume once again.

Converse to this is the take-profit point. It is important to set the take-profit, which is really the price at which a trader exits a trade by selling the security and then takes a profit from the sale. The take point is often the point at which any additional upside will become limited beyond this point. Let us assume the trade approaches a key resistance level after a large upward movement then traders can choose to exit the trade at this point.

Improving the Risk Management Process

1. Setting the Risk: Reward Ratio

When an entry signal is sighted, work out the most appropriate place to locate the stop loss than first take the profit order. As soon as a suitable price level for the orders is noted, the next step is to determine the risk versus reward ratio. Now should the outcome not be satisfactory, then it is advisable to quit the trade. Traders should generally not attempt to reduce the stop loss or widen the profit order. Discipline, at this point, is very important.

Rewards in trade are never certain and are the only potential. It is the risk that traders have control over so it should be seriously considered. A lot of the time, inexperienced traders will take the opposite approach and later suffer the consequences.

2. Traders should Avoid Break-even Stops

Creating a no-risk trade by locating the stop loss close to the entry point is something that should be avoided at all costs. The reason is that this is a dangerous move and most often not profitable. While seeking some protection is advisable, these kinds of moves cause more harm than good and should always be avoided.

3. Fixed Stop Distances should not be used

Sometimes a trader may wish to make use of a fixed number of points on the stop loss then place profit orders on markets and varied instruments. These are essentially shortcuts and should not be used under any circumstances. The reason is that they often neglect price movements and the general operation of the markets.

Also, things such as momentum and volatility are never static but always changing depending on various factors. These will also have an effect on the price movement and will affect fluctuations over time. When volatility is high, profit order points and stop loss points need to be wider to maximize profits during price swings and to prevent any premature stop runs.

4. Risk-Reward and Win-Rate Ratios should be compared together

There are traders who do not believe in the win-rate ratio and consider it irrelevant. This is actually not a wise thought because it is a very important metric. Win-rate on its own is not a very useful metric, but when pitted against the risk vs. reward ratio, then it provides important insights.

Traders should Work Out their expected Returns

Traders need to be able to work out any expected returns from their trades. Now both take-profit and stop-loss points are essential to work out this figure. Expected returns provide an important figure that cannot be underestimated. This figure that results from the calculations causes a trader to think and rationalize their trades. It also ensures that only the most profitable trades are chosen.

How to Set the Stop-Loss Points

It is the technical analysis that mostly helps to determine the take-profit and stop-loss points. However, fundamental analysis of the stocks in question does play a crucial role, especially with the timing. For instance, if a trader is holding stock and the earnings report is around the corner, then such a trader will have to dispose of those shares before the news affects the markets. This is necessary regardless of whether the stock has hit the profit margin or not.

One of the most popular ways of setting up these points is to use the well-known Moving Average. Moving averages are pretty simple to work out and are tracked closely by market players. Some of the important Moving Averages include the 9, 20, 50, 100, and 200-day averages. These should typically be applied to any stock in question and then making a determination as to whether they have had an effect on its price or not.

Also, the support and resistance trend lines can be used to place the take-profit and stop-loss levels. First, the trader needs to draw these lines simply by connecting all the past lows or highs that appeared on the above average and significant volumes. The main aim here is to effectively determine the levels where the stock price is affected by the trend lines when volumes are significantly high.

Traders need to be able to determine at what points they enter and exit any traders that they wish to participate in. This determination needs to be made before the trade is actually entered. When indicators such as the stop-loss are effectively used, then the trader will be able to minimize their losses and also reduce the frequency with which trades are excited unnecessarily. The bottom line here is to prepare early, well ahead of time so as to be sure of success in all trades.

Chapter 12 Managing Risk in Trading and the Role of Journaling

The first thing you need to know as a trader is that you will run volumes of trades and experience a lot of risks. Trading the markets is one of the riskiest investment techniques, and many people go for day trading because they have the potential for higher gains over a short period. If you have a small account, day trading gives you the chance to grow small accounts in such a short timeframe.

Risk comes about because you have to execute hundreds of trades in such a short time. You also have the capacity to place any trade you want, for as low as $500 or as high as $25,000 in a single trade. The trades are also at high speed, which means the market can swing any way – up or down. The direction of the market determines whether you make a loss or a profit.

Day trading gives you two realms of strategies to go with – high risk trading strategies or Lowe risk strategies. The goal of a successful trader is to maximize profit while lowering risks. Every time you place a trade, you need to evaluate the risk of the trade and then weight it against the potential reward. Often times this is made worse by our emotional reaction to various price directions. For instance, since you experienced a loss recently, the next logical step would be to take a higher risk on the next trade so that you can compensate on the loss. Experienced traders have a heightened level of awareness that they use to recognize a loss and reward and will make sure they take the right decision. However, you have to learn the skill over time.

You can develop a sense of decision making by keeping a journal as you trade and then reviewing the notes after the close of the market.

Different Types of risk

When talking about risk, you need to consider the different types in order for you to understand what we are saying. As a day trader, your primary role is to know the distance between the entry and the stop. Stop loss needs to be based on a resistance area on the chart or recent support.

Majority of your losses need to happen when a trade hits the stop price. This means you won't make any profit on whatever you are trading.

The second type of risk id the volatility of the market. As day traders, volatility is a friend to all of us, but it is also risky because markets that are extremely volatile tend to result in higher losses than what you actually planned for. Since there is a sense of inherent risk in trading, you need to try and avoid placing a trade when the volatility cannot be predicted, for instance when there is breaking news.

The other type of risk is exposure risk. Exposure results when you multiply the price of shares by the number of held shares. As an investor, you increase this risk when you hold on positions for a very long time. To mitigate this risk, you need to hold onto shares for a short time.

If you are holding onto large positions for a long time you stand to experience stock halts. Halts can take hours or days, though they are rare. The most common halts are those waiting for the release of news or volatility halts. Anytime a stock halts, it can lead to a different price. The biggest risk is that the stock might reopen at a very different price, which might be lower than the current price of the stock. You can take steps to reduce the effect of the halts by understanding what leads to the halts in the first place.

Journaling

If you are looking at a routine that is easy to implement and that can change the way you trade, then think about keeping a journal. The journal is a little black book that details what you do each day.

The aim of keeping a journal is to help improve your setups so that you use your experiences to analyze and help refine your trading while you improve the whole experience.

Here, we look at all you need to come up with a journal and maintain it.

What is A Journal?

A trading journal is a way to keep track of what you are doing o daily basis as a day trader. You jot down notes of what you do each day especially the different trades (or lack of) and the results of any action you take.

The trading journal needs to be tailored to your trading styles and preferences. You can keep the journal in a physical notebook or a detailed digital document on your computer. Regardless of the format, when maintained with due diligence, the trading journal can be the best way to make you a better day trader.

How Does the Trading Journal Help You Achieve Better Trades?

There are a number of ways in which a trading journal will help you become better at what you do.

Many traders attribute their success to creating and maintaining a trading journal. By noting down the different trades, you are able to check the progress over time. This allows you to find out what is working or not and change or modify them to succeed.

Helps You develop discipline in Trading

Having a trading journal helps you develop discipline as you trade. How does it do so? Well, it forces you to follow the guidelines that you have set down.

The sense of accountability that you get when you have a trading journal makes sure you are responsible for research and trading. If you know what you need to keep a log each day, you do it without fail. Making sure you log your trades and whatever happens requires a lot of discipline. Good habits such as these require you to go straight when executing trades.

Helps You Master Your Emotions

One of the top suggestions to help you run trades the right way is to trade like you are not human. Machines do not have emotions and approach all the processes in a scientific way.

However, this is easier said than done. When you get in a position to lose money, usually you find it tough getting emotion out of the way.

Keeping a journal can help you keep the emotions out of the way. With a journal in place, you get to keep track of how you feel emotionally in various trading stages. This is just to keep the emotions in check.

With time, you realize that there is a pattern that is emerging, for instance, you might find yourself getting calmer and taking orders the right way each time.

Improves Your Risk Management Practices

Day trading comes with a high level of risk. This is something that you cannot change at all because it is the nature of the market for things to run this way.

However, there are various ways in which you can mitigate these risks. For one, you need to invest a large amount of research and study to give you the knowledge that you need to choose the least risky trades possible.

With a journal, you can learn things about risk tolerance. For instance, you might find that you have consistently been able to hold positions for longer and you have been losing profits as a result. You might also find that you have issues getting out of trades because you have been taking positions that are too big for your stage.

By looking at the risks that you have been taking and how they affect the results you return, you get to make adjustments.

For instance, you might exit trades sooner or you might end up taking smaller positions based on the results you return. This way you help reduce risks and improve risk management.

Creating the Perfect Trading Diary

Now that you know how effective the trading journal is, you need to know how to come up with the best one. Here are a few tips for success when coming up with a journal:

- Be consistent

Trading needs you to have a routine. You will probably get the most out of the journal if you have a routine that you follow religiously.

You also need to follow the routine to the latter. This means that you are consistent with what you do day in day out. For instance, you need to wake up early each day to prepare for trading. This allows you to get errands and tasks out of the way early and gives you to do research so that you are ready to roll when the market starts.

This is a directive though because since many traders are doing other responsibilities, you need to come up with the right schedule that works for you. Choose the routine that will work for you and that you can stick to easily.

- Analyze the Market

The more the trades that you track, the more data you have to deal with and the more you get to learn and the faster you do it.

By recording the trades, overall thoughts, market observations and more, you aren't just learning from the mistakes that you are doing, but you are also gaining a sense of how to perform the right market analysis.

For instance, with the right trading data, you get to notice gains and losses in a particular industry or sector. This can give you clues on the trends in the market that you might have missed out.

Once you see what is working and what isn't, you get to have a targeted market analysis.

- Analyze and Come Up with Your Own Setups

A trading journal allows you to come up with the right setups. Here is how this works out:

- Find the setups that trigger trade entry

When do you enter the market? The trading journal helps you figure everything out. You need to go into each trade with a plan. However, if you realize that you are entering trades too soon or too late based on the journal, you can then decide to try something different.

With the perfect trading journal, you have the capacity to determine the setups that trigger the entries.

- Gain Insight into the Market

When you record your own setups, you have the ability to gain insight into the market that you are trading in. you get to notice market trends and how they might end up affecting the setups.

As a trader, understanding the way the market runs is ideal because it helps you to keep up to date. The market is dynamic, and the setups that work in one market condition might not work for other conditions. When you understand the market, you get to navigate around and acclimatize to new markets.

- Know the Appropriate Lot Size

In any market, the lot size means the number of shares which you buy in any transaction. The theory of size allows you to regulate price quotes. It is basically the size of the trade that you place in the financial market.

With price regulation being a part of every market, you need to always be aware of the number of units that you purchase eon contract, and determine the price you pay per unit.

Make sure you keep track of the lot sizes that you deal with in any trade, as it helps you to decide the types of approaches that you take in the future.

- Determine the Style of Trading

Many traders choose to be one type of trader or another. Many of them do it by force, which is a fact that isn't the best. As a trader, you need to naturally gravitate towards a specific trading style, and not force it.

Rather than chasing after what is trendy or what you have seen other traders do, it is advisable to focus on a style of trading that gives you profit, whether you go after long or short positions.

A trading journal can help you determine the type of trade that is best suited for you by giving you a summary of the trades that gave you money.

- Understand Profit Placement

Trading is a probability game, with so many moving pieces that make it work. With so many parts that are needed to make everything work, you need to make sure you get everything right the first time. This isn't easy at all.

Here are a few specifics that you need to master:

- *Cut losses fast*: you need to learn to cut losses quickly, which means you pull out of a position earlier than later, even if it means missing out on a few profits. It is always good to be safe than sorry. Having a trading journal helps you determine when to get out of a trade. If you notice that you are losing constantly, then journaling can help you learn how to cut losses fast. Additionally, if you notice that you are getting out of trades too early, then you can start staying gin the game a little bit longer.

- *Stop losses*: you need to learn how to come up with the best stop loss order. The order can help you release the order when you reach a particular price. With the right stop loss order, you can buy the security rather than selling it when you reach a certain price. Make sure you record the different entry and exit positions; how much you have risked and the results of everything. As the information collects over time, you can determine what your best setups are so that you can focus on replicating the profits you gained in the past to eliminate losses.

Apart from this information, you also need to record other things so that you make the most out of each entry:

- *The date*: this shouldn't be left out of the journal. Not only does it help you to track what you were doing and when you were doing it, but it allows you to go back and look at the performance of the stock on that date in future. Never assume that you will rack everything in your brain!

- *The Time Frame*: do not just record the date, but make sure you know the perfect time for each entry. In the world of trading, minutes matter. Trading in the morning can make a huge difference compared to trading in the afternoon. For instance, the setup that works for you during the morning hours might not work the same way in the afternoon.

- *Price in*: this is the point where the journal starts working well with the trading plan. When coming up with a trading plan, you set the key tactics such as the entry point, the exit and what you plan to gain from this trade. This helps you to stick to the plan and then keep emotions out of things. In the journal, make sure you note the price at which you entered a successful trade.

- *Price out*: don't just mark the time that you entered the trade – also take note of the price that you exit the trade too. The exit is also as vital as the entrance. Keeping this data allows you to analyze whether you are staying in a position for the right amount of time. Note any difficulties that you encounter getting out of the position, as this might affect the level of risk next time.

- *Amount you are risking*: before you enter a trade, you need to determine the amount of money you plan to put into the trade. Note: The money you put tin should be an amount you can risk losing. So, how much money should you risk on a trade? The answer is that you need to always take a cautious position, and never try to risk what you can't lose. You do not want to enter into a trade and blow up the account as this might trigger emotional trading.

Tips for Creating an Efficient Trading Journal

1. Identify the Patterns That lead to Losses

As a trader, you can't eliminate the risk of making losses. For many traders, the success rate is 70 percent, and many of them know that the 100 percent win rate is a myth.

You can never control how much you win, but you can at least control the amount you can lose by cutting losses fast.

You also get to learn from the losses. Once you have a trading journal, you begin to identify patterns that lead to losses and assess what is happening.

2. Identify the Patterns That Have Made You Profit

As a trader, you not only focus on the things that went wrong, but also look at what went right as well. You need to chart patterns in the trades to help you analyze what make you the most money. Many successful traders base their success on being able to identify patterns. Many depend on stock charts, but later realize that even the trading journal gives them an insight into what they need to do.

3. Go for Professional Assistance

Trading classes give you an asset that you will never regret in your trading life. Even with the right data, you might find yourself failing to make profitable trades because you do not have the mechanics to make things work for you. When you take time to learn the mechanics of trading, you find that you have the basis to identify key indicators and add them to the journal.

Just like any other trade, the more you get prepared to execute trades the more successful you become. The knowledge originates from previous traders that have become successful in their efforts.

4. Work With templates

Templates make it easy for you to come up with a plan. There are many platforms online that offer you both paid and free templates that you can use to create the perfect journal, all you need to do is to choose the one that suits you then customize it to your liking. As you become more adept, you find that the journal becomes your best friend, and it also becomes more detailed.

Chapter 13 Tips and Tricks to Make Your Life Easier when Using the MT4 Platform

So far ,we've covered plenty of tips in this book. The idea is to learn them ahead of time, before working intensively with the platform, so you can increase your productivity.

SPEAKING OF PRODUCTIVITY, A QUESTION: WHAT IS THE QUICKEST WAY TO INCREASE PRODUCTIVITY WHEN THE EVERYDAY WORKING TOOL IS A COMPUTER STATION? ANSWER: REDUCE THE NUMBER OF REQUIRED CLICKS.

IF THE SAME JOB CAN BE DONE WITH HALF THE CLICKS, THAT'S A FIFTY-PERCENT TIME SAVING. SO, HERE'S OUR NEXT TIP: THE MT4 HAS AN OPTION TO REDUCE THE NUMBER OF CLICKS REQUIRED TO SELECT OBJECTS ON A CHART.

Go to Tools/Options/Objects, and make sure you check the box that says, "Select object by single mouse click".

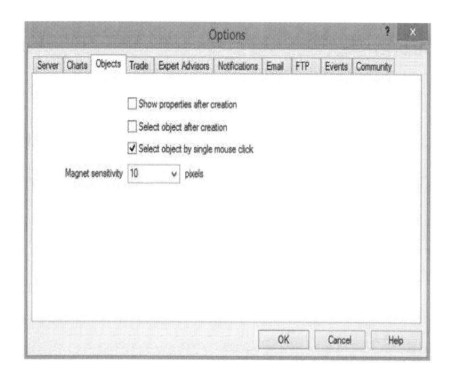

This way, when drawing a trend line, channel, or just counting waves to apply the Elliott Waves Theory, one click is enough to select the object.

Speaking of trend lines... they can use some attention too. The default setting for a trend line has it projecting it indefinitely to the right side of the screen; you'll find that annoying, not to say useless.

Solving this issue is easy. First select a trend line and right-click on it.

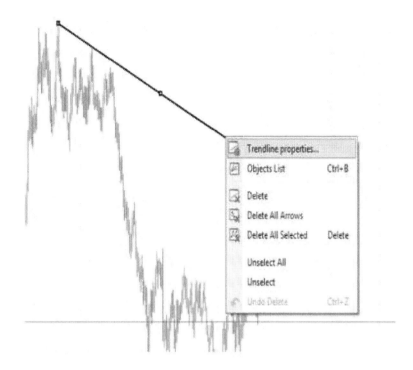

From the popup menu, select the first option: Trend line properties... In the Trend lines dialog box, go to the Parameters tab.

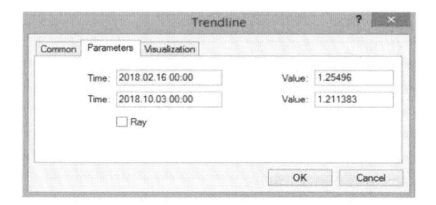

The "Ray" option is what gives the trend line the properties of a ray – i.e., extending it indefinitely. We don't want that, so make sure the box is not checked. This way, the trend line is limited only to what's drawn, or just to the time and price values entered in the dialog.

Still on the topic of trend lines and objects, another handy shortcut is to copy and paste objects. The copied object keeps the same parameters/characteristics of the original one. It's just a replica.

To copy an object, hold down the CTRL key on your keyboard and then click the object to select it. Now drag the new object to use anywhere else on the screen.

This is an essential step for all kinds of strategies. For example, when building a channel from a simple trend line, one needs to keep the angle of the second line exactly the same as the first. So, copy/paste works best.

Moreover, some traders use various colors for different trend lines coming from higher or lower timeframes. Or, as is in the case of top/down analyses with the Elliott Waves Theory, traders use color codes to illustrate various cycles within the theory.

No matter the strategy, the copy/paste function for objects is a time-saving tool you'll love when using the MT4 platform.

Another useful tip when using the MT4 is to save your work. There's nothing more frustrating than working all day on an Elliott count or strategy, making notes on charts and so on, and losing all your work. How is that possible?

Power failures, for instance, do happen. If you work on a desktop station, the MT4 will shut down in an instant, and your work won't be saved.

The MT4 only saves work on normal closing. So, if your strategy is labor-intensive, make sure to restart the MT4 platform from time to time so that the work done remains there for further use.

Conclusion

One of the most important things that you should always remember as you engage in day trading is the notion of developing a trading strategy. Never fall for the myth that your trading strategy will not work. In fact, the best forms of online trading strategies are those that work for you. Don't settle for a strategy simply because your trading partner claimed that it worked for them. Build your strategy from scratch. Test it and find a way of constantly improving it. A strategy which has been proven and tested over time will guarantee that you maximize on getting profits while reducing your risks considerably.

On the issue of risks, another essential thing to remember is having a risk management strategy. It is not surprising to learn that a trader with a 50% success rate could perform better than one with a 75% success rate. If the latter fails to use a risk mitigation strategy, then they could incur huge losses in spite of their profits. So, as part of mitigating your risks, first, know the importance of planning your trade. Without a trading plan, you will be setting yourself to fail. Equally, if you are trading using larger accounts, remember to stick to the one percent rule.

Don't be greedy. Yes, the markets might seem appealing, but there is no guarantee you will continue making profits if the trend is maintained. In line with this, to help you mitigate losses and lock in profits, you should make good use of taking profit and stop loss points. The best traders in the market are using these tools. Therefore, you are not an exception.

Now, with the numerous guides and online tutorials on day trading, one will wonder why most traders fail. Surprisingly, people fail not because they lack capital but because of their mistakes. For instance, a new trader might enter the market without any plan. If the first few traders are successful, they will gain the impression that they don't need a plan to trade. The moment things turn sour, they abandon their randomness and look for other trading strategies. At the end of the day, they will be doing something else which is not trading. They will be gambling. It is important for a new trader to know of the common reasons why most traders fail. This guarantees that they know how to avoid making similar mistakes. Take, for example, the notion where new traders simply begin trading without any formal knowledge about the industry. You need to do your homework before starting to trade. Find out what other traders do on a regular basis to make sure that they close the day with profits.

When trading using a small account, you should not be discouraged by the fact that you have limited funds in your account. Indeed, managing a small account has its challenges including the fact that you will be working under pressure not to make any losses. However, you should look at the bright side. Acknowledge the fact that you are getting something out of the trading activity. Trading in a small account gives you the advantage of learning how to trade with minimal risks. As a new trader, it is imperative to embrace the importance of starting small. With time, the knowledge and experience you get will make a huge difference.

The good news is that there are proven and tested strategies which you could use to improve the small account. For instance, you could choose to risk more for every trade you buy. Also, you should always ensure that more capital is at work. Forget about securing your account. This will take away a bigger portion of the money which should have been used to trade. The idea of swinging big when there is a perfect setup to trade should be at your fingertips. Doing this warrants that you take advantage of a trading opportunity which could increase your capital. Also, you might want to forget about using stops. Using stops might hinder you from making the best out of a trade which would have performed well later on.

You will need a sober mind to succeed in day trading. Unfortunately, there are common mental errors which could affect how well you perform in your trading activity. For instance, if you lack confidence in your plan, how do you expect to stick to it? You have to believe that your plan will lead you to make profits that you anticipate. This mentality will develop a positive attitude about the whole trading activity. Therefore, you will have all the reasons to be disciplined and stick to your plans no matter the circumstances.

If you are going to trade when your mind has deviated, then there are high chances that you will fail. You need to have a clear mind free from any distractions. If you have personal issues you need to attend to, ensure that you sort them out first. Any small mistakes in day trading could cost you a lot of money. Hence, you need to be focused at all times. Still, if you are not feeling well, just stop trading.

Markets are there to stay. Therefore, if you don't trade today, you can still trade tomorrow. The point here is that you need to be healthy enough to give your mind the energy it needs to make sound decisions.

Whether you are trading using a small or a large account, discipline is the key to success. If you can't stick to your strategy, it is better to try something else. Most traders have failed in day trading because of their lack of discipline. It is by being disciplined that you will know when to enter and exit the market. With discipline, you will also understand the importance of using only one percent of your trading capital.

Good luck trading!

OPTIONS TRADING

THE NEW APPROACH TO MARKETS
WHICH INVOLVES INVESTING FOR
CREATING MORE CASHFLOW FOR THE
SAKE OF YOUR FINANCIAL FREEDOM.
WITH THE NEW GUIDE TO MAKE PROFITS
FAST.(FOREX MARKET, SWING)

Description

Options trading is such a unique yet valuable way of making money in the stock market. While there are some risks involved in the trade, these are normally limited, giving you a chance to make some good money from the trade. Adequate market research and knowing when to make a move will help you succeed in options trading. Brokers can also assist too since they can help you trade before you master the business.

Trading in options is a process. The more prepared you are, the better the experience. Of course, the starting point lies in to understand what options trading is. Options are an alternative strategy for Forex investors who do not wish to trade in underlying securities. The basics involve understanding how to purchase and sell calls and puts. This is what constitutes an options contract.

With basic information at hand, you are now ready to attempt your first trade. The power of options lies in their versatility. However, this versatility comes with a cost. If not handled carefully, the trade becomes riskier than stock. That is why you will come across many disclaimers advising you to only engage in options trading using risk capital. This book plays a vital role in helping you appreciate the principle of decaying time and how it applies to options trading. Without understanding how this principle works, any trade that you carry out will be surrounded by diverse risks and uncertainties.

While you can succeed in options trading without carrying out any technical analysis, it may be difficult for you to determine the duration, direction, and range of movement within the market. Since options are always subject to decay, any slight change in the values is very important. Understanding technical analysis indicators such as the RSI, IMI, and MFI can go a long way to ensure that you manage volatility, minimize risks, and close your trades with a profit. As a trader, you must always choose an indicator that complements your trading strategy and style.

This book gives a comprehensive guide on the following:

- Top Reasons to Trade Options
- Ways to Trade
- Covered Calls
- A Step-By-Step Way to Sell Covered calls
- Volatility

- Technical Analysis
- Vertical Call Spreads
- Advanced Strategies and Techniques
- Make Binary Options Trading Simple Through a Broker
- Options Trading Risk Strategies
- Top Mistakes made by New Traders
- Tips for Success... AND MORE!!!

Introduction

An option is an agreement to buy and/or sell some financial assets. We call this asset the underlying.

Options have an expiration date in the United States; the sale could occur on or before that date. There is a pre-arranged asset price.

It is called an option because the buyer of the contract has the option to proceed with the transaction, and is not obligated to do so. If the owner of the contract (the buyer) decides to go through with the transaction, they are said to be exercising their rights under the options contract. While the buyer has the option to do so or not, the other party to the agreement is legally obligated to the terms set out in the agreement. That means they must go ahead and buy or sell the underlying asset if the buyer exercises their rights.

On the stock market, an options contract represents shares of stock. Typically, one contract is for 100 shares. And so the contract gives the buyer the specific rights. If it is a call option, they can buy shares of a stock with a fixed price per share. Meanwhile, for a put option, they are able to sell shares of stock at the pre-arranged price. This is a key point, and it doesn't matter what the current share price is when the buyer decides to exercise their rights. The seller of the options contract is legally obligated to honor the terms of the contract. This means they must buy or sell the shares at the pre-agreed upon price no matter what.

Options also expire in a matter of days, weeks, months, and even years from the present date. It's important to know the expiration date of an option because that has a large influence on the price of the option. Options that only last for one week are called weeklies, while options that last one year or more are called LEAPS.

It's seldom the case that the option remains in force between the seller and the original buyer because options are traded on their own market like stocks. An option is likely to change hands multiple times as options traders seek to profit or avoid losses. Option prices will constantly be fluctuating.

Most options expiration are never exercised, but you need to be on guard about this if you are selling options because if the current owner of the option would benefit by purchasing or selling the shares, there is a risk that they will actually decide to exercise their rights. The risk of this is quite a bit higher than normally portrayed in internet discussions about the topic, where it's often noted that "most" options expire without being exercised.

All of this might sound a bit confusing at first, but as we go along the details will be clarified, and it will start to make sense. Let's begin by exploring the two major types of options.

Strike Price

The price that is pre-agreed upon for the sale is called the strike price. That will be the price per share if it's exercised. So, for example, you could have an options contract for Apple. If the strike price is $180 per share, even though the Apple is actually trading at some other value such as $201 per share, the $180 price would be used if the option was exercised. The strike price is arranged and agreed upon when the contract is written and for the lifetime of the option.

Call Options

A call option is an agreement that gives the buyer the option to purchase stocks. The benefit to the buyer is the agreement contains a pre-arranged price, which is called the strike price.

Remember that all options contracts are optional for the buyer, which is the buyer of a call option is not obligated to purchase the shares. Buying a call option is a long investment, which is you are bullish on the stock and hope to profit from a rise in the share price. This can be done in one of two ways. The first way is to simply purchase the shares at their strike price if the market price of the shares has risen above the strike price. That way, the buyer benefits from being able to purchase the stock on a reduced price after the price of the shares has risen, possibly substantially. Then either they can turn around and sell them at a profit on the stock market or they could be satisfied that they were able to buy stocks at a lower price.

The second, and far more common way to profit would be to trade the option, that is, sell it to another buyer for a profit. An options trader can do this because when share prices rise in comparison to the strike price, demand for that option rises, driving up the price for the option. This is how most traders earn money trading options. So you could buy an option for $100, and then sell it for $150 a few days later.

Premium

This is the fee that is paid to purchase an options contract. The party who writes the options contract receives a fee from the buyer to enter into the contract. This is called the premium. The seller keeps the premium no matter what happens. The premium is quoted as the price per share, but note that an options contract covers 100 shares of stock. So if the quoted price of an option is listed as $2, the actual price you have to pay in order to purchase it is $200 (or $2/share x 100 shares). Although this entitles you to control the shares of stock, you don't actually own them unless you exercise the option.

Why Sell Call Options?

You might ask why someone would sell a call option in the first place since they can end up having to sell shares of stock. The reason is that selling options is a way to generate monthly income. As we will see later, if you already own shares of stock, you can sell options contracts against them and earn money from the sale. Owners of shares of stock that do this are making a bet that they can sell the options contract and earn money without having to sell their shares, but if you decide to sell options contracts be aware that in some cases the right to buy the shares will be exercised. So while you will profit from the premium you earned from the sale of the options contract, you may be forced to sell your shares of stock.

Advanced options traders can sell options contracts without having to actually own the shares of stock. These are called naked options, and we will discuss this more advanced method later in the book. By "naked," we mean that the options contract is not backed by anything. The danger is that the owner of the option (the buyer) will exercise it.

In that case, the seller of the naked call will lose money, because they would have to buy the shares of stock at the market price, and then sell them to the owner of the options contract at the lower strike price. So they would lose the difference: (market price – strike price + premium paid per share) x 100 shares.

If the party who writes the options contract owns the share of stock, it's best to enter into this type of arrangement when you can set a high strike price. In other words, choose a price that is higher than the price you originally paid to obtain the shares. That way even though you might be forced to sell the shares, at least you will make a profit on the deal. However, you won't make as much profit as you could have had you sold the shares on the open market. We say that you missed out on the upside.

In the end, selling options contracts is a bet against the stock, in the sense that you don't think the share price is going to go as high as the buyer believes it will go. If it fails to do so, the option will reach the expiration date, and it will "expire worthless" because nobody would buy shares that were more expensive than the going rate.

Call options have this name because the originator of the options contract might have to sell the shares of stock that they own; in other words, the shares will be "called away."

Break Even Point for Call Options

If you are buying call options, it's a good idea to have the break-even price in mind. In this case, it would be the premium + strike price:

Call option break-even point = premium + strike price

Suppose the market price is $50 per share.

Then, if you buy an option for $1 with a strike price of $51, the break-even point is $51 + $1 = $52 a share. So in the event you exercise the option, the break-even price would be $52 a share, and you'd want the stock price to go higher than that in order to make a profit.

However, if you are only buying options in the hope of selling them as the price of the options contract rises with rising stock prices, then the break-even price isn't really relevant. In that case, you only want the price of the option to go higher than the premium you paid for it. If you bought an option for $1 a share, then if the option price goes above $1 a share, you have a chance to profit, depending on what your broker's commission structure is.

Example: Buying a Call Option

Let's say a particular stock is trading at $50 a share. You buy a $50 call option (the strike is $50) for the stock with 45 days left to expiration. The price of the put option is quoted at $1.41, which means to buy the option it cost you $1.41 x 100 shares = $141. At 30 days remaining until expiration, the price of the stock has risen to $55 a share. Under these conditions and everything else being equal, the price of the call option is now $5.07, so you can sell it for $5.07 x 100 = $507, earning a profit of $366, less any commissions.

If you really wanted to buy the shares, you have the option to purchase the stock from the originator of the call option for $50 x 100 = $5,000 (remember 100 shares), which would save you $500 off the price you'd pay on the open market. Since you had paid $141 to buy the options contract, your net savings would be $359.

If you wanted to, you could then turn around and sell on the open market. This means you could sell them at the market price of $55 a share, for $5,500, leaving a profit of $5,500 - $5,000 - $141 = $359.

This serves to illustrate why under these circumstances the option is unlikely to be exercised since that is slightly less profit than you'd get simply selling the option to someone else. Where that circumstance might change was if the option was about to expire and you couldn't find a buyer for the option. That would still leave you with the ability to exercise your rights under the options contract and buy the shares at the reduced price, and then you could sell them immediately to get the profit.

Why Buy Call Options?

If you aren't interested in buying the shares, the main reason to buy call options is to profit by selling the option at a later date so that you can profit from price moves in the underlying shares. As we saw from our example, the price moves can sometimes cause dramatic increases in the price of the option. It isn't often that a stock is going to move $5 one way or the other, however, even a $1 or $2 rise in stock price can have dramatic effects. Consider an option on a stock trading at $51 a share with a strike price of $50 and 30 days to expiration. You could buy that option for $1.77 a share (total price - $1.77 x 100 = $177). If the share price increased to $52 the following day, you could sell the option for $2.42 (total price $2.42 x 100 = $242), making a quick $65.

With a call option, the benefit comes when the share price is higher than the strike price.

Even when call options have strike prices that are above the share price, they can appreciate in value when the share price of the underlying stock increases. So this also provides opportunities to earn profits.

Here are some recent moves that stocks made that would have led to enormous profit margins for people holding call options contracts:

Between June 17, 2019, and June 18, 2019, Apple increased from $194 per share to $200 per share.

On June 3, 2019, AMD was trading for $27.40 a share. By June 6, 2019, it was $31.84 a share.

On June 6, 2019, Amazon closed at $1,754.63. By June 18, 2019, it was up to $1,914 a share.

Between May 31, 2019, and June 11, 2019, IBM went from $127 a share to $135 a share.

Of course, stocks are not always going up, and you have to study the market closely to find opportunities. The point is that these opportunities are out there.

Put Options

The second class of options is called a put option. Like any option, it has a strike price with an expiration date. But in this case, the buyer has the option to sell 100 shares of the underlying stock. The transaction would take place at the pre-arranged strike price before or during the expiration date of the option. These are called "puts," and this stems from the fact that the originator of the contract is forced to buy shares of stock, so the shares are "put to" the party who wrote the contract.

Put options can be used in different ways. One way to profit from put options is by essentially shorting the stock. So when you buy a put option, you are short, believing that the stock will decline in price. Put options allow the owner to sell shares above the ongoing price on the market. That means they increase in value when the stock market declines.

Imagine that you buy a put options contract at $2 a share, for a stock trading at $50 a share. We could set the strike price to $48.

If the share price dropped to $46 a share or lower, you could buy the shares on the open market and then sell them to the originator of the put option at $48 a share.

Many options traders never exercise options but instead rely on being able to sell them at a profit to other traders before they expire. In the case of a put, you are still essentially shorting the stock because the price of the option will rise as stock price drops. In this case, you wouldn't buy the shares to sell to the writer of the put option, and you'd simply sell the put on the options market at a price that was higher than what you paid for it.

Example: Buying a Put Option

Let's say a particular stock is trading at $50 a share. You buy a $50 put option for the stock with 45 days left to expiration. The market price of the put option is quoted at $1.39, which means to buy the option it cost you $1.39 x 100 shares = $139. At 30 days left until expiry, the price of the stock has dropped to $45 a share. The price of a put option is now $5.02, and so the total price you could get selling the put option would be $5.02 x 100 = $502, fewer commissions.

Just like with a call option, if you buy a put option, you can exercise your rights, which, in this case, means selling the stock at a higher price than it's trading for on the market. If you already owned the shares, then the put option actually saves you from having to eat too many losses. That is, as the owner of the options, you can use sell the stock at $50 a share, even though it is trading at $45 a share. But remember you'd lose the price you paid for the premium, and so your net would be $5 - $1.39 = $3.61.

Some people buy put options to protect their investments in large numbers of shares. Owning a put option and being able to sell someone your shares at a much higher price than they are trading for in the market in the event a stock has a major downturn can be reassuring.

Even for those not currently owning the stock, you could buy them at the reduced market price, that is currently $45 a share, and then exercise your rights and sell the shares to the originator of the options contract at the strike price of $50 a share.

Why Sell Put Options?

Suppose that the party who writes or is the writer of the option has to buy shares of stock at an inflated price. This is because the strike price would be higher than the market price if the option were to be exercised. So you might be wondering why anyone would enter into such a contract. Again, there is a bit of speculation going on here. In this case, the seller of the option is speculating that the price of the stock is going to remain above the strike price of the option before it expires. In that case, they can earn money from the premium, which is the fee they received for the option.

Also, unless the stock is in a catastrophic situation, it might not be such a bad deal having to buy the stock. If it goes up in price again, then you can either break even or possibly see the stock price go high enough so that you can earn a profit.

Put options can be "protected," meaning that you reserve enough cash in your brokerage account just in case you need to purchase the shares. Remember they would be sold at the strike price. For example, with a strike at $40, you'd have to have $4,000 in your account in order to sell a "protected" put.

On the other hand, with brokerage approval, you could sell a "naked" put. This is equivalent to selling a naked call, meaning that the options contract isn't backed by anything.

How Many Options Are Actually Exercised

The big rub in this is that the vast majority of options are never exercised. In fact, only 10% of options are exercised. The others expire worthlessly or are closed out. That means that people who write options contracts have good odds that they can make a monthly income selling either calls or puts. Since most options aren't exercised, many traders earn monthly incomes selling naked puts. But if a put option is exercised, you had better be able to come up with the cash in order to purchase the shares at the strike price.

Put options give you the opportunity to profit from drops in the share price. Any $1 move in share price can mean big pricing changes in options.

Between April 23, 2019, and April 25, 2019 SNAP declined from $11.99 a share to $10.79 a share.

Between May 3, 2019, and May 14, 2019, SPY dropped from $294 a share to $280 a share.

- On April 24, 2019, Intel was trading at $58.72 a share. By May 1, it was trading at $50.76.

Knowing When to Buy Puts and Calls

The trick, of course, is to know when the stock will rise, which means buy a call option, or if the stock declines, which means buy a put option.

Knowing how to make your trades isn't going to be something you're going to be successful at very often simply going off gut feelings. Instead, you're going to have to put some time into studying the companies you plan to invest in, just like you would if you were building a personal stock portfolio, but in this case, you're going to be more interested in short term news that can move the stock. That means you're going to be looking for upcoming earnings reports and what the expectations are. You'll want to pay attention to news about products the company has on the market or plans to release. One earnings report that failed to meet expectations can send stocks tumbling; on the other hand, if it exceeds expectations, the shares will rise dramatically in price. Any product recall or failure can send shares tumbling, the release of an exciting new product like a new model iPhone that wows critics can send shares skyrocketing.

You can't predict everything ahead of time so you can't expect to win on every single trade, but by studying company fundamentals and keeping up with financial news, you can make reasonable bets that make for more wins than losses on your trades.

Options Pricing

Don't confuse strike price with options pricing. You will see options listed by strike price, but the price for the option is listed for one share. Remember that the option is for 100 shares, so the price you have to pay for the option is the option price x 100.

For example, SPY is a fund that tracks the S & P 500. The current share price is $293.17 a share. Looking at options, we see that they are listed as calls or puts by strike price. So we see a $294 call expiring in 2 weeks, with a price of $3.23. This means that the price to buy one options contract would be $323. If we wanted to buy 5 options contracts, it would cost $3.23 x 100 x 5 = $1,615.

In The Money

In this case, the strike price of the option is positioned favorably, in comparison to the current share price of the stock on the market. Call options are in the money when the strike price is below the trading price of the stock. For example, IBM is currently trading at $139.20 a share. That means a call option that has a strike price of $137 would be "in the money."

We say it's in the money because someone would benefit by owning the call option, because they would have the ability to exercise the option and therefore buy shares of IBM at $137 a share, which is cheaper than the $139.20 per share they would have to pay simply buying the shares on the market. In the money call options are worth considerably more than those options that are not in the money. For example, a

$137 option on IBM option would cost a total of $377, while an IBM option with a strike price of $142 would cost $97.

Put options are in the money when the strike is higher than the market price. In that case, anyone who owns an option contract would benefit because they could sell shares of IBM at the strike price. Since they're higher than the price currently going on the market, they benefit.

In the money options always have a higher value. If the share price is $139.20, a $140 IBM put is in the money and costs $233. A $138 put option is not in the money, and so costs less, at $160.

At the Money

In this case, the share price is exactly equal to the strike price. You can buy at the money options as a strategy to save some money. This can be a good strategy because they may have a good probability of moving in the money in the coming days or weeks.

Out of the Money

In this case, for a call option, the market price is below the strike.

These options will be priced lower when compared to "in the money" options and "at the money" options. If there is a strong reason to believe that prices will move enough so it will be in the money at some point before the option expires since the prices are low, they can be a good bargain. But that depends on the specifics of market conditions and what's going on with the company at that particular time.

Now, consider puts. We say it's "out of the money" when it's market price is higher than its strike price.

When an option is out of the money, it can't be exercised, and so it's why they are cheaper. The main thing to remember about out of the money options is that they expire worthlessly.

To see how it works for a call, suppose the share price of some stock is $135 a share. Now consider is an option that has a strike price set to $140, for 100 shares. Then, if the share price remained constant:

At 30 days remaining, the price of a call option would be $71.

At 20 days remaining, the price of the option would be $41.

At 10 days remaining, the price of a call option would be $12.

With just five days left, the price of the call would be $2.

You can see that out of the money options rapidly lose value. This is because the pricing of the option when it's out of the money is tied up in the time value. Of course, if the price of the stock suddenly reversed, which it could in 5 days, this would turn into a profitable scenario. If the share price jumped to $140 3 days to expiration, then the option price would jump to $79. If later that afternoon it went to $141, then the price of the call option would jump to $139.

Of course, if you were to purchase an "out of the money" option close to expiration, you'd have to have good reason to believe the stock price was going up. Of course, if you were right, you'd probably be seeing some movement in the share price already because other traders would be bidding up the price. Also, it is unlikely you're going to have the kind of information the "smart money" or big institutional investors have before regular individual investors know what is going on.

Chapter 1 Top Reasons to Trade Options

We've seen that trading options are an activity that has its upsides and its downsides. In this chapter, we are going to look at the top reasons that you want to trade options. Keep in mind that you can personalize your portfolio and investment strategy, so it's not necessary to go "all in" when it comes to trading options. You can have options trading as one part of a diverse investment strategy. In fact, many people use options to cover risks in other parts of their overall portfolio.

1. Trading Options provides an investment opportunity with limited capital

We then expanded on that and saw what kind of possibilities existed when investing larger amounts. However, if you are just starting out with investing, it's not necessary to buy more than one options contract at a time. You can invest for a relatively small amount of money depending on the stock. Trading doesn't have to be approached with an all or nothing mentality. You can start with small investments and work your way up by reinvesting your profits.

2. You can hedge your risks with index funds

Most people who invest in stocks will be investing in index funds in order to have a diversified portfolio. By utilizing options, you can hedge your risks with index funds. Index puts can help you mitigate losses if the market experiences a major downturn. Smart investors will utilize index puts so that the next recession doesn't leave them with huge losses.

3. Profit off of other losses

OK, it sounds bad when phrased that way. This is an opportunity that simply isn't available when doing regular stock trading.

4. Collect Premiums

This is another way to earn money in an overall investment portfolio that uses diverse strategies as well as diverse investments.

5. Capitalize on outsized gains

One of the biggest benefits that come with trading options is being able to control large amounts of stock that could have a huge upside if there is a major increase in stock price by purchasing a large number of call options. Of course, being a fortune teller isn't generally a lucrative income, but you can increase your chances of success by carefully studying the markets and the companies behind the individual stocks. Look for dynamic areas where new companies could see a huge gain in the stock price over a short period. The risk is that you'll lose your premium if the strike price isn't surpassed, but if it is then you'll have a chance to score big.

Chapter 2 Ways to Trade

The main method for investing in the forex market, therefore, remains the classic forex market. When you operate on the forex market, you are actually buying and selling currencies.

However, over the years, other financial instruments have been introduced to invest in forex and currencies indices on the forex exchange. We are talking about CFD (contract for difference) and binary options. The main feature of these two financial instruments is the following: when you use them to invest in forex, you will not actually own the lots you are investing in.

That said, for those who do not intend to trading online, it could make little sense. Let's try to clarify. Both CFDs and binary options are contracts between investors and brokers. It's not like the classic forex market, where traders buy and sell among themselves. In CFDs and binary options, the asset movement (in this case the buying and selling of currencies) does not take place.

CFDs and binary options are used to speculate on the performance of the value of equity securities. If the trader's forecast is correct, the operation will lead to a profit; vice versa, if the trader's prediction is wrong, the operation will lead to a loss. So the mode of operation is similar to the stock market: if I invest on the upside, whether I do it with CFDs or actually buy currencies, I only earn money if the value increases.

As we explained in the previous paragraphs, CFDs are also derivative instruments, so they are used to speculate on the performance of asset values. This means that when you buy and sell CFDs, you will never own the asset traded (as opposed to classic forex trading).

Moreover, as with binary options, with CFDs it is possible to trade on:

- Equity securities
- Equity indices
- Forex currencies pairs
- Commodities
- ETF

Leverage plays an important role in CFD trading: through leverage, we can literally multiply the value of our investment. Just to give an example, if you use a lever of 1: 100 and invest € 100, thanks to this lever you can move well € 10,000 (using only your hundred!). All this is made possible thanks to the leverage, which is a sort of "loan" (if we can define it) by the broker, thanks to which you can invest more money than you really have.

But if we talk about eToro, we can't avoid talking about Social Trading. For those who do not know, eToro was the first broker to have introduced Social Trading in CFDs. Thanks to Social trading it is possible to invest by copying (automatically) the operations carried out by the other traders registered on the eToro platform. All you need is a couple of clicks to find the traders to follow, choose the amount to invest, and you're done. In this way, even novice traders can exploit the knowledge and experience of professional traders, copying their operations.

The online trading strategies are based on the study of mathematical and graphic analysis that can suggest the trader the best moment to buy and sell. As we have seen today, it is possible to invest in the stock market thanks to online trading, choosing between trading binary options and trading with the forex market.

Precise right away that there is no suitable trading strategy for all traders, but there are different trading strategies, based on traders and their style of trading.

Therefore, it is possible to customize different online trading strategies on the basis of their trading objectives, their intellectual and psychological abilities.

We also recommend using 2 proven techniques not to turn winnings into losses:

stop loss: it establishes a maximum loss that you are willing to suffer;

take profit: you place a dynamic exit level that rises slowly.

Stocks vs. other investments

In this historical moment, the search for high returns has become almost spasmodic. Unfortunately, the expansionary policy of central banks has caused the collapse of yields (now virtually 0). Anyone who wants to get a positive return must take risks.

In this context, many are deciding to invest in stocks. What we are wondering with this chapter is whether it is really worth investing in stocks. The answer? It certainly is worth it, but it all depends on the modality of the investment.

This is an investment that can still guarantee very high performance, provided, however, to follow some guidelines.

The first tip is to use only really affordable platforms to invest in stocks. Among the best, we can definitely remember Plus500 or Markets. These platforms are characterized by the fact that they are very easy to use, even for those who have never worked with the actions but, at the same time, guarantee advanced tools, suitable even for the most experienced and needs. At the time of registration, you receive a free bonus that amounts to 7,000 euros for Plus500 and 4,000 euros for Markets. This is additional capital that can be used to operate on the stock markets but cannot be directly withdrawn. If you use the bonus and you get profits, these profits can instead be taken without problems and constraints.

Both Plus500 and Markets are Trading Contracts for Difference (CFD) trading platforms: this is a particularly flexible and easy-to-understand derivative instrument that guarantees the possibility of obtaining high profits both when markets rise, and markets fall. This is the second condition that makes it worthwhile to invest in stocks: if you buy shares directly, you earn only when the markets go up. And in today's financial conditions, it's an immense gamble. At this time, it is absolutely not convenient to buy shares, the thing that must be done is to subscribe derivatives (such as CFDs that are very simple) that have underlying actions. Plus500 and Markets are the ideal solution for investing in stocks and, incidentally, they also allow investing in forex, indices, commodities, bitcoins, etc.

If you want to invest in shares and you want to earn money, the advice is to open an account on Markets or Plus500.

The big advantage of stock investing: leverage

Through the use of financial leverage (or simply "leverage") a person has the possibility to buy or sell financial assets for an amount higher than the capital held and, consequently, to benefit from a higher potential return than that deriving from a direct investment in the underlying and, conversely, to expose yourself to the risk of very significant losses.

Let's see how the concept of leverage works starting from a simple case. Let's assume you have $ 100 available to invest Leverage financial in a stock. Let's assume that the gain or loss expectations are equal to

30%: if things go well, we will have $ 130. Otherwise, we will have $ 70. This is a simple speculation in which we bet on a particular event.

In case we decide to risk more investing, in addition to our $ 100, also another $ 900 borrowed, then the investment would take a different articulation because we use a leverage of 10 to 1 (we invest $ 1000 having a capital initial only of 100). If things go well and the stock goes up 30%, we will receive $ 1300; we return the 900 borrowed with a gain of $ 300 on initial capital of 100. So we get a 300% profit with a stock that in he gave a 30% return. Obviously, on the $ 900 borrowed we will have to pay interest, but the general principle remains valid: the leverage allows to increase the possible gains.

Considering the further case of the investment in derivatives. Let's assume we buy a derivative that, within a month, gives the right to buy 100 grams of gold at a price set today of $ 5,000. We could physically buy the gold with an outlay of 5000 $ and keep it waiting for the price to rise and then sell it back. If we decide instead to use derivatives, we should not have $ 5,000, but only the capital needed to buy the derivative. Let's say that a bank sells for

100 $ the derivative that allows us to buy the same 100 grams of gold in a month to $ 5,000. If in a month the gold is worth 5,500, we can buy it and sell it immediately, realizing a gain of 500 $. With the 100 $ of the price of the derivative, we make a profit of $ 400, or 400%, at $ 100.

Without using derivatives and leverage, the same $500, I could have earned them only against an investment of $ 5,000, making a profit of 10%.

What are the potentials of its use?

The potential of leveraging is clear. But be careful: the leverage multiplier effect, described with the previous examples, works even if the investment goes wrong. For example, if we decide to invest $ 100 in our possession plus an additional sum of $ 900 borrowed, if the stock depreciated by 30%, we would remain with only $ 700 in hand; having to return the $ 900 borrowed plus interest and considering the $ 100 of our initial investment we would have a loss of over $ 300 on an initial capital of $ 100. As a percentage, the loss would, therefore, be 300% against a reduction in the value of the share of 30%.

Another element to keep in mind is that the different financial levers can be combined: in this way speculation operations are carried out using a "squared lever" with clear reflections on potential potentials.

What may appear to be an interesting tool with positive potential for the investor, on the other hand, presents risks that must, therefore, be taken into due consideration. In fact, if the financial system as a whole works with a very high leverage and financial institutions lend money to each other to multiply the possible profits, the loss of an individual investor can trigger a domino effect by infecting the entire financial market.

Banks are typically entities that operate with a more or less high degree of leverage: against a certain net capital, the total assets in which the resources are invested is generally much higher. For example, a bank with equity of $ 100 and leverage of 20 manages assets for $ 2,000. A loss of 1% of the assets entails the loss of 20% of the equity capital.

The development of the market for the transfer of credit risk (from financial intermediaries to the market) has meant that the traditional bank model, called "originate-and-hold" ("create and hold": the bank that provided the loan it remains in the balance sheet until maturity), has been substituted for many operators from the "originate-to-distribute" ("create and distribute": the intermediary selects the debtors, but then transfers the loan to others, recovering the liquidity and the regulatory capital previously committed or the pure credit risk (credit derivatives), with benefits only on capital requirements), with the effect of a further increase in leverage. The spread of this second bank model is one of the factors that explain the crisis triggered on the sub-prime mortgage market.

Chapter 3 Covered Calls

In this chapter, we'll investigate a trading strategy that is a good way to get started selling options for beginners. This strategy is called covered calls. By covered, we mean that you've got an asset that you own that covers the potential sale of the underlying stocks. In other words, you already own the shares of stocks. Now, why would you want to write a call option on stocks you already own? The basis of this strategy is that you don't expect the stock price to move very much during the lifetime of the options contract, but you want to generate money over the short term in the form of premiums that you can collect. This can help you generate a short-term income stream; you must structure your calls carefully.

Setting up covered calls is relatively low risk and will help you get familiar with many of the aspects of options trading. While it's probably not going to make you rich overnight, it's a good way to learn the tools of the trade.

Covered Calls involve a long position

In order to create a covered call, you need to own at least 100 shares of stock in one underlying equity.

When you create a call, you're going to be offering potential buyers a chance to buy these shares from you. Of course, the strategy is that you're only going to sell high, but your real goal is to get the income stream from the premium.

The premium is a one-time non-refundable fee. If a buyer purchases your call option and pays you the premium, that money is yours. No matter what happens after that, you've got that cash to keep. In the event that the stock doesn't reach the strike price, the contract will expire, and you can create a new call option on the same underlying shares. Of course, if the stock price does pass the strike price, the buyer of the contract will probably exercise their right to buy the shares. You will still earn money on the trade, but the risk is you're giving up the potential to earn as much money that could have been earned on the trade.

You write a covered call option that has a strike price of $67. Suppose that for some unforeseen reason the shares skyrocket to $90 a share. The buyer of your call option will be able to purchase the shares from you at $67. So, you've gained $2 a share. However, you've missed out on the chance to sell the shares at a profit of $35 a share. Instead, the investor who purchased the call option from you will turn around and sell the shares on the markets for the actual spot price and they will reap the benefits.

However, you really haven't lost anything. You have earned the premium plus sold your shares of stock for a modest profit.

That risk – that the stocks will rise to a price that is much higher than the strike price - always exists, but if you do your homework, you're going to be offering stocks that you don't expect to change much in price over the lifetime of your call. So, suppose instead that the price only rose to $68. The price exceeded the strike price so the buyer may exercise their option. In that case, you are still missing out on some profit that you could have had otherwise, but it's a small amount and we're not taking into account the premium.

In the event that the stock price doesn't exceed the strike price over the length of the contract, then you get to keep the premium and you get to keep the shares. The premium is yours to keep no matter what.

In reality, in most situations, a covered call is going to be a win-win situation for you.

Covered Calls are a Neutral Strategy

A covered call is known as a "neutral" strategy. Investors create covered calls for stocks in their portfolio where they only expect small moves over the lifetime of the contract. Moreover, investors will use covered calls on stocks that they expect to hold for the long term. It's a way to earn money on the stocks during a period in which the investor expects that the stock won't move much at price and so have no earning potential from selling.

An Example of a Covered Call

Let's say that you own 100 shares of Acme Communications. It's currently trading at $40 a share. Over the next several months, nobody is expecting the stock to move very much, but as an investor, you feel Acme Communications has solid long-term growth potential. To make a little bit of money, you sell a call option on Acme Communications with a strike price of $43. Suppose that the premium is $0.78 and that the call option lasts 3 months.

For 100 shares, you'll earn a total premium payment of $0.78 x 100 = $78. No matter what happens, you pocket the $78.

Now let's say that over the next three months the stock drops a bit in price so that it never comes close to the strike price, and at the end of the three-month period, it's trading at $39 a share.

The options contract will expire, and it's worthless. The buyer of the options contract ends up empty-handed. You have a win-win situation. You've earned the extra $78 per 100 shares, and you still own your shares at the end of the contract.

Now let's say that the stock does increase a bit in value. Over time, it jumps up to $42, and then to $42.75, but then drops down to $41.80 by the time the options contract expires. In this scenario, you're finding yourself in a much better position. In this case, the strike price of $43 was never reached, so the buyer of the call option is again left out in the cold. You, on the other hand, keep the premium of $78, and you still get to keep the shares of stock. This time since the shares have increased in value, you're a lot better off than you were before, so it's really a win-win situation for YOU, even though it's a losing situation for the poor soul who purchased your call.

Sadly, there is another possibility, that the stock price exceeds the strike price before the contract expires.

In that case, you're required to sell the stock. You still end up in a position that isn't all that bad, however. You didn't lose any actual money, but you lost a potential profit. You still get the premium of $78, plus the earnings from the sale of the 100 shares at the strike price of $43.

A covered call is almost a zero-risk situation because you never actually lose money even though if the stock price soars, you obviously missed out on an opportunity. You can minimize that risk by choosing stocks you use for a covered call option carefully. For example, if you hold shares in a pharmaceutical company that is rumored to be announcing a cure for cancer in two months, you probably don't want to use those shares for a covered call. A company that has more long-term prospects but probably isn't going anywhere in the next few months is a better bet.

How to go about creating a covered call

To create a covered call, you'll need to own 100 shares of stock. While you don't want to risk a stock that is likely to take off in the near future, you don't want to pick a total dud either. There is always someone willing to buy something – at the right price. But you want to go with a decent stock so that you can earn a decent premium.

You start by getting online at your brokerage and looking up the stock online. When you look up stocks online, you'll be able to look at their "option chain" which will give you information from a table on premiums that are available for calls on this stock. You can see these listed under bid price. The bid price is given on a per share basis, but a call contract has 100 shares. If your bid price is $1.75, then the actual premium you're going to get is $1.75 x 100 = $175.

An important note is that the further out the expiration date, the higher the premium. A good rule of thumb is to pick an expiry that is between two and three months from the present date. Remember that the longer you go, the higher the risk because that increases the odds that the stock price will exceed the strike price and you'll end up having to sell the shares.

You have an option (no pun intended) with the premium you want to charge. Theoretically, you can set any price you want. Of course, that requires a buyer willing to pay that price for you to actually make the money. A more reasonable strategy is to look at prices people are currently requesting for call options on this stock. You can do this by checking the asking price for the call options on the stock. You can also see prices that buyers are currently offering by looking at the bid prices. For an instant sale, you can simply set your price to a bid price that is already out there. If you want to go a little bit higher, you can submit the order and then wait until someone comes along to buy your call option at the bid price.

To sell a covered call, you select "sell to open."

Benefits of Covered Calls

- A covered call is a relatively low-risk option. The worst-case scenario is that you'll be out of your shares but earn a small profit, a smaller profit than you could have made if you had not created the call contract and simply sold your shares. However, you also get the premium.
- A covered call allows you to generate income from your portfolio in the form of premiums.
- If you don't expect any price moves on the stock in the near term and you plan on holding it long term, it's a reasonable strategy to generate income without taking much risk.

Risks of Covered Calls

- Covered calls can be a risk if you're bullish on the stock, and your expectations are realized, and there is a price spike. In that case, you've traded the small amount of income of the premium with a voluntary cap of the strike price for the potential upside you could have had if you had simply held the stock and sold it at the high price.

- If the stock price plummets, while you still get the premium, the stocks will be worthless unless they rebound over the long term. You shouldn't use a call option on stocks that you expect to be on the path to a major drop in the coming months. In that case, rather than writing a covered call, you should simply sell the stocks and take your losses. Alternatively, you can continue holding the stocks to see if they rebound over the long term.

Chapter 4 A Step-By-Step Way to Sell Covered calls

Now that you know about how important it is to sell covered calls, and how they can help you, let's take a moment to go through the different options and how you can sell covered calls effectively. Here, we'll take you through each of the steps, and why they matter.

Step One: Beginning with Choosing the Underlying Security

The first thing that you need to make sure that you have is, of course, the underlying security, which is what you're going to sell to investors in order to have them try to purchase for lower, or higher than what it is on the market. The call option essentially allows for the person to potentially buy it in the future. The seller would be the one with the options that don't get rid of them until the person decides to buy the stock.

First, you need to choose security that works for you. Look at the different stocks that you own and look to see the ones that have good dividends, that you're willing to keep for a while, but if you did sell them, there wouldn't be much love lost. You should, for example, choose 100 shares of a stock that you own, and you can see that the stock is getting close to the price that you'd sell it. One option does equal 100 shares, so you'd write a single covered call on the stock that you have. Of course, not all stocks have underlying options, and usually, the stocks with underlying options are ones with a higher value.

Step Two: Calculating Before Writing

Before you execute this trade, you should make sure that you always make sure that you do look at how much you're going to get from this. If you feel like this covered call should be done at a certain time period, you should wait.

When you're back here, you'll want to put into the covered call calculator the stock price, options price, and the number of shares, and you may need to add in commission fees and margins, and you should make sure that you choose for the options excised to be there, and you can calculate. You should also choose whether the option exercised is set to *no* to see the difference. You can also look to buy-write or overwrite the stock that you have, and the broker can also add some instructions onto these too. Do put your covered call through the calculator before you begin.

While the sheet is relatively easy to fill out on your brokerage site, this prevents a lot of issues from coming about, and can also give you a good idea of what you're going to do next.

Step Three: Heading to the Brokerage to Fill Out the Sheet

Next, you got to your brokerage and go to the options order entry form, which is where you look at the contract you're putting together, the limit price, the stop price, the transaction, order type, duration, and also the expiration date.

Next, remember that options expire every third Friday, so you should always make sure that you do this. Now, you should look at the stock itself, see what the strike price for this, and what you're willing to sell for, and the premium price on this. Let's say that if it does close higher, it will get exercised, so you lose the stock, but the thing is, you're still making money. But if it's lower, you get to keep the shares, and the premium, which means that it's literally just posting, having people purchase options, and then rinse and repeat.

Remember that one contract equals 100 shares of stock, so if you have 300 shares of stock, only do one at a time. The limit price and order type are also important to make sure that you have a limit there to prevent them from selling or falling to a different price.

There is also the transactions tab, which is where investors get confused. This is usually the "sell to open" option, which means that you're selling this to open the position. If you want to buy back the one that you sold, or buy long, you choose the option of buy to close.

You can then choose the duration, and how long it will stay, and you can also choose all-or-none with this, and you choose whether or not you can trade this. You can't usually choose the preferred ECN but leave it on auto.

Step Four: Watching the Market

At this point, you've got three options for well, your option and covered call, and they're important to note. The first is the stock goes down, so the call will be worthless, and you have to sell it for the price of the option. If you notice that it takes a dive before the expiration date, don't freak out. While there might be some losses, you'll notice that the stock itself goes down in value, so you can buy it back for less money than you got to sell it. If the option on the stock is changed, you close the position, buy back the call contract, and go from there.

So let's say that you have an options contract that's going for $100 and the strike price is $105. If the price goes all the way down to 20, you might have to sell the stock at that price if someone bought a contract for it, but if you still have the premium, you can then buy it again for that low price. You will have to sell if the option is exercised, but again, this is something that you can decide for yourself, and if someone buys a contract.

There is also the option that it stays the same or goes up but doesn't reach too high. This isn't that bad, because the call option will expire, so you pocket the premium, and you will still have the stock that you initially had. Not something that you can complain about.

Finally, you have scenario 3, and that is that the stock rises above what the strike price is. If this happens, then you're going to assign the call option to this stock, and that means you will be forced to share those 100 shares of stock. So, unfortunately, you still lose the stock. Most of the time though, since you're still netting a profit, there isn't as much love lost as you might think.

But, there is another issue that comes about with this. That is, if the stock skyrockets after you sell the shares, you're probably going to notice that you could've netted a huge profit from this. This is when a lot of investors tend to kick themselves for this, but the truth is, you shouldn't do that. This is actually a decision that you made when you chose to part with the stock at the strike price that you desired, and you still achieved profit from this.

That is the common problem a lot of investors face when it comes to selling stocks. They think that they shouldn't have done it just because the price for it skyrocketed to a whole different height. But, that's not always the case. You shouldn't feel down about this, and it can be a bit disheartening, but realize that you're not terrible for choosing the option to part with this. Sometimes, you may not even realize that the stock is going to fluctuate with time, and that is why, when you're choosing stocks for covered calls, they should be stocks that would very rarely have that much of a rise in price, and while having that volatility is good, you should also make sure that it isn't so volatile that you can't predict how it may go next.

When it comes to improving your covered calls, the best thing to do is to research and hold onto the stock. If you do have older stock that you just don't want to hold onto anymore, then I do suggest that you consider the option of writing covered calls on them. Remember, there are always times when you can buy these back too, so if you want to get the stock back and cash in on those dividends, it can be quite worth your while to do this.

Chapter 5 Volatility

There's one final factor that affects the prices of contracts on a fundamental basis, though it's not really something we've touched on so far. The volatility of a contract is, however, an incredibly important concept to grasp for an options trader.

Volatility refers to the movement of the underlying stock. Some stocks will slowly wend their way up and down in a predictable manner – those are not very volatile. Others change on a day to day basis and change between up and down along the way.

To sum up the effect of volatility in a single sentence: the more volatile the stock, the more that an options trader is willing to pay for it. A volatile stock has a better chance of reaching the strike price and perhaps shooting far beyond it before the expiration date.

However, it's also the most dangerous of the factors that you need to bear in mind because it's arguably the most likely one to force you into a bad decision. A volatile stock, for example, can lead to a much higher premium and therefore a higher contract price; unless that stock shoots through the roof, you could actually end up losing money even when you should be making it.

One way to estimate the volatility of a stock is to take a look at what it has done in the recent past. This tells you how much it has moved up and down already, which some use as an indicator of how much it will move up and down in the future.

Unfortunately, it's not always true that the past repeats itself and you can't predict the future based on what's already happened. Instead, options traders use "implied volatility" to make their guesses: the value that the market believes the option is worth.

You can see this reflected in the activity on the options for that stock. Buyers will be keen to get their hands on options before a certain event takes place, such as the announcement of a new product or a release about the company's earnings. Because of this, options increase in price because there is implied volatility – the market thinks the stock is going to shoot up.

You'll see lower demand on a stock that's flat or moving gently, because there is no implied volatility and therefore no hurry to get in on the action. You'll also see correspondingly low prices for the option.

Volatility is obviously a good thing – as a buyer, you want the stock to be volatile, because you need it to climb to the strike price and beyond. However, there is also such a thing as too much volatility. It's at that point the contracts become popular, the prices rise and you stand to pay more for a contract than you will ultimately profit.

Your brokers will likely be able to provide you with a program that will help you determine implied volatility, asking you to enter certain factors and then calculating it for you. However, it's only through experience that you'll learn how to spot a stock that's just volatile enough to justify its higher price – again, practice is key.

It's also worth noting that a lot of the risk in options trading comes from volatility, largely because it's impossible to be accurate in your estimates. What happens if an earthquake destroys that company's headquarters? Stocks are going to plummet, and you had absolutely no way to see it coming.

That's why options traders are forced to accept that their fancy formulas are not going to be perfect predictors. They will help, but you should still be conservative in your trading and avoid the temptation to sink everything into a trade you believe could make your fortune thanks to its volatility.

Strategies for a Volatile Market

Long Straddle

This strategy is essentially an amalgamation of the long call and long put trading strategies. You will be using the money options for executing the strategy. You are required to purchase at the money calls along with at the money puts of the same amount. Execute both these transactions simultaneously and ensure that the expiry date for them stays the same. Given that the expiry date is long-term, it gives the underlying security sufficient time to show a price movement and increases your chances of earning a profit. A short-term expiration date doesn't provide much scope for any changes in the price of an asset, so the profitability is also relatively low.

Long Strangle

This is also known as the strangle strategy, and you must place simultaneous orders with your broker. You must purchase calls on relevant security and then by the same number of puts on the security. The options contracts you execute must be out of the money and must be made simultaneously. The best way to go about it is to purchase those securities that are just out of the money instead of ones which are far out of the money. Make sure that the strike prices in both these transactions are equidistant from the existing trading price of the underlying asset.

Strip Straddle

This strategy is quite similar to a long straddle- you will be purchasing at the money calls and at the money puts. The only difference is that the number of puts you purchase will be higher than the calls your purchase. The expiry date and the underlying asset for both these transactions you make will be the same. The only factor upon which your profitability lies on is the ratio of puts to calls you use. The best ratio is to purchase two puts for every call you make.

Strip Strangle

You stand to earn a profit if the underlying asset makes a big price movement in either direction is. However, your profitability increases if the price movement is downwards instead of upwards. You will be required to purchase out of the money calls and out of the money puts. Ensure that the number of out of the money puts you make are greater than the out of the money calls you to decide to make. So, to begin with, the ratio of 2:1 will work well for you.

Strap Straddle

This is quite similar to the long straddle strategy- you are required to purchase at the money calls along with at the money puts for the same date of expiry. You are required to purchase more calls than ports, and the basic ratio to start with is 2:1. User strategy for certain that there will be an upward movement in the price of the underlying asset instead of a downward price movement.

Strap Strangle

This is quite similar to the Long strangle strategy and uses it when you're quite confident that there will be a dramatic movement in the price of the underlying strategy. You tend to earn a profit if the price moves in either direction, but your profitability increases in the price movement are upward. There are two transactions you must execute- purchase out of the money puts and purchase out of the money calls options. However, the number of out of the money calls you to make must be greater than the out of the money puts. The ratio of out of the money puts out of the money calls must be two to one. So, you will essentially be purchasing twice as many calls as sports.

Long Gut

You are required to purchase in the money call options along with an equal number of in the money put options. All of these will be based on the same underlying security along with the same date of expiration. The decisions you are required to make while using the strategy are related to the strike price you want to use and the date of expiration. It is suggested that to increase your profitability, and reduce the upfront costs, the strike price you must opt for must be closely related to the current trading price of the underlying asset.

Call Ratio Back spread

You are required to purchase calls and right calls to create a call ratio back spread. Since it is a ratio spread, the number of options you execute in each of these transactions will not be the same. As a rule of thumb, try to purchase two calls for every call you write. Always ensure that the total credit for the contracts you've written must be higher than the total debit for the contracts you have acquired.

Put Ratio Back spread

You will earn a profit if the price of the underlying asset moves in either direction; however, your profitability increases if the price of the underlying asset's price goes down instead of going up. You are required to purchase puts and write puts simultaneously. As is obvious, both of these transactions will be based on the same underlying asset. The only difference is that instead of purchasing an equal number of puts, you will be purchasing to puts for every put you right. The puts you purchase must be at the money while the once you write must be in the money. The expiry date, along with the underlying security, must be the same.

Short Calendar Call Spread

The strategy is best used when you are certain that there will be a significant price movement in the value of the underlying security. However, you are uncertain of the direction in which the security will swing. Instead of spending a lot of time trying to analyze the direction of the price change, you can use the strategy. The strategy is likely complicated, and beginners must not attempt it in the first try. There are two transactions you must make. The first transaction is to purchase at the money calls, and the second transaction is to write at the money calls. Since it is a calendar spread, the expiry date is used for both these transactions must be different. The options you decide to purchase must be short-term with a relatively close expiry date while the options you write must be long term with a longer date of expiration.

Short Calendar Put Spread

There are two transactions that are required to execute in this strategy- purchase at the money puts while writing at the money puts. The date of expiration for both these transactions will be different since it is a calendar spread. The price of the contracts that have a longer expiry date will be quite high as compared to the ones with a shorter expiration date. It is based on the basic idea that a substantial movement in the value of the underlying security will mean that the extrinsic value of both the sets of options will end up being equal or close to being full. The initial credit you receive is because of the higher extrinsic value of the options written. So, if the extrinsic value becomes equal on both sites, then that credit which will be created is your profits.

Short Butterfly Spread

There are three transactions you are required to execute while using the strategy. You can either opt for calls or puts. However, for the purpose of illustration, let us consider using calls instead of puts. The principle used will stay the same. The first transaction you are required to make is sold in the money calls, then sell the same number of out of the money calls and finally purchase twice as many at the money calls. You are free to select varying dates of expiration, but it is a good idea to stick with the same date. The only major decision you required to make is related to the strike price. Ensure that the distance between the strike price and the current price is equal. It means that the in the money calls must be as in the money as the out of the money calls are out of the money.

Short Condor Spread

You are free to adjust the strike prices of the options you execute for optimizing your preferences of profitability along with the breakeven ranges. Only use this strategy after you gained some experience as an options trader. There are four transactions you required to execute in a short condor spread. You can use either calls or spreads, but in this example, we'll talk about using calls. Once again, the principle of execution stays the same regardless of it being a call or a put option. The first transaction you are required to execute is right deep in the money calls, and the second transaction is to purchase in the money calls at a higher strike price than the previous calls. The third transaction is to write far out of the money calls and then purchase out of the money calls at a lower strike price than the previous one. The number of options in each set of sale and purchase must be the same along with the date of expiration. The only decision you required to make is related to the strike price you use. The potential of your profitability depends on the strike price you use. The greater is the difference between the strikes and the current price; the higher is your potential to earn a profit. If this range of difference is high, then the strategy is known as a short albatross spread.

Reverse Iron Butterfly Spread

You are required to place for doors while executing the strategy. For the sake of simplicity, always execute these transactions simultaneously. You're required to purchase and write both calls as well as put options.

Write out of the money calls, purchase at the money calls, write out of the money puts, and then purchase at the money puts. The number of options you execute while purchasing and buying the sets of calls or puts must be the same. Also, the expiration date must stay the same.

Reverse Iron Condor Spread

There are four transactions you are required to perform simultaneously to maximize your profitability while using this technique. You must purchase out of the money puts, then sell out of the money puts at a lower strike price stands the put in the previous transaction. You must purchase out of the money calls and then sell out of the money calls at a higher strike price than the ones used in the previous transaction. The number of contracts you purchase or write in each of the four transactions must be the same, along with their expiration date. The transactions very are selling the contracts; ensure that they are further out of the money than the transactions where you are purchasing the contracts. If the difference in these strike prices is quite significant, it is known as a reverse iron albatross spread.

Chapter 6 Technical Analysis

Technical analysis is the method of using charts and other recording methods to analyze various data in options trading. Using these visual instruments, you have the chance to determine the direction of the market because they give you a trend.

This method focuses on studying the supply and demand of a market. The price will be seen to rise when the investor realizes the market is undervalued, and this leads to buying. If they think that the market is overvalued, the prices will start falling, and this is deemed the perfect time to sell.

You need to understand the movement of the various indicators to make the perfect decision. This method works on the premise that history usually repeats itself – a huge change in the prices affects the investors in any situation.

History

Technical analysis has been used over the years in trades. The technical analysis methods have been used for over a hundred years to come up with deductions regarding the market.

In Asia, the use of technical analysis led to the development of candlestick techniques, and it forms the main charting techniques.

Over time, more tools and techniques have come up to help traders come up with predictions of the prices in various markets.

There are many indicators that you can use to determine the direction of the market, but only a few are valuable to your course. Let us look at the various indicators and how to use them.

Support and Resistance

These levels occur at points where both the buyer and the seller aren't dormant. These levels are displayed on the chart using a horizontal line extended in the past to the future.

The different prices reach at the support and resistance points in the future.

How to Apply Support and Resistance

• Using these points allows you to know when to call or put.

• Support and resistance give you a way to determine the entry point to use for a directional trade.

The Significance of Trends in Option Trading

Technical analysis works on the premise of the trend. These trends come by due to the interaction of the buyer and the seller. The aggressiveness of one of the parties in the market will determine how steep the trend becomes. To make a profit, you have to take advantage of the changes in the price movement.

To understand the direction of the trend, you ought to look at the troughs and peaks and how they relate to each other.

When looking for money in options trading, you ought to trade with a trend. The trend is what determines the decision you make when faced with a situation – whether to buy or to sell. You need to know the various signs that a prevailing trend is soon ending so that you can manage the risks and exit the trades the right way.

Characteristics of Technical Analysis

This analysis makes use of models and trading rules using different price and volume changes. These include the volume, price, and other different market info.

Technical analysis is applied among financial professionals and traders and is used by many option traders.

The Principles of Technical analysis

Many traders on the market use the price to come up with information that affects the decision you make ultimately. The analysis looks at the trading pattern and what information it offers you rather than looking at drivers such as news events, economic and fundamental events.

Price action usually tends to change every time because the investor leans towards a certain pattern, which in turn predicts trends and conditions.

Prices Determine Trends

Technical analysts know that the price in the market determines the trend of the market. The trend can be up, down, or move sideways.

History Usually Repeats Itself

Analysts believe that an investor repeats the behavior of the people that traded before them. The investor sentiment usually repeats itself. Due to the fact that the behavior repeats itself, traders know that using a price pattern can lead to predictions.

The investor uses the research to determine if the trend will continue or if the reversal will stop eventually and will anticipate a change when the charts show a lot of investor sentiment.

Combination with Other Analysis Methods

To make the most out of the technical analysis, you need to combine it with other charting methods on the market. You also need to use secondary data, such as sentiment analysis and indicators.

To achieve this, you need to go beyond pure technical analysis, and combine other market forecast methods in line with technical work. You can use technical analysis along with fundamental analysis to improve the performance of your portfolio.

You can also combine technical analysis with economics and quantitative analysis. For instance, you can use neural networks along with technical analysis to identify the relationships in the market. Other traders make use of technical analysis with astrology.

Other traders go for newspaper polls, sentiment indicators to come with deductions.

The Different Types of Charts Used in Technical Analysis

Candlestick Chart

This is a charting method that came from the Japanese. The method fills the interval between opening and closing prices to show a relationship. These candles use color coding to show the closing points. You will come across black, red, white, blue, or green candles to represent the closing point at any time.

Open-high-low-close Chart (OHLC)

These are also referred to as bar charts, and they give you a connection between the maximum and minimum prices in a trading period. They usually feature a tick on the left side to show the open price and one on the right to show the closing price.

Line Chart

This is a chart that maps the closing price values using a line segment.

Point and Figure Chart

This employs numerical filters that reference times without fully using the time to construct the chart.

Overlays

These are usually used on the main price charts and come in different ways:

• *Resistance* – refers to a price level that acts as the maximum level above the usual price

• *Support* – the opposite of resistance, and it shows as the lowest value of the price

• *Trend line* – this is a line that connects two troughs or peaks.

• *Channel* – refers to two trend lines that are parallel to each other

• *Moving average* – a kind of dynamic trend line that looks at the average price in the market

• *Bollinger bands* – these are charts that show the rate of volatility in a market.

• *Pivot point* – this refers to the average of the high, low, and closing price averages for a certain stock or currency.

Price-based Indicators

These analyze the price values of the market. These include:

• *Advance decline line* – this is an indicator of the market breadth

• *Average directional index* – shows the strength of a trend in the market

• *Commodity channel index* – helps you to identify cyclical trends in the market

• *Relative strength index* – this is a chart that shows you the strength of the price

• *Moving average convergence (MACD)* – this shows the point where two trend line converge or diverge.

• *Stochastic oscillator* – this shows the close position that has happened within the recent trading range

• *Momentum* – this is a chart that tells you how fast the price changes

The Benefits of Technical Analysis in Options Trading

There are a variety of benefits that you enjoy when you use technical analysis in trading options. The benefits arise from the fact that traders are usually asking a lot of questions touching on the price of the market and entry points. While the forecast for prices is a huge task, the use of technical analysis makes it easier to handle.

The major advantages of technical analysis include

Expert Trend Analysis

This is the biggest advantage of technical analysis in any market. With this method, you can predict the direction of the market at any time. You can determine whether the market will move up, down or sideways easily.

Entry and Exit Points

As a trader, you need to know when to place a trade and when to opt out. The entry point is all about knowing the right time to enter the trade for good returns. Exiting a trade is also vital because it allows you to reduce losses.

Leverage Early Signals

Every trader looks for ways to get early signals to assist them in making decisions. Technical analysis gives you signals to trigger a decision on your part.

This is usually ideal when you suspect that a trend will reverse soon. Remember the time the trend reverses are when you need to make crucial decisions.

It Is Quick

In options trading, you need to go with techniques that give you fast results. Additionally, getting technical analysis data is cheaper than other techniques in fundamental analysis, with some companies offering free charting programs. If you are in the market to make use of short time intervals such as 1-minute, 5-minute, 30 minute or 1-hour charts, you can get this using technical analysis.

It Gives You A Lot of Information

Technical analysis gives you a lot of information that you can use to make trading decisions. You can easily build a position depending on the information you get then take or exit trades. You have access to information such as chart pattern, trends, support, resistance, market momentum, and other information.

The current price of an asset usually reflects every known information of an asset. While the market might be rife with rumors that the prices might surge or plummet, the current price represents the final point for all information. As the traders and investors change their bearing from one part to another, the changes in asset reflect the current value perception.

If all this turns out to be true, then the only info you require is a price chart that gives all the price reflections and predictions. There isn't any need for you to worry yourself with the reasons why the price is rising or falling when you can use a chart to determine everything.

With the right technical analysis information, you can make trading easier and faster because you make decisions based not on hearsay but facts. You don't have to spend your time reading and trying to make headway in financial news. All you need us to check what the chart tells you.

You Understand Trends

If the prices on the market were to gyrate randomly without any direction, you would find it hard to make money. While these trends run in all directions, the prices always move in trends. Directional bias allows you to leverage the benefits of making money. Technical analysis allows you to determine when a trend occurs and when it doesn't occur, or when it is in reversal.

Many of the profitable techniques that are used by the traders to make money follow trends. This means that you find the right trend and then look for opportunities that allow you to enter the market in the same direction as the trend. This helps you to capitalize on the price movement.

Trends run in various degrees. The degree of the trend determines how much money you make, whether in the short term or long-term trading. Technical analysis gives you all the tools that make it possible for you to do this.

History Always Repeats Itself

Technical analysis uses common patterns to give you the information to trade. However, you need to understand that history will not be exact when it repeats itself, though. The current analysis will be either bigger or smaller, depending on the existing market conditions. The only thing is that it won't be a replica of the prior pattern.

This pans out easily because most human psychology doesn't change so much, and you will see that the emotions have a hand in making sure that prices rise and fall. The emotions that traders exhibit create a lot of patterns that lead to changes in prices all the time. As a trader, you need to identify these patterns and then use them for trading. Use prior history to guide you and then the current price as a trigger of the trade.

Enjoy Proper Timing

Do you know that without proper timing you will not be able to make money at all? One of the major advantages of technical analysis is that you get the chance to time the trades. Using technical analysis, you get to wait, then place your money in other opportunities until it is the right time to place a trade.

Applicable Over a Wide Time Frame

When you learn technical analysis, you get to apply it to many areas in different markets, including options. All the trading in a market is based mostly on the patters that are as a result of human behavior. These patterns can then be mapped out on a chart to be used across the markets.

While there is some difference between analyzing different securities, you will be able to use technical analysis in most of the markets.

Additionally, you can use the analysis in any timeframe, which is applicable whether you use hourly, daily, or weekly charts. These markets are usually taken to be fractal, which essentially means that patterns that appear on a small scale will also be present on a large scale as well.

Technical Analysis Secrets to Become the Best Trader

To make use of technical analysis the right way, you need to follow time-testing approaches that have made the technique a gold mine for many traders. Let us look at the various tips that will take you from novice to pro in just a few days:

Use More than One Indicator

Numbers make trading easy, but it also applies to the way you apply your techniques. For one, you need to know that just because one technical indicator is better than using one, applying a second indicator is better than using just one. The use of more than one indicator is one of the best ways to confirm a trend. It also increases the odds of being right.

As a trader, you will never be 100 percent right at all times, and you might even find that the odds are stashed against you when everything is plain to see. However, don't demand too much from your indicators such that you end up with analysis paralysis.

To achieve this, make use of indicators that complement each other rather than the ones that clash against each other.

Go For Multiple Time Frames

Using the same buy signal every day allows you to have confidence that the indicator is giving you all you need to know to trade. However, make sure you look for a way to use multiple timeframes to confirm a trend. When you have a doubt, it is wise that you increase the timeframe from an hour to a day or from a daily chart to a weekly chart.

Understand that No Indicator Measures Everything

You need to know that indicators are supposed to show how strong a trend is, they won't tell you much more. So, you need to understand and focus on what the indicator is supposed to communicate instead of working with assumptions.

Go With the Trend

If you notice that an option is trading upward, then go ahead and buy it. Conversely when the trend stops trending, then it is time to sell it. If you aren't sure of what is going on in the market at that time, then don't make a move.

However, waiting might make you lose profitable trades as opposed to trading. You also miss out on opportunities to create more capital.

Have the Right Skills

It really takes superior analytical capabilities and real skill to be successful at trading, just like any other endeavor. Many people think that it is hard to make money with options trading, but with the right approach, you can make extraordinary profits.

You need to learn and understand the various skills so that you know what the market seeks from you and how to achieve your goals.

Trade with a Purpose

Many traders go into options trading with the main aim of having a hobby. Well, this way you won't be able to make any money at all. What you need to do is to trade for the money – strive to make profits unlike those who try to make money as a hobby.

Always Opt for High value

Well, no one tells you to trade any security that comes your way – it is purely a matter of choice. Try and go for high-value options so that you can trade them the right way. Make use of fundamental analysis to choose the best options to trade in.

Be Disciplined

When using technical analysis, you might find yourself in situations that require you to make a decision fast. To achieve success, you need to have strict risk management protocols. Don't base on your track record to come up with choices; instead, make sure you follow what the analysis tells you.

Don't Overlook Your Trading Plan

The trading plan is in place to guide you when things go awry. Coming up with the plan is easy, but many people find it hard to implement the plan the right way. The trading plan has various components – the signals and the take-profit/stop-loss rules. Once you get into the market, you need to control yourself because you have already taken a leap. Remember you cannot control the indicators once they start running – all you can do is to prevent yourself from messing up everything.

Come up with the trading rules when you are unemotional to try and mitigate the effects of making bad decisions.

Accept Losses

Many people trade with one thing in mind – losses aren't part of their plan. This is a huge mistake because you need to understand that every trade has two sides to it – a loss and a profit. Remember that the biggest mistake that leads to losses isn't anything to do with bad indicators rather using them the wrong way. Always have a stop-loss order when you trade to prevent loss of money.

Have a Target When You Trade

So, what do you plan to achieve today? Remember, trading is a way to grow your capital as opposed to saving. Options trading is a business that has probable outcomes that you get to estimate. When you make a profit, make sure you take some money from the table and then put it in a safe place.

How to Apply Technical Analysis

Many traders have heard of technical analysis, but they don't know how to use it to make deductions and come up with decisions that impact their trades. Here are the different steps to make sure you have the right decision when you use technical analysis.

1. Identify a Trend

You need to identify an option and then see whether there is a trend or not. The trend might be driving the options up or down. The market is bullish if it is moving up and bearish when it is moving down. As a trader, you need to go along with the trend instead of fighting it. When you fight against the trend, you incur unnecessary losses that will make it hard to achieve the rewards that you seek.

You also need to have good ways to identify the trend; this is because the market has the capacity to move in a certain direction. It is not all about identifying the direction of the trend but also when the trend is moving out of the trend.

So, how can you identify a trend the right way? Here are some tools to use so as to get the right trend:

Chapter 7 Vertical Call Spreads

Call spreads require less upfront capital than the previous strategies we've looked at, the collar and the covered call. While the covered call is a steady income earner for the main long position and the collar works with speculative and investment positions, call spreads are purely speculative.

The vertical in the name refers to the way the trade is structured and how it presents itself when viewed as part of the option chain. Options spread trades are a slightly more advanced form of trading and prior to getting into these strategies, it is best if you gain a thorough understanding of the collar and make steady income with it.

Bull Call Spread

The bull call spread enables you to make money in up trending markets. The beauty of this strategy is that you can adjust your spread on the basis of the level of market bullishness, with more bullish markets requiring a high speed and mildly bullish ones requiring a lower spread.

The trade consists of two legs, a long call and a short call with the same expiration month. The long call should be close to or at the money and is the primary instrument for profit in this strategy. The short call should be decided on the same principles as the short on the covered call, with a strike price just far enough to provide a good premium but not too close that the market price would breach it.

As you can imagine the strike price levels depend heavily on the level of bullishness of the market. Generally speaking, it is a good idea to place your short call just beyond a strong resistance level. Let's look at how the numbers work with an example.

Profit and Loss Numbers

Walmart, WMT, is currently trading at $110.62. Let's assume a bullish outlook for the stock but not a heavily bullish one. Assuming we set an exit time of a month for this trade to work out within, the August 110 call, which is technically at the money will cost us $2.44 to purchase. Alternatively, you could also purchase the 112 call which can be had for $1.41. Let's go with the latter since this reduces our cost basis.

For the short call, given that our outlook is only for a month, a strike price of 120 seems reasonable since to hit this level a gain of 9% is necessary which seems unlikely to happen in just a month. The premium we receive for this option is $0.04. Thus, our numbers are:

Cost of trade entry= Premium paid for 112 call - premium received for 120 call = 1.41-.04= $1.37.

This also happens to be our maximum risk on this trade. If the market price of the stock decreases, the long call will expire worthless but the short call premium will remain the same and thus cap our risk.

Maximum reward= Strike price of short call - Strike price of long call - Premium paid for long call + Premium received for short call = 120-112-1.41+0.04= $6.63

This gives us a very tidy 4.43 reward to risk ratio which any directional trader would give an arm and a leg for. You can increase the profit potential by laying around with the long call strike price but remember that your short call strike has to be taken into account as well.

Furthermore, you will also need to place your strike prices at sensible levels with respect to S/R zones. Your short call should ideally be beyond a strong resistance level or if your outlook is a month or less, beyond some level which is sure to give pause to price and delay its advance past it. The best level for a short call would be right at the resistance level since any price beyond this will result in an opportunity loss and any level below this will result in a less than maximum reward.

What if the market turns out to behave in the exact opposite manner than what you predicted? Well, in that case, you will need to adjust your trade by either moving your spread to lower levels, that is, picking lower strike prices for both legs and switching to a bear call spread strategy which we'll look at in the next section.

All in all, the bull call spread relies on you reading market conditions correctly and more importantly, picking the right strike prices in line with S/R zones. If you happen to see price in a range, then using the bottom boundary as the long strike price and the top boundary as the short strike price is an excellent method to make money every month.

Start by implementing this in ranges and then progress to slow moving trends. Only once you've mastered these should you move onto fast trends.

Bear Call Spread

The bear call spread is designed to take advantage of bearish market situations. Now, keep in mind that in addition to bearish overall conditions, you can also make use of this strategy in ranging conditions, such as at the top of the range.

If you find a price at or near the top boundary of a range then implementing this strategy with a shorter term expectation for it to work will bring you good profits in the short run. The key as always is to ensure that your risk is covered and that your strike prices are in line with S/R environment.

The bear call, just like the bull call, has two legs to it. There is a short call and a long call but in the bear call spread's case, the short call is below the long call. The higher strike price long call caps our maximum risk while the short leg functions as the primary profit generator.

The short call should be at the money or as close to it as possible with the long call just beyond a strong S/R level. Let's look via an example how the numbers work for this strategy.

Profit and Loss Numbers

Sticking with good old' WMT, we have a market price of $110.62 as of previous close. Let's assume this is at the top of a range currently and we expect the range to hold. Mind you, we don't know for sure which is why every trade needs risk mitigation.

You first step is to buy a call with a strike price beyond the resistance level. This will give you premium income and obviously, the closer it is to the market price, the more income you will earn. Of course, the danger of having it too close is that a momentary spike might jeopardize your strategy so you need to balance it out.

Let's say that 115 is a good level and that we expect this to hold for at least a month. The August 115 call costs us $0.50 to buy.

Next, we sell a call which is as close to the money as possible. As with the bull call spread, let's pick the 112 level which will provide us with $1.32 in premium income. As a side note: the prices I've quoted for the 112 strike price option is different because remember that when you buy, you pay the ask price and when you sell, you pay the bid. In this case $1.32 is the bid price.

Our number work out as:

Maximum gain/cost of trade entry= Premium from short call - Premium from long call = 1.32-0.4= $0.92

Maximum loss= Strike price of long call - Strike price of short call - cost of trade entry = 115-112-0.92=$2.08

As you can see, this trade has a reward risk ratio of just 0.44. However, this is still a profitable strategy due to the fact that the win rate is usually quite high with this strategy. Recall the win rate and average win calculations we performed in the chapter on risk and you can figure out what win rate is required to break even and profit on this strategy.

Even this strategy can be adjusted to higher spread levels should you choose but this should be done only if the S/R and the market environment supports readjustment. If you misread a bear trend and the market starts becoming bullish, adjustment is not going to do anything for you.

Both the spread trades require you to read market conditions thoroughly and this why I recommend starting out with covered calls and collars which are market neutral. Despite the lower risk levels of the vertical spread trades, you will have to incur a higher level of directionality with them and this exposes you to further risk.

The bear call spread is a good example of this. Given the high win rate it needs to make you money, it is far less forgiving of mistakes than other strategies. Thus, you need to have a very high level of market and order flow deciphering skills, coupled with the right mindset.

There is money to be made but you need to build the correct foundation before progressing forward.

Chapter 8 Advanced Strategies and Techniques

Some things to know about Calls and Puts:

Calls are used for bullish markets. They are utilized when you assume the option is going up.

Puts are used during a bearish market. They work best when you believe the stock is going lower and you need to protect yourself from a great loss.

It can mean the difference between a $50,000 loss and a $5,000 loss. You're getting out before the story gets even rougher. You can even make money with a Put. Your strike can ensure that you sell a stock at a certain price, which ends up being a higher amount than what the stock is actually worth. The one main rule to this strategy is that the investor never forgets that everything in Options Trading has an expiration date. If you fail to handle your Call or Put within the specified time, everything expires.

Image of a Call Option in action

(Courtesy, www.investorglossary.com)

Grow A Small Account into Something Bigger:

There are a couple of ways of building your portfolio by using Options Trading. The first one is by purchasing a large number of contracts, maybe 10 to 20, at a low price. This is very important, that the stocks must be low-priced stocks, because Putting an Option on one large stock isn't likely to yield much for you. Variety here is very important. Think of it like this: When a contractor goes to work on a home does he take only a hammer with him? No. He takes an entire toolbox. He might even take several truckloads of tools and other workers to assist him. Why? Because the success of his business depends on the variety of tools he has at the ready. If he only has one great hammer, he can only do one thing at a time. It's the same with Options Trading. If you're going to make a living doing this, or if you're going to grow your portfolio to a size that benefits you financially, you're going to need to Put Options on a large number of low price stocks, in the same way the housing contractor invests in a lot of small tools to make a much bigger business success for himself than one expertly designed hammer can do.

So, what's a low priced stock? Maybe a stock that moves up about $1.00 within a thirty day period. Purchase smaller contracts for those stocks that seem to be moving quickly, but steadily. You don't want to purchase something that has fallen sharply, picked up quickly, and fallen sharply again. Another great analogy for assessing whether or not a stock is a decent one is to think of dieting. Research shows us that those people who diet extremely, who lose more than 10lbs in a week's time, gain it back twice as fast when the diet is over. Stocks can be measured in a similar way. The sudden loss and gain is always something to measure with caution. Did the stock fall sharply in the last 30 days? Is it climbing back up in a measured pattern? Maybe by $1.00 to $3.00 every thirty day period? Then this is probably a stock that's worth taking a look at, and maybe, even Putting an Option on.

Remember, an Option is just a contract. We use Options in all sorts of areas in our everyday lives. We pay a monthly premium on health insurance. Maybe we spend $150-$300 a month on a health insurance plan that covers our check-ups, emergency room visits, and surgeries. Most of the time, nothing serious happens, but does this mean that most people are fine without having health insurance? No way. Why? Because everything could be fine for 25 years of your life. You could, literally, only ever had a cold, but when you fall down the stairs one day and break your arm, you suddenly find yourself needing to make an emergency room visit. Just to get in the door, it's several hundred dollars. The initial nurse triage is another hundred dollars. Then, after hours of waiting, you get into one of the emergency room beds and a new nurse sees you and hooks you up to an IV. Gives you some pain meds. Another doctor comes in to see you. Orders more tests. Now your bill has skyrocketed into the thousands. The person who has health insurance may complain that they have to pay a monthly premium of $300 just to cover one 25-year-old who's never sick, but that complaining ends the day they break their arm and, $10,000 later, they walk out of the emergency room only having to pay the $100 copay.

Sample of exercising the Put Option

(Courtesy, www.learn-stock-options-trading.com)

This is why insurance is so important. It's the same with Options Trading. Why would you throw $10,000 at a stock, watch it crash, and maybe walk away another $20,000 in the hole a month later? This is why Options are important. Yes, they come with risk, but only as much risk as you contract yourself to lose. If you've placed a $100 Put on a Strike, then when that stock falls, you're out only $100 per share, and not, say $500 like someone else.

Another good example of why Options are important when protecting your portfolio is to think of real estate. Say you're looking for a new home and you've been pre-approved for a $300,000 loan. The guy across the street is going to sell his home for exactly $300,000. Awesome. But you're not sure that you want to buy the house for that amount yet. You don't want to be roped into several hundred thousand dollars of debt until you see how other things are selling around the neighborhood. Maybe, you can end up buying the house for less in the end. So, you offer your neighbor a contract, an Option. You say, "I'll pay $3,000 today, non-refundable, if you promise not to sell this house to anyone else within the next 30 days, and you sell this house to me for $300,000 no matter what else is happening to the housing market in this neighborhood at the end of that time period." You tell your neighbor that this contract binds you to buy this house within 30 days or to walk away having lost

$3,000. Your neighbor considers the offer, thinks it makes pretty good sense, and you sign on the dotted line.

This could go one of two ways: In the next thirty days, the house next door to your neighbor's could be sold, without a realtor, to a family member just for the price of the mortgage, and there's only $20,000 left on the mortgage. No profit is made because of this low sale, and it brings down the value of every home on the street. This includes your neighbor's house, which is now only worth $250,000, but if you really love it, and you buy it, you're going to pay $50,000 above market and you'll be throwing much of your money away. So, what do you do? You safely walk away. Yes, you're losing that $3,000 that you saved up all last summer, but you're not stuck in a $300,000 upside down mortgage. Now which one would give you greater heartburn? The upside down mortgage in a neighborhood that's going down in value, or the loss of $3,000 which, if you saved it last summer, you could save it again this summer?

The other thing that could happen in this Options scenario is that the guy's house you're interested in buying could have a windfall. The house next to it could sell to, not a family member but a stranger, and this person could be absolutely in love with the place. She could offer the seller $450,000 just for the gift of living in your neighborhood, and now you can purchase your dream home within that 30 day timeframe for only $300,000. That house has gone up in value now, too, maybe even by $100,000. You can buy that house for a steal, sell it at a much higher price, and make a profit. Options protect your financial future in much the same way that insurance does. So, now that you see how Options are used in everyday life, you can get a better insider understanding of how they work in the financial world as well.

Chapter 9 Make Binary Options Trading Simple Through a Broker

With the idea of globalization, the development of the business substances has come to even the country and remove fragments of the globe. In this day and age, it has turned out to be especially apparent for a nation to go into international exchanging for worldwide acknowledgment. The equivalent is the situation with the paired choices exchanging which trading is performed on the stocks and items in the financial markets. The benefit just as misfortune circumstance in the twofold exchanging is subject to the development in the cost of the shares or products. As the world's economy is creating a wide margin, the parallel transferring can be a worthwhile exchanging if execute with a careful examination by the speculator.

The capacity of Binary Trading Brokers
Paired exchanging has turned into the most common exchanging platform, and because of the quick thriving of this business, development in parallel alternatives intermediaries' quality is occurring. The significance of the representatives can't be

disregarded as the real job of the agent is to deliberately deal with the exchange of the speculator by managing him through each thick and slender of twofold exchange. Behind the achievement of each transaction, the binary choices intermediary is the first column. With the appearance of new representative elements in the international business platform, it has turned out to be much simpler to choose the best specialist as indicated by the inclination. The agent enables the financial specialist in taking the best choice at the ideal planning to keep away from the misfortune and limit the dangers.

Cash and Risk Management by The Binary Options Broker

Merchant in parallel alternatives exchanging has the total specialist to choose the benefit and plan the cash the executive's strategy. It is the parallel alternatives dealer who directs the broker in the best conceivable manner concerning the advantage type that is best for exchanging. The help of the agent has a great deal of significant worth as he is knowledgeable about the field of exchanging and is proficient in his methodology. For the long haul advantages and benefits to the financial specialist, it would be the best plan to take help from the representative. Double alternatives agent diminishes the merchant in great occasions by furnishing with the best counter-strategies to make tremendous result from each exchange. Dealers, who are particularly keen on building up a fruitful career in parallel exchanging world, never stay away from the administrations and help of the best twofold agent.

Winning In The Currency Options Trading Market

When trading monetary standards on the Forex showcase, an incredible method to shield yourself from unexpected, unpredictable changes in the market is to purchase currency alternatives. When you are buying a choice from an intermediary, you agree with that handle that gives the privilege or "choice" to buy sell or do nothing at a foreordained cost. Currency choices can have extraordinary potential for noteworthy increases with restricted hazard. In the accompanying part, we will investigate a couple of the procedures that make options trading so appealing.

Before we plunge into currency choices trading systems, you should realize that trading in a universal market, for example, the forex, includes trillions of dollars consistently. The universe of the global fund can and is a confused organization with incredible opportunities to make and lose a lot of cash quick. I implore you to master everything that you can about the market you choose to enter and make a few papers or practice exchanges "sham" account before taking a chance with your assets. You can discover numerous books, instructive courses, and essential data online or however your intermediary or venture instructor.

System #1

Keep time on your side.

Purchase choices in large slanting markets with additional time. The extra time you have in the decision the better possibility you need to make counter "puts" or "calls" supporting your position. You will pay a premium for these choices at the same time, the time you put resources into can receive extraordinary benefits.

Methodology #2

Purchase at or close to the cash with almost 90 percent of all alternatives terminating out of the money each day, be one of the 10% and purchase choices that are "in cash" or at the cash. Keep in mind a long shot can make pleasant increases, however until that cash is in your record, that is all that it is, potential. Purchasing in or at the money will enable you to set aside a few minutes.

I trust these procedures give you a superior thought of how to approach currency alternatives. These techniques are over improved and only two of numerous ways you can use to expand your chances of getting more cash in the outside currency showcase. At whatever point conceivable you ought to receive the mentality; it is smarter to take numerous little increases over a significant lot of time than hazard it all on a long shot.

Currency Forex Online Trading For Newbies
This is kind of an amateur's manual for the Forex showcase, for any individual who is keen on dunking their hands in a trillion dollar daily venture commercial center that can profit for anybody willing enough to buckle down out it an attempt. While the Forex advertises is viewed as a standout amongst the best contributing choices for merchants of products, there are as yet inborn entanglements and things that

everybody ought to keep away from before they begin developing their venture portfolio. Getting off on the right foot will imply that the remainder of your adventure will be smooth and inconvenience free. This is the manual for currency Forex online trading for novices.

Right off the bat, you need to comprehend the market, which implies understanding the ware you will manage; currency. The Forex showcase manages a single action - the purchasing and selling of money for the express reason for profiting. This is done when you do spot purchasing of currency (or any purchasing). Your cash goes into the nation or the nation's stakes; which implies your money can go the world over in only seconds and it very well may be utilized for any one thing which incorporates; reinforcing of speculative stock investments, infrastructural support, supporting financial activities or even primarily as a formative activity. The conceivable outcomes are unfathomable; however, what happens is that you will reinforce the nation's financial position and accordingly raise the estimation of their dollar. When that occurs, you make a moment benefit from the PIP (rate in point) increment. The more positive PIPs you click, the more cash you are likely going to make. More or less, a straightforward nutshell; this is the essential apparatus of the Forex trading market.

The Forex showcase works 24 hours every day and this implies contributing has no rest assigned to it. Be set up to be woken up by your agent at some odd hour to let you know of a venture chance of the century. Online trading likewise implies that you can get to the market from anyplace and wherever on the planet; all using a PC. I think the most comfortable route for a novice to begin is to agree to accept anybody of the realized financier firms online. They give thorough preparing to anybody needing to gain proficiency with the essentials of Forex trading and have even sham records with phony cash and reenacted circumstances for you to tinker around with before you plunge into the genuine article. Likewise, a significant number of these organizations will also either give or offer you a Forex Trading Systems programming, which is essentially a stage that makes trading even more straightforward. With a professional layout, callouts and data showed ergonomically; these frameworks are indispensable for the beginner to discover his or her way around the commercial center. Further developed structures exhort novices on their speculation moves and right their wrongs on the spot.

Trading Options - Learn How to Trade Options

Today the quantity of examiners who attempt their karma in choice exchanging is unmistakably uncovering an ascent. Dissimilar to stocks that may result in a noteworthy hit to your financial position, the most extreme misfortune while transferring opportunities are restricted to the sum you paid for the chance. To begin with, online choices exchanging contact an intermediary who charges a sensible commission for his administrations and offer clues on the ideal approach to perform decisions exchanging. A portion of the representatives provides you with a stage to figure out how to trade alternatives utilizing sham instruments until you figure out how to ace it. This is without a doubt an incredible method to increase most extreme financial influence while managing the genuine devices.

Making a benefit in the present volatile market is intense and testing. With the swing to be taken by the market staying unusual to a more significant degree to many, it is continuously smarter to move to exchange investment opportunities. Exchanging alternatives carefully pursue some essential methodologies that make supernatural occurrences even in the fluctuating business sector situation. The players of choice exchanging can incorporate the different techniques implied for the bearish just as the bullish markets to appreciate most extreme influence. A portion of the significant decisions exchanging methodologies included bull call spread, and the bull put spread techniques in the bullish markets; short straddle, short choke, proportion spreads, long condor and long butterfly in a precarious bearish market situation; and guts, butterfly, condor, straddle, choke, or hazard inversion where one wants to play a nonpartisan turn in exchanging choice when he is unconscious of the contort to be taken by the market.

It isn't only the methodologies that characterize the accomplishment of alternative dealers, for both the essayist and examiner of choice exchanging. Different components that control the progression of exchanging alternatives are:

1. One when to purchase or sell the options as past its expiry, the other options

are nothing, yet a squandering resource with zero esteem.

2. Volatile supplies of reliable organizations that are certain to yield more significant premium instead of different organizations.

Highly fluid alternatives that are exchanged with most extreme energy in the market moving over various hands to appreciate most enormous influence, not at all like illiquid resources that are to stamp a hit to the financial situation.

Continuously play with the cash you can manage the cost of as too hazardous an endeavor will make a gap to your current financial standing. Each stock picked by you for the alternative needs to appreciate more prominent value movements offer most extreme unpredictability, or more all, must be reasonable to make it an active exchange.

The Non-Directional Trading Formula and Other Types of Trading

A few people may discover financial market exchanging, for example, outside trade exchanging, and fates advertise exchanging, forex choices exchanging, securities exchange exchanging, and so forth., as something terrifying. This is for the straightforward reason that the terminologies and the procedures may sound excessively mind-boggling. Notwithstanding, exchanging comes down to just three sorts. The dimensions of trouble likewise vary.

The most popular sort, additionally the least demanding of the three is the sort that goes with the pattern. This is likewise considered the directional exchanging technique that is additionally viewed as the customary methodology. It trusts that movement in the financial market takes just a single direction thereby making it unsurprising. Brokers oblige the pattern as dependent on the past information assembled. A few methodologies that fall under this sort are the "Sacred Grail" set up, the spurious exchanging, retracement type and a break-out variety.

The following kind is the one that counters the pattern. It conflicts with the group and anticipates an adjustment in direction. Many would not consent to a sort that battles the model yet this has demonstrated to have worked for some merchants especially those that pick tops and bottoms, as it were. This is a real method for gaining benefits in the exchanging industry and many sticks to this technique.

The last and most convoluted sort is the utilization of the non directional exchanging equations and methodologies. This is the most developed; however numerous speculators discover it very unpredictable. It is likewise tough to execute and needs much computerization. It is hard to understand yet learning it will be to the financial specialist's advantage since it is the perfect sort for a market that moves in numerous direction and is very erratic. The present economic situation of the world makes this chaotic movement in the market conceivable. Let that not hose your spirits and keep making benefits with the utilization of a non directional exchanging recipe.

Aspects of Currency Online Trading That Can Benefit You

This is the most fluid market on the planet. This is the reason you ought to consider going into currency online trading. The more significant part of the more traditional markets on the earth today have an element which can be very inconvenient to trading, and this is the way that it has a lot of formality and procedures that will back you off somewhat. These red tapes can now and then bind you and see the market move past you. When you have a fluid market, you can then settle on the choice and after that examine the market responds to your preference. Making cash is always about speed and speed is something that isn't an element of a portion of the markets out there. This is the reason you ought to consider the Forex market, the liquidity and the over the counter nature will make it an excellent choice for you.

Next, the online currency trading is additionally a lose-lose situation which implies that there will dependably be a champ and dependably be a failure. What isolates the two gatherings of speculators is that one gathering buckles down and has a decent methodology set up. This implies you will dependably get the opportunity to profit on the Forex market. Buckle down, have an adequate framework set up and pick the correct merchant. You likewise need to settle on which sort of venture strategy you are OK with. When you have this in your grasp, at that point, you will have a decent day at the market, and you will before long end up the correct way. In the most noticeably awful and the best of times, there will dependably be champs in the Forex market. You should put yourself in the correct market bearing, and soon you will profit.

The exact opposite thing you ought to consider about the Forex market is that there are incredible frameworks of help out there, regardless of whether you are a novice financial specialist who has no clue about the market. These can be considered under the class of dummy accounts, guidebooks, and intermediary preparing accounts. These things will assist you with gaining close information about the market and therefore, commit the errors you need and learn from them without losing genuine cash. When you take a few to get back some composure on the market, something you can do is to see it or not the market is directly for you. Likewise, you will also have the option to find out about the market and base your system (starting) on these dummy accounts.

These are a portion of the things that you should think about currency trading. One of the words about this market is that it considers the easygoing and the retail financial specialist to turn out and profit that full-time brokers are in the market. Along these lines, while thinking about which stage to get into and put your cash at, at that point the Forex market ought to be one of the alternatives you consider.

Find out About the Basics OF Forex Trading

Forex or Foreign Exchange Trading alludes to the trading of monetary standards of various nations against one another. The trading is regularly done through specialists in a relentless money market. The dealers make or free cash out of synchronous purchasing and selling of monetary forms in worldwide just as neighborhood markets. The instrument utilized for the exchange is a proportion between the estimations of the two financial types to be exchanged, ordinarily known as the conversion standard or the forex rate.

Forex trading is directed in a market which gloats of exceptionally high liquidity. There is no time limit - the market is open 24 hours every day amid all the working days. This is a worldwide market which encourages trading with every free currency of the world. The idea of the market is precariously making it conceivable to profit, exploiting the quickly evolving prospects. The progressions are generally achieved by specific components like dangerous obligations and so forth.

Like in some other business, dangers are natural in such trading too. This is because trading here depends on the theory which in no uncertainty increases the hazard. There is a wellbeing statement here which you can work out, for example by setting a breaking point which as it were is to characterize the most extreme misfortune when the markets conflict with you.

Zero commission trading gives different choices, and there is a plausibility for substantial volume trading regardless of whether your capital base is generally low. Today such trading is significantly progressively rearranged with the appearance of the web and the online forex trading alternatives. You can get a ton of information online and furthermore set up a dummy record and work on trading with it before you choose to go live.

Forex-trading is embraced by corporate gatherings who exchange millions and furthermore by little scale brokers who begin off with a few hundred and enjoy forex smaller than expected trading. A great deal can be picked up from the world's largest currency trading market with a touch of tolerance and understanding.

Chapter 10 Options Trading Risk Strategies

Partaking in options trading, there are some risk management options that can help you invest better and will make things better for you. This chapter will go over nine specific things to watch out for when options trading, and why each of these nine options are important in options trading. You should be able to use this in order to obtain consistency in options trading, along with considerable success.

Allocation Flows Downstream

The first concept is to go over asset allocation. You should make sure that you aren't putting everything intone thing. You should make sure that you're not putting your entire investment portfolio into equities, but also into bonds, real estate, and commodities. You should also work to make sure that the diversification applies to classes as well.

Many start thinking that they are going to only put their options into equities such as Apple or Google. However, if you're not putting it in other places, it will make your portfolio become too weighted in one area. You should also make sure that it's not overlapping with one another as well, such as if you own both stocks and mutual funds. You should look at the company and what they hold before investing in it, because you might end up investing too much into one area.

The reason why you should watch for this and make sure that you allocate effectively is because the more diverse a portfolio means that there will be less swings or losses when volatility happens. In recent years however, the downturns can be correlated, so make sure that if you're investing, don't put everything into one market. If you put everything in real estate, it can end up ruining you, such as the case of many investors during the 2008 housing bubble burst.

The Importance of Differences

Options that are diversified actually can make a difference in a portfolio. Options, especially ones that are volatile, can be seen as a class. They can also be used to protect you overall. You can use ETFs to help with this, and it can be helpful when it comes to hedging. Having a different portfolio can help you prevent anything awry from happening, and it can also show that you're in a good position in case if things go bad.

Watching Overall Risk Capital

You need to watch out for the overall risk capital. If you're trading options, you should watch for it increasing above 15-20% of the overall risk capital. This is because if you let it exceed, you're putting yourself at risk and you might have too much on the table. You will also need to plan in case if the stop-loss happens to you, you might lose more of your capital than expected. That's why you should make sure that your portfolio only has that much, and if it exceeds act accordingly.

Watch Option Account

If you have an option account, you need to watch how much is on the market. You should make sure that no more than 50% is on the market at any time. It's risky to even have 50% on the market, so it might be best to have less than that when you can.

Watch Singularities

For a single option, you should make sure that it doesn't represent more than 5% of the options portfolio on the risk side. If that position starts to fail, it will not hurt you if it's that number. That's because it can usually go down to about 2.5%, which is only a

50% loss. It's better to make sure you don't put too much into one area than to rely on one option to save it all.

Trade How You're Comfortable

The problem with many beginner traders, is that they don't trade with what they're comfortable with. Many credit products are hard to understand, but the bigger issue at hand is that they are double-leveraged products. Many who are beginning are not comfortable with their construction and behavior. You should make sure that you know how you're working with the product, because if you're not familiar enough with it, you're not going to get anywhere with it. It can save you if you keep this risk management strategy in, and as you combine this with learning, it can make your ability to trade options that much better.

Manage your Money

Managing money is vital for this. You only have a certain amount to use, so you have to keep control of it in order to prevent it from being lost forever. The best thing to do is to position-size, which is when you decide how much you want to enter into any options trade. By doing this, you can determine how much you want to invest, and how much of a percentage you will put into something. You should only use a small amount so you're not relying on one outcome. Some trades can turn out bad, but if you manage it right and only put a certain amount into it, you'll be able to decide how much you're going to put in and how bad the possible risks can be.

Chapter 11 Top Mistakes made by New Traders

Swing trading isn't as risky as day trading, but it does still carry risks. Let's look at the top mistakes made by new swing traders.

Failing to use a stop-loss

Always use a stop loss on your orders so that you minimize potential losses.

Risking too much on a trade

Remember to only risk 1-2% of the capital in your investment account on an individual trade.

Not being careful with leverage

Remember swing traders can use 2:1 leverage. If you're careless, this can get you into big financial trouble.

Letting yourself be driven by emotion

Many new traders get worked up with emotion watching securities move. During this experience, they can get impatient or find themselves fearing they will miss out on a big win. However, this leads to bad moves by the trader, selling too soon or throwing too much money after something they think is a sure thing that turns out to be a bust. Or maybe they enter the trade too early. Instead of being driven by emotions in the heat of the moment new traders need to stay focused on using the analysis and techniques described in this book and go into deeper research to learn more.

Unrealistic Expectations

Swing trading is not a get rich quick scheme. Many new traders have unrealistic expectations that they will become a millionaire overnight. Not only does it take time to become a successful trader and build wealth, but it takes an awful lot of hard work. To become a successful trader, you have to spend a lot of time studying the markets, paying attention to financial news, learning how to read charts, studying the companies and so on. None of this is easy, it takes work.

Giving in to panic

Panic can lead traders to sell and take losses or fail to realize gains they could have had. Again, this is an emotional response. Instead of fearing that you'll lose everything you should follow the suggested rules for risk and always use stop loss orders to minimize potential losses.

Greed

Staying in a trade too long in the hopes of getting rich quick has undone many new investors. A new trader should set profit goals for each trade and stick with them. Use OCO orders so that the order takes care of the profits as well as the losses for you so that you don't stay in a position too long and then miss out on profits, losing money instead as the stock price declines.

Getting arrogant after a few wins

In the event that you rack up a few successful trades, you might get cocky about it and become overconfident. But be aware, if you are not careful the bad trades will find you and the losses will come. Getting arrogant rather than maintaining a humble attitude which will lead you to carefully study the markets and taking precautions while shooting for realistic profits can lead to big trouble over the longer term.

Failing to Plan

Trading for the hell of it is not a plan. Neither is trading hoping that millions will come, so trading as if you are playing the lottery, this is not a good strategy to follow. You need to lay out a specific plan before you place your first trade. Have realistic goals and always know what your goals are. Once you meet the goals then you can readjust. Your goals should be modest in the beginning, that way they will be easier to meet. Set out ahead of time how much capital you are going to risk and what your specific goals for profit are going to be. When you meet your goals, don't blow it by losing focus. Set more realistic and attainable goals with reasonable levels of risk.

Failing to take time to learn

Congratulations! No, I mean that seriously. By reading this book, you have already shown that you are the kind of person who is willing to sit down and take the time to learn about the markets before diving in. However, there is a lot to learn about stocks, trading, and options. You should be constantly learning, reading as many books as possible, watching YouTube videos, and taking a training course. You may also benefit from personally getting to know other traders in your area to learn from them and trade experiences. The stock market is very complicated, and even seasoned veterans make large mistakes and lose a lot of money. You can never learn enough about it so be sure to keep putting in the time to improve your knowledge. When it comes to the stock market, trading, and options, you should consider yourself a lifelong learner.

Don't buy out of the money options

Out of the money options are cheap, however, remember that the probability of the stock moving enough to turn an out of the money option to one that is in the money is relatively low. An out of the money option is a bad way to invest.

Ignoring Time Value

Remember that the three things that impact the price of an option are whether it's in the money or out of the money, that is what the strike price is relative to the current stock price, volatility, and time value. Time value always decreases with each passing day, so you need to know where the option stands with respect to time value.

Buying options close to expiration

This is somewhat similar to buying options that are out of the money. As an option gets closer to expiration, they get cheaper. New traders think they are snapping up bargains by buying options that are close to expiration. However, the closer an option gets to expiration, the more worthless it becomes especially if it's out of the money. Buying an option that is both out of the money and close to expiration would be a really bad move.

Trade in the right time frames

Swing trading is a short-term activity, but it's not day trading. How long a time frame is involved depends on whom you ask. Many swing traders will be trading on a 2-6-day time frame. If that isn't comfortable for you, that's fine. You can always stretch it out further, even out to 100 days or so. But don't be so risk averse that you fail to exit your positions. If that becomes an issue maybe long-term investing is more your style. On the other hand, if you find that swing trading isn't exciting enough when you've put together enough capital to open an account (you are going to need $25,000 at a minimum) then maybe day trading is where you belong. The reality is that you are going to have more success trading at a level that is most comfortable for you. Don't swing trade because other people think day trading is too dangerous or do it because you're a long term investor who's getting mocked by their trading friends.

Chapter 12 Tips for Success

Stay away from calls that are Out of the Money: If a call is not at least at the money then it is not worth your time. While you have likely heard the old adage, buy low and sell high, that is never the right choice in this case as calls that are out of the money are much less likely to get back to where they need to be if you hope to turn a profit on them. This, in turn, amounts to little more than gambling because there are always going to be relatively few indicators that you can rely on to determine if the price is going to stabilize in the time allotted.

It is important to keep in mind that buying an option means knowing what direction an underlying stock is going to move in, but it is just as important to know when it is going to move in that direction. If you misjudge either, then you are likely to lose out on the commission in addition to not being able to use that money in other more profitable ways until the option expires. Don't forget, in order to make money you need the option to increase all the way from out of the money to the strike price if you want to make a profit.

Work out multiple strategies: Eventually you will start to feel constrained by the system or plan that you are utilizing and want to expand into a wider variety of options. When this happens it is important that you work out new plans and strategies instead of trying to force your existing strategy to work in ways that it was not designed to. Certain strategies are always only going to work in certain scenarios and trying to force them to do otherwise is just asking for trouble. What's worse, these faulty decisions are going to taint your overall trade average, making your plan seem worse than it actually is.

Utilize a spread: A long spread is comprised of a pair of options, one with a higher cost and the other with a lower cost. The higher cost option is the one that you will buy and the other is the one that you will sell. Everything about the pair of options should be the same except for their strike prices. When using a spread, it is important that you always keep the time value in mind or else you will find yourself in a scenario where it serves to limit your profits.

Always be clear on when you will be entering or exiting: Ensuring that you know exactly when you want to start a trade or to exit an existing trade can become more difficult the more your emotions begin to come into play. While it will be difficult to leave money on the table at first, having limits to your trade will keep you from losing much more money than it will ultimately cost you. What's more, when you think about the amount of money that you are likely to gain in the short period between when you should exit a trade and when you ultimately do, the amount saved is typically going to be negligible.

Don't double up: If a trade that appears as though it is going to turn a profit suddenly and unexpectedly moves in the wrong direction, the reaction of many novice options traders is going to be let emotion get the better of you and possibly double down on what is rapidly becoming a bad investment in hopes of making back all of the money that was previously lost. If you find yourself in a situation where you are thinking about doubling down on something questionable you can keep yourself from making the wrong decision by first asking yourself if you would have made the decision if things had gone your way from the start. In nearly all scenarios, cutting your losses and moving forward with a clear head is the preferable action. Remember, there are always more profitable trades on the horizon.

Keep earnings dates in mind: When it comes to maximizing your earnings potential it is important to have a clear idea of when any of the underlying stocks related to your options are going to have to disclose their earnings for the past quarter. Regardless of what the outcome of these calls is going to be, they are sure to generate a fair amount of movement when it comes to the stock in question which means being caught unaware can leave you trading based on information that is suddenly extremely outdated. Option prices typically tend to spike around earnings time as a result.

Additionally, it is important to keep in mind when any underlying stock is going to be paying dividends as well. This is extremely important because unless you exercise the options related to the stocks that are going to be paying dividends then you won't make any money in the process. These dividends can sometimes be assigned earlier than expected which is why you always want to have a firm grasp on the newest information available regarding the dates in question.

Understand the risk of early assignment: It is common for new traders to sell options or months without realizing they are putting themselves at risk until they are handed their first early assignment and are forced to deal with it in any way possible. The early assignment occurs when a holder exercises their rights well before the expiration date of the option in question that you are the writer on and it means you have to fulfill your obligation even if the terms aren't as much in your favor as you would like. If this happens to you the best thing you can do is not to let your emotions get the better of you and instead look for ways to make the best of a bad situation before committing to anything specific.

Commit to spreads only when appropriate: When you are first starting out it can be easy to start a spread, consider all available options and then setting up the remainder of the spread. If you typically find yourself buying a call, finding the best possible moment, and then setting up a sell call then you will likely find yourself in a situation where a sudden change of fortune between the two makes seeing even a marginal return on your investment more difficult than you previously intended. This can easily be presented by committing to a spread all at once as this will provide fewer chances for various variables to sneak in and ruin your calculations.

Trade what you can afford to lose: One of the most difficult lessons for many new options traders to learn is that you must never put more into a trade than you can realistically afford to lose, regardless of how good of a deal the trade appears to be at the time. There is never, ever going to be a trade that is a sure thing which means that luck will always play a factor no matter how airtight your system may have appeared to be in the past. If you typically take bigger risks than you can realistically afford, it isn't a question of if you will learn your lesson, it is a matter of when.

Conclusion

Options trading is a great way to enter the market with a small amount of capital. The premiums keep changing and you can make a lot of money if you trade wisely and do not take unnecessary risks.

This book has explained all the important facts about the options trade. It has tried to throw light on all the aspects of options trading so that you understand the functioning of the market. Trading is just a psychological game. Both parties are trying to guess the direction of the wind. The seller is taking a bigger risk but the profit of the seller is also sturdy as the seller is an experienced player. You have to understand the psyche of the seller.

Knowledge is power when it comes to trading. It is not a guessing game. You are speculating about the rates and the way the market will behave, yet you must have a plan and reasoning behind the actions. Once in the trade, this knowledge will help you in figuring the market will move and the kind of profits you can expect to make.

The biggest mistake new traders make is not calculating the real value hidden in the trade. A contract that may look attractive might not have any real value at all. You must pay special attention to that part.

The aim of this book is to explain the main concepts of options trading and how it works. You will have to form strategies to move into the market and you will definitely make a profit.

SWING TRADING

THE ULTIMATE BEGINNERS GUIDE WITH STRATEGIES ON HOW TO INVESTING IN OPTIONS, CURRENCY FOREX AND FUTURES TO GENERATE PASSIVE INCOME FROM HOME EVERY DAY WITH THE RIGHT MONEY MANAGEMENT

Description

The amazing thing about trading and competing in the stock market is the sheer number of opportunities available. At any given time, there are new profitable positions that are waiting to be discovered. If you genuinely enjoy reading about new companies and current events, then it will be easier to identify opportunities as they appear.

Remember that the best way to find opportunities is to research stocks and sectors that you already have a personal interest in. The knowledge you have already is a useful tool for staying ahead of the market. If you have an interest in cars, then you'll probably enjoy reading about automotive companies; what new car models are being introduced and how do you think they will perform? If you have an interest in computers and tech; what types of technology have you read about that you think could be groundbreaking? Out of all the new companies producing these technologies, which ones have the most promising fundamentals, and are more likely to succeed? If you approach to research this way, then you'll no doubt find opportunities for stocks to trade and invest with.

This book gives a comprehensive guide on the following:

- Why is Swing Trading Better Than Day Trading?
- The Daily Routine of a Swing Trader
- How Greeks Predict Option Pricing
- Swing Trading with Call Options
- Candlestick Chart Patterns and Technical Indicators
- Fundamental Analysis
- Technical Analysis
- Watch for Counter Trends
- Breakout & Breakdown trading
- Predicting the Market
- Having the Right Mindset for Trading
- The Secret of Profitable Trading
- Commandments of Swing Trading
- The Top Mistakes That Beginners Make... AND MORE!!!

Introducing

The Definition of Swing Trading

There is a lot of confusion out there about what swing trading really is. So, let me be very clear on what it is.

Swing trading is a short-term trading style that involves you taking a position in the financial markets and staying with it for a number of days, perhaps weeks. So, you could watch American Express stock today and decide that you are going to buy it, then after you place your trade, you let it stay for a day or two, perhaps even more depending on how fast the market action is and the time frame you are watching.

Swing trading is different from other types of trading such as position trading, day trading, high frequency trading or scalping mainly because of the period of time that a trade is held. On one hand, some trading styles such as position trading allow you to take a position and then hold it for a longer period of time such as a couple of months or even years. On the other hand, a style such as scalping can involve holding a position for a few minutes, perhaps even seconds. Therefore, a good way to think about swing trading is, a style that strikes a balance between both sides, offering more flexibility.

As a swing trader, you are mainly looking to profit from short term price changes or what is known as price swings in the markets. Now that we have fully defined what swing trading is, let us compare it to "Day trading."

Swing trading vs. Day trading

As I said before, many people who are new to trading ask themselves, "What is the difference between Swing trading and Day trading?" So, let's talk about it. Day trading is a completely different trading style. And the difference between the two comes down to the length of time that positions are held. Day trading is a trading style in which you execute a number of positions in a day, but at the end of the day, you close all of them out. So, you may open a number of trades, say 10 of them in a day, but at the end of the day, you are flat.

You will never find a day trader holding a position overnight, the way you may find swing traders or position traders doing. A day trader prefers to take small daily gains from the market consistently but not hold his positions for any longer than a day. Because of this, you will often find day traders seeking opportunities in short time frames such as one minute, five minutes, ten minutes or even 30 minutes.

If you think about it, day trading is more like a day job. As a matter of fact, most hot shot day traders simply regard it as their main source of income.

Swing trading is regarded as more of a part time activity. In swing trading, you will be typically looking at longer time frames such as 3 hours, 4 hours, daily or weekly to spot swing trading opportunities. Therefore, this type of trading can be adopted by people who are or already employed in a different job.

If for instance you are a swing trader who is looking at a 4-hour chart to trade, this means that a single candlestick in a candlestick chart will be formed every four hours. This means that you only need to check up your chart every four hours to see what is going on. So, if you are an employee, even with a busy schedule, my guess is you can still afford to check up a chart every four hours. So, this type of trading style can suit you.

Another thing to keep in mind is that, since day trading involves placing trades every now and then, the natural ups and downs of the markets can end up being very stressful indeed. A small mistake in this type of trading can end up wiping you out on all your profits. So, day trading can only suit you if you are someone who very disciplined and can withstand short term ups and downs in your portfolio.

Swing trading allows you take a more laidback approach. You can place a trade and walk away from your computer and not have to worry about it until may be the next day. So, if your goal is to seek a source of income that is more passive, then swing trading is the way to go. It is also good for you if you are a person of mild temperament who doesn't like lots of action.

Truth be told, none of these trading styles is better than the other. It is just a matter of picking the trading style that fits you as a person and your current situation in life. You may want to consider the following before you make a decision:

- The amount of time that you can set aside for trading: If you are a busy person, you may want to consider swing trading.

- The amount of money that you have: Day trading may require that you start out with a lot of money since you will end up being dependent on it for your means of livelihood.

- Your personality: If you are more of a person who likes to take things nice and slow, you may want to stay away from day trading and opt for swing trading instead.

- Risk tolerance: Day trading is for you if you can withstand watching several trades going against you and still maintain your calmness. Swing trading is better if you are more of the calculating type who can only stand taking a loss once in a while.

- Trading experience: Trading experience matters a lot in trading. If you are new to trading, you may need to start as a swing trader and take your time to learn the ropes. After you start mastering the business, you can then slowly graduate to day trading. Day trading is meant for competent professionals who have a lot of experience in this business and therefore know what they are doing.

Now that you have fully understood what Swing trading is and how different it is from Day trading; it is time that we began looking into a number of Swing trading strategies that you can apply.

Chapter 1 Why is Swing Trading Better Than Day Trading?

As you are looking through these two options, you may notice that swing trading seems very similar to working with day trading. While there are some similarities between these two, and there are many times that they will use some of the same strategies in the same way, they are two very different forms of investing. In many cases, investors tend to favor working with swing trading because it gives them more time to make decisions and can help them to earn more profit on each trade. Some of the advantages of working with swing trading compared to day trading include:

- *Temperament:* If you are not a fan of making split-second decisions, then swing trading may be a better option for you.
- *Availability:* If you don't have all day to watch the market and do the research and trading, then swing trading is a better option for you.
- *Lifestyle balance:* Day trading can take up a lot of time and can take away from the balance of your work and your leisure

activities. Swing trading doesn't cause quite a much of a hassle.

- *Financial demands:* Swing trading is often less demanding financially when compared to day trading. This is especially true when you are a beginner who doesn't have a lot of money to invest.
- *Less idle time:* You won't need to sit around and wait as long for a trade or an alert before you can set it up.

These are just a few of the benefits that you can get when you decide to get started with swing trading rather than relying on day trading. Let's take a closer look at each of these reasons to get a better understanding of why swing trading may be the strategy that you need.

Temperament

If you are someone who doesn't really like to make snap decisions, then day trading is often not the best idea, and swing trading can work better for you. One advantage of this kind of trading is that you have more time luxury than others. You can take some more time to consider the trades that you want to take before you make a trade. You can use a variety of tools and analyze the trade a bit before using the strategy. You also have more time to determine your rewards and your risks, which can be very important when you want to be a successful trader.

Swing trading is a much better option for those who see themselves as methodical thinkers, the ones who like to plan out a trade in advance, the ones who like to determine the best entry points, analyze the upside and the downside, and the ones who want to settle on an exit strategy. Moreover, they want to have plenty of time to do all of this before they push to either purchase or sell the security they want to trade.

To keep it simple, if you are someone who likes to have some time to figure out if a specific approach is the best for you, then swing trading is the best option. In some cases, you may find that you are well adapted to doing both swing trading and day trading. But, for those who want to have more time to think through their decisions and those who want to be able to enjoy the trading a bit more, then swing trading is the better option.

Availability

The next thing that you need to look at is your availability. All of the exchanges in North America are going to open up at 9:30 am Eastern Time and then will go until 4 pm Eastern Time as well. The chances that you get to trade outside of these hours are known as pre-market and after-market, but trading during these periods is usually not recommended because there is less predictability and higher volatility during these times.

The amount of time that you have to trade the market during certain times of the day can depend on a few factors but mostly on where you live or your specific time zone. If you live on the west coast, for example, you would have to trade between 6:30 and 1:00 each day. This may work a bit for you because you could get a few hours of trading in before heading to work.

But, if you live on the east coast and you have to be at work by 9:00 in the morning, you may find that there aren't many hours for you to trade with. In this case, swing trading may be the best option for you. You will have the luxury of trading in the evening or even during your lunch break. You can use this time to check your stocks, view the market action, and then get back to work.

With day trading, you would have to watch the market all day. But, with swing trading, you could just check in on occasion and see how the market is doing when it works for you. Just make sure that you put in the right entry and exit orders. If you do this, then the price movements of the securities will come to you and fill your orders during the day, even when you are doing other obligations during the day.

Lifestyle Balance

Now, we are going to spend some time looking at how swing trading is better for a lifestyle balance. Everyone is different when it comes down to how much time they want to set aside for work, and how much they want to set aside for play. Some like to work all of the time, but most people like to have at least a little time for fun activities in their days. You also have to figure out how much time you need to devote to your family and other commitments on top of the work that you want to do with trading.

Again, one of the advantages of doing swing trading is that there is a lot of flexibility for the trader to enjoy. You don't have to sit in front of the computer all day, so you get some freedom to come and go. Yes, you do need to sit down each day and review your position, look for some new opportunities to take care of, and pay attention to what the market is doing. But you don't have a requirement for what time to sit and watch the market, and you don't have to stay there all day long.

Financial Demands

With swing trading, you won't need to have as much money ready to get started. Ideally, you will start at about $5000 in your account. If you can, it is better to start with more, but it is possible to start with less depending on the trades that you want to do. Just remember that the less capital you put into your trading account to start, the more limited number of choices you will have when it comes to stocks you can trade with.

If you want to open up a margin account, the amount of capital that you need to start can be a little bit less. Government regulations state that these margin accounts need to have a minimum of $2000 in them. The deposit can be done in cash or in other negotiable securities, like bonds or stocks that you hold onto. You will have to talk with your broker about using those first.

When compared to doing day trading, the US requires that you deposit a minimum of $25,000 in the account before you can even take a look at trading. This amount is pretty high, and it is going to be more than what most people are able to do. This alone can be a big advantage when it comes to trading with swing trading.

Less Idle Time

Most people have better things to do than just sit around and wait to see something happen. You have other obligations, work, chores, family, and more that you want to spend your time on. But, when you are a day trader, you will have to spend a lot of time sitting, watching, and waiting in between all of your tradeable opportunities, and this can be a lot of wasted time, which most people don't want.

When it comes to swing trading, though, you can still monitor your positions while doing some of your other responsibilities and duties for the day. You don't have to keep yourself tied to a computer screen, waiting to see an alert from your scanning program, or waiting for a big market event to take place that will help you see that a security is going to move in one direction or another. This can free up a lot of your time compared to what day traders have to deal with to make any profits.

As you can see, there are a lot of benefits that come with swing trading. It is a short-term strategy, so you don't have to stay in the market for too long, but it still provides you with the benefits that you are looking for when you want to earn a good profit in the process. You still get more time to do the trades, you don't have to stay connected to a computer all day, and swing trading is usually seen as an easier option compared to other trading strategies.

Chapter 2 The Daily Routine of a Swing Trader

Swing traders differ from investors in various ways. Investors buy shares and hold on to them for lengthy periods of time. They often hope to generate annual returns, like 10% to 20% per annum on their investments. This is a different approach from traders who enter the markets and exit after a very short while. Traders hope to make small but frequent profits in the course of a few days or weeks. Their aim is to make between 10% - 15% or more each month. This translates into big returns over time.

Swing traders use both fundamental analysis and technical analysis to determine stocks with an upward trend and with momentum. A swing trader's work includes the identification of financial instruments such as stocks that have a well-defined trend.

The aim of a swing trader is to purchase securities when the prices are low, hold the securities for a couple of days, and then exit when the prices are high. This way, they exit trades profitably, and it is the method that they use to earn their profits. It makes sense to enter trades when prices are low and then sell when the prices go up.

As a retail trader, you may be at a disadvantage compared to professional traders. Professional traders are generally more experienced, have a lot of leverage, access to more information, and pay lower commissions. However, you do have some advantages in some instances because you are not limited to the risks that you can take, size of investment, and types of trades. As a retail swing trader, you need to ensure that you have all the knowledge necessary to take full advantage of the markets.

Trading Techniques

Swing trading techniques are easy to learn. They are also straightforward and simple to demonstrate. After learning these techniques, it is advisable to put them to practice for a couple of days until you get confident enough to trade live. If your practice trades were largely successful, then trading the real markets will also likely prove to be successful.

As a swing trader, you do not have to focus your energies using complicated formulas and learning complex techniques. You also do not need to buy and hold stocks or other financial instruments like currencies. Instead, you only need your trading charts.

Beginning of the Trading Day

As a swing trader, you need to be up early before the markets open. Most traders are awake by 6.00 in the morning and start preparing for their trading day. The few moments just before the opening of the markets are crucial as you get the feel of the market.

One of the first things that you need to focus on is finding a potential trade. You should spend your time finding securities that are on a sure trend. Another thing you should focus during these early morning moments is creating a watch list of stocks and securities. Also, check out all your other positions.

Current News and Developments

You should take time in the morning to catch up with the latest developments and news, especially those that directly impact businesses. One of the best sources of financial and business news is CNBC, which is a cable news channel. Another great source of market information is the website www.marketwatch.com. This is an informative website that provides the latest and most reliable market news.

As a swing trader, you need to be on the lookout for three things in the news. These are different sentiments in various market sectors, current news reports such as earnings reports, and the overall market outlook. Are there sectors that are in the news? Is the news considered good or bad? What significant thing is happening in other sectors? If something significant or of concern happens, then you are likely to come across it in the news.

Identifying Potential Trades

So how do you find trades that you'd be interested in? As a swing trader, you may want to find a catalyst. A fundamental catalyst will enable you to enter a trade with sufficient momentum. Then all you will need is technical analysis to confirm your exit and profit points.

1. Special Opportunities

There are different ways of entering the market. One of these is to find a great opportunity with so much potential. Great opportunities can be found through companies planning an IPO, those ready to file for bankruptcy, situations of takeovers, buyouts, insider buying, mergers, acquisitions, and restructuring. These and other similar events provide excellent trading opportunities, especially for swing traders.

To find these opportunities, you need to check out the SEC website or filings from companies. Certain forms such as 13-D and S-4 contain all the relevant information that you need. You can also subscribe to the website www.SECFilings.com so as to receive notifications whenever companies file reports. While these opportunities carry some inherent risks, the possible rewards are too great to ignore.

2. Sector or Industry Opportunities

Apart from the rare opportunities, we also have opportunities that are specific to a given sector. These are opportunities that you will find on certain websites regarding sectors whose performance is well above average. For instance, we can determine that sectors such as energy are doing exceptionally well by observing energy ETFs. There are certain sectors that pose a high risk but have high returns and can be very profitable.

3. Chart Breaks

We can also rely on chart breaks to find opportunity. Chart breaks are especially suitable for swing traders. Chart breaks are really stocks or securities that have been traded so heavily such that they are very close to major resistance or support levels. As a swing trader, you will search for opportunities out there by identifying patterns indicating breakdowns or breakouts.

These identifying patterns can be Gann or Fibonacci levels, Wolfe Waves, channels, and triangles. However, please note that these chart breaks are only useful when there is huge interest in the stock. This way, you can easily enter and exit trades. Therefore, whenever you note this chart breaks, you should also focus on factors such as price and volumes.

Securities Watch List

One of the things that you really should embark on is building a list of stocks or other securities to watch closely. The stocks that should constitute this list include those with a great chance at high volumes and upward price movement. It should also include stocks with a major catalyst.

Checking Your Current Positions

It is important to keep tabs on your current positions. You probably have other trades so take a look at these and see if there is anything needed on your part. This is something that you should focus on early before the trading day begins. You should review these positions with the benefit of foresight based on the information obtained from news sources and online sites. See if any news items will affect your current positions.

Checking this out is pretty easy and straight forward. All that you need to do is to enter the stock symbol into websites such as www.news.google.com. This will reveal plenty of essential information that you need to be successful. Should you come across any material information that can directly affect your trades, then consider what you should do, such as adjusting the different points like take profit and stop loss.

Market Hours

Now that the markets are open, it is time to get busy as a trader. During this time, you will mostly be trading and watching your screen. Check the market makers of the day and also be aware of any fake bids and asks.

Find a viable trade and apply all the skills and knowledge you have acquired to identify entry and exit points. There are plenty of techniques you can apply to arrive at these points. Think about Fibonacci extensions, for example. These can help you identify entry and exit points; you can also use price by volume and resistance levels.

As the trading day proceeds, you may need to make certain adjustments to your positions. These adjustments will depend on a number of factors. However, it is not advisable to adjust positions once you enter a trade, especially if you are planning on taking on additional risks. If you have to make adjustments, then it is better to focus more on adjusting the take profit points and stop loss levels.

After Hours

Most swing traders are largely inactive after the normal trading day is over. At this point in time, the market is not liquid at all and the available spread not suitable to enter any trades. Therefore, take this time to do some evaluation of your earlier trades and your positions. Examine your trades and see where you could do better. Focus on any open positions you may have and consider all material events that could have some effect on your positions.

Summary

To be an efficient trader, you need to have a routine. You should learn to wake up early before the beginning of the trading day and to get prepared. You also need to automate as many processes as possible. The crucial step is learning how to set up your workstation and your trading computer. Doing this ensures that you are totally ready for the trading day.

As a trader, you really need to learn how to separate charting from trading. There needs to be a different platform for charting, and in our case, www.tradingview.com comes highly recommended. It is just when you are ready to begin trading that you will log onto your trading platform.

There is a good reason for this. If you use the same platform for both charting and trading, you may fall into the trap of impulse decision. You will clearly view your orders right in front of your face. This will create a sense of panic and urgency, and you may do things in a hurry. When they are on different platforms, you create a thin layer that prevents impulsive action.

It is advisable to learn how to use templates a lot more effectively. This helps especially with the charting. Charting becomes an extremely effective and efficient process when you come up with different templates with varying colors. For instance, you can come up with a different color for resistance and support levels and other tools. The next time that you trade, it will be easy to track each tool individually based on its color code.

Also, remember to come with relevant alerts. Some traders prefer using multiple screens in order to monitor multiple developments at the same time. Instead of multiple screens, you can choose to create specific alerts so that should something relevant occur somewhere, then you will get to hear about it on time. Alerts are crucial and will ensure that you get to find out when there is a price movement and so on.

You can use the weekends to plan the coming trading week. You can do this without the worry or concern of active markets. You can also take the time to come up with different trading strategies and styles that can help you attain your trading goals.

Think up of different situations that can arise as you trade and then come up with suitable solutions for each. This way, should any situation happen in the course of the trading week then you will be well prepared to handle it. Sometimes, though, you may feel the need to use a trading template already designed. These can be found online and are easy to download. However, you can also come up with your own trading plan and strategy to implement. In brief, you should always enter a trade with a plan in hand. This means that you should plan your trade and then trade your plan.

Chapter 3 How Greeks Predict Option Pricing

The Greeks, as they are known as, can be daunting mathematics filled with formulas necessary to measure an options position exposure to risk. Fortunately for you and me, today these are calculated for us on trading platforms used to trade options. I'll define each of the Greeks, but we are going to focus on Delta. Delta is the option Greek you will want to become familiar with because it helps you to understand how an option's premium will rise or fall in comparison to the price of the underlying stock.

Since our main goal in trading options is to make money, the most important thing you need to know ahead of time is how the security we're trading will move at price. When it comes to options, this knowledge is found in "Delta."

Delta is a mathematical formula to measure the magnitude of change of an option's price as the underlying Stock moves in price. Here is what that formula looks like, but don't worry if it makes your eyes cross, your broker will do the calculations and list each options current delta within the trading platform.

You will merely need to look it up, know what the number means and how it affects the trade.

- ABC stock trading at $50
- A call option with a Delta reading of .60

☐ A .60 Delta reading for a call option for ABC stock would mean that for every $1 upward move in ABC's stock price, the call option premium would increase by .60 cents or $60 (.60 x 100 = $60).

☐ A -.60 Delta reading on a put option for ABC stock would mean that for every $1 downward move in ABC's stock price, the put option premium would increase by .60 cents or $60 (.60 x 100 = $60).

However, the Delta will also work against you should the stock move in the opposite direction by the same amount. A call with a .60 delta will lose $60 in value for every $1 downward move in the underlying stock and a put option with a -.60 Delta would lose $60 in value for every upward move in the underlying stock.

How to Use Delta to Calculate Potential Gains

Using the Delta alone you will be able to guesstimate (you'll have to use Gamma to be accurate) how many $1 moves a stock must make to double or triple your investment, and when you might want to sell the option for maximum profit if the underlying security is likely to reach the move you are expecting. Here is another example of a practical application:

- ABC stock trading at $50
- Call option Delta reading at .60
- Call option premium at $4.00

How many .60 ($60 increase in option price) moves would it take to double your money? The option increases by $60 for every $1 move up in the underlying stock, so it would roughly take a $6 move upward at ABC's stock price to double your money ($4.00/.60 = 6.666) ($60 x 6.66 = $399.6) our option premium price would need to be at $7.99 before we sold it to double your investment.

You might ask yourself if ABC stock is likely to make a $6 move upwards or lower your sell target. Would this information be helpful in trading options? Absolutely! Knowing where you are going will aid you in knowing when to sell for greater profits on a trade, without this knowledge you would be hoping and praying it doubled when in fact from the beginning it was not likely to double at all.

What happens to traders who don't practice this calculation and apply it to their trades? They hold on to a declining asset, hoping it will return and surpass the previous highs, when in fact it has hit its support and resistance levels and is now headed in the opposite direction. By the time it returns to those levels again, the option is near its expiration and time decay has substantially diminished the option price, or it's almost worthless. Don't let this happen to you; practice the calculation on any options you are considering buying. You might not get it down your first couple of trades, but you will soon see the value, and you will have an edge that the majority of options traders fail to understand.

Now you are ready to learn about Delta's buddy, Gamma. While Delta is usually sufficient, adding Gamma to the calculation will make your Delta more accurate instead of just roughly accurate. Yet, if adding Gamma blows up your brain, you can do good with Delta and add Gamma later if you want a more accurate sell target calculation.

The Only Other Greek You'll Ever Need is Gamma

Gamma measures how much the option's Delta changes in response to the changes in price to the underlying asset. More simply stated, Gamma shows you how much the Delta will change with each $1 move in the underlying stock price. Here is another example so you can fully understand how it makes delta calculations more accurate:

If Gamma is reading 0.05, it means Delta will increase by .05 for every dollar move. In our earlier example, Delta was at .60 and meant the premium would increase by $60 for every $1 move up in the underlying stock price. We calculated that we would need a $6 move in the stock price to double our investment with a current option premium of $4 when we add Gamma to the mix it changes our calculations to the better. Using Gamma, we know that for every $1 move up our delta calculation will increase .05 and our profit on the option if the stock moves up $6 is now $435 vs. 399.60 when we merely use our Delta calculation. It's not necessary to use Gamma if you are fine with Delta calculations only, but you can see that you could adjust your sell target to $425, $430 of $433, etc., earning slightly more from your investment by using Gamma.

Chapter 4 Swing Trading with Call Options

Now it's time to go into the "how's" of swing trading. This chapter will discuss how to swing trade stocks and options, as well as how to look at charts to find patterns, and how to make a trading plan. Once you are finished with this chapter, please, don't just leave the book and start trading! Instead, take what you've learned and use some practice simulators to do some practice trades. You should spend time practicing before using your money to swing trade.

How to Swing Trade

Let's review some of the basics of swing trading. Swing trading is buying an asset during a "swing" in the chart. If you're looking at a chart, the swings are those short rises up and the short rises back down. They make the small hills and valleys in the chart. They're pretty small, so you're not looking for a larger trend, you're simply looking for those changes that occur during a week-long period. In swing trading, you need to analyze the chart, find the support and the resistance of the asset, and then determine a good area to enter and exit the trade. Your analysis will also show you where to place your stop-loss. A stop-loss is incredibly important because it can help you prevent you from over-investing in the trade. This sounds really simple, but there's more to it, so this section will cover these topics.

How to find the support and resistance

As a swing trader, you should sell the asset before it reaches the resistance. Resistance is the highest point reached before a reversal or swing low. It is the point at which most people start selling their stock, and thus, it starts a new dip in the trend. Support is the lowest point it reaches before going up. Support is the point at which many people start buying the stock, so the stock prices rise.

Take, for example, a person throwing a ball in the air. The point of your hands holding the ball before the throw is your support point. It is the lowest point that the ball reaches before you throw it. After throwing the ball, the highest point in its arch, before it falls again, is the resistance. When swing trading, you want to sell the asset before it reaches resistance.

The reason why you want to sell your stock before you reach resistance is because resistance is the area where most people start selling. This means that your stock price might dip soon after so it's a good idea to sell before you hit resistance. Resistance can be calculated by analyzing a chart. Look at the chart's history for the last year. What is the highest point the stock is valued at, and how consistent is that? For example, if you're trading stock ABC, and you look back at their last 12 months on the market, you want to find at which points they were selling the highest. Maybe for a couple of months out of the year, the highest value the stocks had was $20. If it's a consistent pattern, then that is your resistance level. It's unlikely that the stock will break out of this pattern. This means that you want to plan your exit before this number is reached.

Resistance can be a useful tool for determining the peak price of a stock, but so can be other tools like moving averages. Whichever tool you choose in order to find the topmost point, make sure you stick with it and don't trade beyond that point. One thing with swing trading is that you won't know if the stock will go beyond the resistance point, but you still need to have your exit plan and follow it.

Support is the point at which you may want to buy the stock. Remember, support is the historically lowest point on the chart where the stock has been placed. Using the same strategy as the resistance one, you want to look at a chart's history for the last twelve months and find the areas where the stock has traded the lowest. For example, if you're trading stock ABC and you see that for the last year, the stock never dipped below $10, then that would be your support line. You don't want to trade below these points. In fact, it would be better to enter the trade somewhere a bit higher and ride the wave of the swing to your exit point. Remember, the goal is to find small profits in a short period of time, so once you've planned your exit within a few days, take it. Even if the market is doing well, it's better to bow out early than mistime it and lose your profits.

Again, just like with resistance, you can combine the support line with the moving averages tool to help you find the points that are best to enter in. Most charts that you'll find online will include the choice to see the moving averages for both the highs and the lows. You can use resistance and support to help you calculate from there.

Now that you understand the basics of resistance and support, it's time to practice. Find a sample stock chart online. You can use stockchart.com or other websites. Stock charts are free, so you don't need to pay to see the data. Using your sample chart, draw your lines for support and resistance during a given point in time. As you draw your lines, keep some things in mind: support and resistance lines are often slanting, going in the direction of the trend. They're not always horizontal, though they can be if the market is neutral and there is no prevailing trend. Find the areas on the chart where there are multiple touches. For example, maybe the lines touch the price point $120 multiple times in the last year. This is a good place to put your resistance or support line (depending on how the rest of the chart looks). Within these two lines is now your zone for purchasing. You can find an area that you would enter the trade and an area that you would exit based on what you're seeing. This is just a practice, furthermore you have the benefit of seeing a past chart.

To apply this to a future trade, try the same thing, but this time analyze the charts of three different securities you're interested in. Map out your support and resistance, and then choose a place that you would enter into the trade and where you would like to exit the trade. Remember to exit before resistance, and enter after support. Using a simulator (remember, practice first), or just by following the chart for a couple of days, you can see how your trade would have panned out if you had put money on the trade. Keep practicing this way, and you'll be able to find patterns in the markets. Since, as mentioned before, history repeats itself when it comes to trades. You can also adjust your strategies regarding resistance and support after some trial and error.

Remember to take lots of time to practice trades with a simulator, or just by following your own charts for a while before using your capital. Once you're ready to actually start trading, you want to follow the strategy that you developed, and map out your resistance and support. In the next section, we're going to talk about pinpointing the best areas to enter and exit a trade.

Chapter 5 Candlestick Chart Patterns and Technical Indicators

These patterns are really easy to detect when you're looking at candlestick charts while utilizing the correct technical indicator. Now, using technical indicators isn't always easy, but it's pretty much a 2-step process:

1. Apply Technical Indicators To The Price Of Your Stock- Here, you'll be applying technical indicators (which are simply math formulae) which will show you whether or not the stock is displaying buy or sell signals.

Technical indicators generally remove all subjectivity from analyzing a chart pattern. Technical indicators are one of two kinds- trending and non-trending.

- Trending technical indicators will show you the most significant changes in a given direction and mostly filter out the chart noise (irrelevant changes which don't contribute to the overall trend.) Now, this can easily happen over a few days, and the indicators will help measure the trends as well as signal when the trend is about to reverse, which will let you sell out at an ample time.

- Non-trending technical indicators tend to work with the buyers and sellers of a security. It determines how much the strength of the other investors in the market are affecting the stock movement. These indicators will often use a standardized price history by establishing the lowest and highest prices within a given time period. After that, they will be measuring the securities position in reference to that range. These indicators will also tell you when a stock is being over or under bought. When a stock is overbought that means it's overdue for a reversal in the trend, as the stock has risen too high. Oversold means the same thing but implies the stock will rise.

While you'll find that many swing traders are looking for the one system of indicators that will always give them the correct result that just doesn't exist. Unfortunately, every indicator can be wrong, swing trading isn't just a concrete science that will always give you profits. If it was everyone would do it, and more importantly, we'd use computer programs for it.

This is why fundamental analysis is so important, it helps you figure out when the technical indicators you're observing are actually correct, rather than simply leaving it to guesswork. You'll find that many swing traders will neglect fundamental analysis even though it is what can help you really get ahead of the market.

2. Compare the Stock to the Rest of the Overall Market- This step, also known as relative strength analysis involves the comparison of the performance of a stock to its market or industry. By looking at the disparity between these two, you'll be able to tell whether or not the stock you've chosen is performing good or bad.

Divergences are extremely good signals because they show you how well the stock of your choice is performing regardless of the way the industry, in particular, is performing.

The Wider View-Fundamental Analysis

If fundamental analysis sounds like a 9-headed hydra to you, and you aren't feeling very much like Heracles, don't be afraid. We'll be using the KISS approach to fundamental analysis in this book. Which is to say we'll "Keep It Simple Stupid."

Now, I'm not going to try to set you up for your MBA in economics. What I'm trying to do here is present you the actually important bits. That is to say that we'll be looking at the most important, key parts of a firm's fundamentals. Only those that affect stock prices are really important to us. After all, we're traders, not economists.

Fundamental analysis is about constantly asking questions. You'll be asking questions like how fast is this company growing, what is its position in relation to the competition, what about the returns?

Through repeatedly answering these questions over and over again, you'll begin to have an idea of what the company's shares should be trading at. Often, you'll find that they aren't trading at that point, which is where you make your entry.

You're not going to find the intrinsic value of a stock that institutions like Wall Street are trying to calculate (the intrinsic value is the true value of the company, rather than simply being the value that the market arrives at.) On the other hand, you don't need the intrinsic value. You're not trying to find the value of the shares down to a singular cent. On the other hand, if you determine their value is between $30 and $50 but they're trading at $20 then you don't need much more to invest.

Getting To Grips with Why It Works

There's much less debate on whether or not fundamental analysis works compared to technical analysis working. After all, the whole field of investing is rooted in it. The more a company earns the more people are willing to pay to have a share of it. Let's say you rent out an apartment for $500 a month, regardless of how much you think the true value of a $500 a month apartment is, it'll be half of the value of a $1000 apartment.

Naturally, fundamental analysis is a bit more complex than this in practice. You'll be looking at quarterly earnings rather than $500 or $1000 a month. The point, however, is that fundamental analysis tries to get the value of a company from its projected future earning potential.

Arbitrageurs are a vital component of why fundamental analysis works. They are generally looking for riskless profits for themselves. For example, if a share is, say $20 a pop, and the firm is valued at $1 billion, then if the firm has $2 billion on their bank, with no debt then an Arbitrageur will pop in and buy a ton of those shares.

The Arbitrageurs taking advantage of such miss-pricings is what helps the market stay afloat. The Arbitrageur might even buy the company for $1 billion and pay for it using the money that the company had on its pricing books.

The bottom line is- fundamental analysis works because entities such as investors, firms or governments pursue riskless profits endlessly.

How to Start Trading

In this chapter, I'll guide you through selecting a quality broker for yourself and opening a trading account. In addition to that, we'll be looking at service providers, starting a trading journal, as well as how to maintain a good mentality to succeed as one.

Brokers

Much like every other kind of trader, swing traders rely on brokers. On the other hand, a swing trader needs to use a different kind of broker from the rest of them. This will depend on a variety of factors we'll be going through in this chapter.

Those factors will be broken down step by step in this chapter, in addition to a variety of details needed to open a brokerage account. After you're done with that, all you need to do is grab a few services to conduct analysis for you.

While some services are useful for conducting market screening, others will chart stocks etc. It's important to decide how much you want to invest in your setup, and I'll recommend some quality services so you can make your pick based on your needs. In addition to this, we'll be making a trading journal, which is, as you'll soon find, one of the most useful tools for a trader out there.

Now, why is the firm that's executing all of your trades being called a broker? It doesn't precisely sound like the best of names and quite frankly sounds much shadier than it should. Brokers really aren't a complicated subject.

Even though their name sounds a bit intimidating, you need a broker in order to become a swing trader...or well, to be a trader in any capacity. On the other hand, due to the wonderful capitalistic market we have, not all brokers are the same. Some will give you highly customized advice while others specialize much more in wealth-management. Some of the highest net-worth people out there participate in these trades. After all, these brokers are quite worth it. Naturally, some of these higher-quality brokers will charge massive fees, because, well, they can simply afford to do it? Generally, they'd tell you that the massive fees they offer are reflective of their advice.

You don't need this. Well, unless you're a billionaire, in which case I think you already know all you need about trading. The brokers that use swing traders use are much lower costed. They are so called no-frill brokers. The good thing about these brokers is that due to competition, even they are giving ATM card access, check-writing privileges etc.

Now, with all of those factors, how do you pick one?

The most common factor I see aspiring traders looking at is commissions. After all, nobody wants a broker to take any sum of their profits. This is a mistake.

Now, now, before you rush me down and put me on a pike, I am not trying to say they don't matter. Naturally, fees do matter. Swing trading wasn't even possible in the olden days due to the massive commissions that were everywhere.

Today, it's different. Fees these days really aren't that much, you'll be paying something like a flat $5-12 per trade that you make, which can easily be less than 0.1% of your trading volume. The difference between $5 and $12 isn't large to you, however, it might mean that you get some extra perks you otherwise wouldn't.

Now, some of the other factors are:

- *Charting systems- If you rely a lot on technical analysis when you're making your trades then you'll be wanting a broker that's good at charting. The charting quality and ease of reading can make the difference between success and failure.*

- *Customer service- In my opinion, this is the single most important factor to look at when selecting a broker. Keep in mind these are people that will be handling massive amounts of your money. You don't want to put it in the hands of someone who you can't properly reach when you need them. Every trader will also sometimes run into problems with their broker, and in those times, this really counts.*

- Ease of Deposits and Withdrawals- How easy it is to get money from your broker is only important when you're trading for a living. If it's hard, you won't have an easy time getting that monthly paycheck. On the other hand deposits are very important when making time-sensitive trades.

Which brokers you're going to choose also depends on how much you're planning to spend, fundamentally, there are two kinds of brokers:

1. Discount Brokers: These brokers are those that instead of offering quality and high-tier services, simply focus on executing trades. You tell them what you want bought and sold, they do that. Naturally, most of these trades will be made through the PC, unless you pay extra for phone support. These brokers are generally cheaper, and offer fewer services.

2. Direct access firms- Direct access firms are those companies that let you go past a broker and trade with an exchange or market without a middleman. The advantage of doing this is that you'll have way more

control due to being able to see who's offering what and for how much.

Usually, these brokers will require you to get some software that will give you very high-speed data, usually superior to streaming sites. While some discount brokers are offering direct access trading, these are generally worse at it than dedicated companies.

2.5 Full Service Brokers- This isn't really on the list because it's not for you. These are brokers like Merrill Lynch, they will offer you a bazillion different services, and charge you just about as much. A swing trader shouldn't need anyone whispering down their ear about what trades to make. Swing trading is a road of independence, you don't need someone else telling you what trades to take and what trades you shouldn't take.

I'm not going to recommend a single broker to you in this book, after all, the quality of brokers easily changes over time. Because of that, I can't really tell you which brokers are good or bad. On the other hand, I also can't know which country you're in, and while most of this book is US-driven, the fundamentals I want to apply everywhere. Just keep in mind to select quality brokers that offer everything you need!

You Need Some Standards Girl

Now, much like a girl that's just entered college, and is faced with the abundance of guys hitting on her, you'll need some standards to pick up the diamonds from the rough.

So, let me give you some baseline things to look for in a broker, like an older girl in a sorority.

Commissions: Never overpay, anything above $10 flat is a bit of a rip-off - that also shouldn't be more than 1-2c off of every share you're buying. Anything higher than this is pretty much just the broker preying on new people like you. It's also important to note that the higher your fees are, the more money you need to earn before you break even. While I've recommended some specific rates just now, too many people look only at rates and nothing else. That is the biggest noob trap in the whole world of trading, and there are a lot of noob traps. Commission rates are important but not as important as some other things.

Versatility: In this day and age, it's very important for your broker to offer to trade more securities than just stocks. Naturally, while most of us start off at stocks, trading other markets is also very popular. If your broker can figure out how to get you trading international securities, currencies etc. then that's a big plus. Naturally, you should be expecting to pay a small premium on top of the standard fee for services like this.

Various Banking Services: You'll find that some brokers are willing to give you services like check-writing or ATM transactions. These are generally just hassle-free measures to get your money. If you aren't trading seriously I'd recommend fetching one of these. With that being said, pretty much every broker will let you get your stuff to your PayPal card, so it shouldn't be all that hard getting your money.

Usability: This refers to your broker's UI and is possibly one of the most important thing about a broker. Think about it like looks in a guy, while they may not be the most important thing, everyone has a baseline of what they'll accept, and if he's pretty enough, most other things won't matter. Well, similarly to that, don't forget to check under the hood of the pretty ones, as they often don't contain everything else you need. On the other hand, a user-friendly and usable UI can make trading much easier, or even increase your profits. If it's quick and easy to place orders you're much less likely to get stressed out and make a bad trade or several. Also note that some brokers will let you test out a demo version of their platform before signing up.

Varied Amenities: Amenities are things that include services conductive to research and charting services. Let's give you an example, a discount broker may be willing to give you level 2 quotes- these will give you the access to order books for Nasdaq stocks. You will also get stock reports from Wall Street, as well as other research reports. On the other hand, these aren't really useful when swing trading due to the short-term nature of it.

Customer Service: This is the one thing I can't stress enough. It's the equivalent of a guy's core values. Sure, you can make do without them for a time, but after some time, you'll find that you're simply incompatible and nothing else can make up for them. It's very hard to determine how responsive a broker will be unless you rely on the internet, so check reviews and do a detailed analysis of every one of them when it comes to customer service. You want to be able to get your broker on the phone whenever you need them, rather than waiting for when it may be too late.

Reports and Analysis: This is the part of a broker that determines how well they can present you your data. Do they provide you year-to-date portfolio index returns? While sure, you could calculate this all yourself, having a broker do it is much easier. It's also great to have tax services in countries that have manual tax reports like the US.

The First Step-Opening an Account

After you've made your pick as to which broker you want to do business with, you'll need to decide on the kind of account you want to open with them.

Here you've got a variety of options, based on whether borrowing money to trade from your broker sounds appealing, as well as your position on trading futures or placing the account on your name or your spouse. You can even make the account a retirement account, or a traditional investing account. The next two questions will answer this, well except the spouse one, that one's to be had between the two of you...I'm not good at relationship counseling.

Cash or Margin Account

Whether you want to get a cash or margin account will depend on you after selecting, which broker you, want to do business with. When you get this choice, keep in mind that cash restricts you to trading with funds you have available, while margin accounts allow you to borrow from your broker to trade. Picking an account is also necessary if you want trading options.

A swing trader with say, $30 000 can borrow up to $30 000 usually, now, this is a double edged sword. Let's say you invest all of it...and you lose 10%, instead of losing 3000 you'll be losing 6000 due to the money you borrowed. Margin accounts tend to make traders much more reckless. By being allowed to trade with money that isn't really yours the dealership is trying to get you to pay a fee on the money you borrowed. These can easily lead to you getting in way over your head.

If you're a new trader (as you probably are) you should be sticking exclusively to cash accounts.

Traditional vs Retirement Account

The second account division is traditional and retirement. The difference is really quite self-explanatory.

Now, the biggest difference here is well, taxes. Traditional accounts will let you take your money whenever you want, and however much of it you want to take out. On the other hand, they also mean that you have to report this as taxable income. In the US at least, if you get classified as a full time trader you can make less taxes by turning these gains from capital to ordinary. This is important because if you aren't classified as a full time trader then you're going to have to pay the full capital tax.

A retirement account stops these problems, however, the government doesn't like this idea, and hence stops you from putting as much money as you'd like into it. Your IRA caps out at $5000 a year if you're under 49. The government also limits you when it comes to taking that money out, in most countries you can only do it after turning 59.

These kinds of inconveniences tend to be why people elect to not open a retirement account. If you just want to max out your retirement, then opening a retirement account is definitely the best idea.

Picking a Service Provider

Unfortunately, trading without a service provider is pretty much impossible. On the other hand, these are all different from each other, so a newbie might get overwhelmed by choice when selecting them.

These differ in a few ways but mainly its timelines, quality, and breadth of data that makes the final decision. What you want in one of these is all the services that you need. Primarily, you'll want charting and access to a database. You'll need those to conduct both technical and fundamental analysis. Now we're going to go over the main things you'll want to look for in a service provider.

Now, let's sit down and take a short lesson on the service provider business model first. They make money by making a deal with a data provider, and then providing you with the data that is relevant for you.

Service providers will be giving you the tools to find and chart the stocks that you want, which will increase the amount of info you have on the market. Using tools such as these is flexible enough to let you change all of your inputs. Ranging from what indicators to use to which criteria to pay attention to.

Providers are classified into two main categories. You've probably guessed it, it's those that provide technical data, and those that provide fundamental data. Those that provide both are therefore classed as unicorns.

A strong charting system is, well, pretty much necessary if you want to be a successful swing trader. They simply do way too much for you to be successful without them. That isn't to say it's straight-up impossible, but it will be far more difficult compared to just taking a provider and going with it.

You will absolutely require real time charts and quotes. Real time here means that they are of live market data, and are not being delayed by an external cause. If your plans are to trade interday, then when you enter your orders, you don't really need real time charting. After all, you'll be entering orders after-market hours. The market has a ludicrous amount of charting providers, and most of these cater to the active traders that are in their system. This is to say that most discount brokers will have connections with some charting systems. In fact, order entry is often integrated with charting, allowing you to make automatic buys and sells, which is a great feature.

While there are a lot of excellent charting services online, I can't really recommend any off the tip of the hat, because I don't know what country you're in and what the rules there might be. With that being said, I would check it out online and then determine if you need additional charting.

Now, charting systems themselves can be difficult to select from. After all, every provider will try to make themselves look different. Spoiler alert: Most of them aren't all that different. All you need to do is pay attention to what you need, the primary concern will be ease of use. After all, you won't have all day to fish out charts, you need them to be available pretty much at the snap of your fingers. Consider their visual appeal and clarity as well, you don't want to spend hours on just reading a chart.

Features such as being able to input your own indicators are excellent for advanced traders. If your plan is to stick with a single one for all of your career, then try to look for one that lets you insert custom indicators. You'll be thanking me later.

When it comes to selecting these programs I recommend checking the rankings made by Technical Analysis of Stocks & Commodities in its yearly Reader's Choice Awards. I use two charting systems: one, which is specially provided by my broker and another one in which I make the bulk of my personal research.

Fundamental analysis software lets traders who decide upon using fundamental analysis in investing as a process need to get a subscription to data providers that can assist them in their research.

It's lucky that most of a company's fundamental data, ranging from historical earnings to expected growth, is available... for free... online, God bless the internet. Honestly, it's amazing how far trading has come, and how easy it is to come across this stuff online these days.

Like seriously, just open Google Finance and look at all it gives you. Ten years ago, my broker couldn't have given me that much information. And this is all FREE, in this age of digitalization, it's important to remember that most of the things you need are available online, if you know how to look for it.

Let's look at, say, Yahoo! Finance (God that's a name I haven't heard in a long time.)

The site will give you:

- *Rudimentary charts to help out your trades*

- *Headlines which the stock of your choice has made in recent days*

- *The company profile of the owner company of your stock*

- *The information on the company's main competitors*

- *The estimates of other analysts as to where the value will go*

- *The companies income statement*

- *The balance sheet of the company you're looking at*

This and many other things are all available for free. Beware, though, that it does have a message board.

Run away from those, for reasons we'll discuss soon, you don't want to be getting into any message boards just yet (or, well, ever really.)

Reuters is another site you can use. While sites like Yahoo! and Google will give you aggregate data, Reuters makes its own data. The main categories available on the website are Stock Overview, Financial Highlights, Estimates, Officers and Directors, Financial Statements, Recommendations, and Analyst Research. All of these have some of their uses, though as a swing trader you'll be primarily looking at Ratios.

The excellent thing about this site is the variety of data it provides. It will give you data on a company vs its peers as well as other things. Such as whether the company is going through good or bad times, as well as free research services. On the other hand, the paid subs are also quite great.

Chapter 6 Fundamental Analysis

When you are trying to find the best stock to take on, you want to focus on different analyses which will help you make an informed decision. One of these types of analysis is fundamental analysis. Fundamental analysis is performed when you are doing general research on a company. For example, if you are interested in purchasing Amazon stock, you will start to look into the company. You might start with the company's history to get a sense of the overall growth of the entity itself. You might decide that looking over the last few years will give you enough history to help you make an informed decision. While how much research you do is more of your personal preference and how serious you take your career as a trader, I believe that the more information you have on a company, the better chance you have of becoming successful.

Fundamental Variables

There are going to be several questions that come to your mind immediately as you start to perform research on a company. For example, you might ask yourself how long the company has been successful.

You might ask yourself if this is a company you believe will give you a good profit or if this company has a history of getting traders high returns. Whatever questions you ask yourself, you need to realize that you have to do more than just ask the basic questions. In fact, you have to make sure you take time to look at the fundamental variables.

Positive Earnings Adjustment

In the trading world, there are people who are known as market analysts. These are people who will often analyze how well companies are doing and then give the companies a review or a forecast, which allows other people to notice where the company is sitting. Market reviewers are typically known as cautious people and don't tend to believe that companies will pass their forecast. However, this does happen and when it does, it brings us into positive earnings adjustment.

Basically, this states that we need to look for stocks which have surprised the market analysts. This is because if companies pass their forecast, they will continue to succeed. Therefore, they become known as one of the best companies to gain a profit from, which is always a great thing for a trader to know.

However, you will still want to make sure that you do your deep analysis before making any moves on a stock.

Positive Earning Revision

This is the process that market analysts go through when they are evaluating how well a company is doing so they can give them a forecast. As stated above, these analysts are cautious and very careful to note where they think the company is going. Therefore, when the company goes farther than what they initially thought, they need to re-evaluate the company. Of course, admitting they are wrong is not an easy thing for analysts to do as it isn't easy for anyone. However, when they do need to admit this, people can quickly learn what companies they should start paying attention to.

Earnings Momentum

While there are many important fundamental variables to look at when you are making an analysis, earnings momentum holds a special place. This variable is very important, especially when it comes to bull markets. Earnings momentum is the variable which looks at the year to year growth of earnings. Therefore, this is what will often set the price for stocks.

Strong Cash Flow

This is another fundamental variable that will tell you how much free cash a company has. This is a very important variable because it will let you know where a company financially sits after it has paid all of its bills and expenses. When you are getting into trading, you want to pay attention to the companies who are financially stable. You want to make sure that a company can grow because the more they grow, the more profit that you can make. Think about it – if you put your money into a stock where the company could barely pay the electric bill, do you think that your money would be secure, if even for a period of time? You want to make place your money in companies which are financially secure.

Earnings Growth

Another variable you want to pay attention to is how much more money the company is making as the years go on. When you look at this variable, you will be looking at the earnings growth variable. This is another company that you would think of investing in because you know that they have seen considerable growth for a certain number of years. Therefore, you analyze that the company will only continue to grow.

Chapter 7 Technical Analysis

Technical analysis is as important as fundamental analysis, especially when it comes to swing trading. However, you could view technical analysis as the more serious of the two types of analysis. Instead of just looking at the basics of the company and the fundamental variables which focus on your potential stock's company, you will focus more on the technical side of your stock when you look at technical analysis.

By definition, technical analysis is measuring the historical trends of the stock. Because many people feel that technical analysis is trickier than fundamental analysis, it might be wise to do more research about the topic before you start analyzing any stocks. There are a few online classes and books that are available for you, if you feel the need to become well educated on technical analysis.

One of the biggest factors to remember when you are focusing on technical analysis is you want to make sure to study every detail of your stock's history. You want to make sure you understand the trend, have made any notes you needed to, and that you believe you see the trend giving you the best profit before you decide to take on the stock. Technical analysis is going to take time and patience. However, you also don't want to spend too much time trying to decide if you want to take on a specific stock or not. This is a special time balance that you will figure out once have opened your account and on your way to trading stocks.

What You Will Study Through Technical Analysis

There are several details of the stock's history that you will look at when you are focusing on the technical analysis part of your trading schedule. This is something that you will do with every stock as it will help you decide if this stock is going to be worth your energy and time.

In order to give you a better view of what type of things you will look for, I will briefly discuss them below.

Study of Charts

Of course, one of the main pieces of the stock you will look at are the historical charts. These charts will give you some of the most detailed information that will help you make the best decision possible for your swing trading journey.

One of the most common charts are known as candlestick charts. These charts received this name because they are shaped like a candlestick. On top of that, the information you will find in the chart is designed through the candlestick. There are two main reasons why traders like candlestick charts so much. First, these charts are fairly easy to read and understand. Not only do they give you the information you need to know but they will also show off colors. The second reason is because these charts are known to give you an indication that the trend is about to change. For many people, this is extremely helpful because it decreases the amount of research that you need to do. However, there are other people that still say you should always perform your own research to make sure that the candlestick chart is correct on its assumption.

In general, the candlestick chart will tell you what the opening price was for the stock, the highest price, the lowest price, and the closing price. By getting these prices, you will start to analyze the chart to see what type of trend this stock is following. By looking at the history of the stock, you can start to get a sense of what the average prices are throughout the day. On top of this, you will also be able to get a sense of how much the stock tends to jump up and down during the day. On top of this, the candlestick chart will change colors in the center, depending on if the stock made a profit that day between the opening and closing price.

Of course, you will want to do this type of analysis for any chart that you come across, whether it is a line or pie chart. While each chart will look a bit different, they will all have the same valuable information within them. They will all tell you what the prices were throughout the day. However, not all of the charts will give you a prediction to what the trend will be doing next.

Volume

Another major part of technical analysis is the volume of a stock. The reasons why the volume is so important is because you will be able to get a sense of the intensity of the stock's movement in price. What this means is you will be able to take a certain amount of time, whether it is a few hours or a few months and get an idea of how many shares were traded during this time. Of course, the more shares that you find are traded, the better the stock is for trading. Stocks tend to reach high volume for many reasons. For example, they could be considered one of the more popular trading stocks on the market, such as Apple or Target. Another reason is because higher volume tends to mean a better profit. Think about it – people don't often take on trades where they are less likely to make a profit. Therefore, if the volume is high you know that most traders have found this stock to be successful.

Analyzing the Trend Line

I have already discussed a lot of information about trend lines in this book. By now, you should know that it is one of the main factors that will help you determine the success rate of a stock and whether you want to take on this stock or not. However, I feel it is important to mention that whenever you are analyzing a trend line, you are using technical analysis. You are not only analyzing what the trend line has done the previous day or the last couple of days, but you are most likely looking at the trend line over a period of months. The farther back you go, the more you will be able to learn details about the stock's trends.

Chapter 8 Watch for Counter Trends

A counter trend is an opposing move that is a part of an overall, larger trend in one direction. For example, a stock of successful and growing tech company is going to spend a lot of time moving upward. As part of that larger upward trend, there will be counter-trends that temporarily move in the opposite direction. Counter trends can represent buying opportunities.

ABCD Patterns

The so-called A-B-C-D chart pattern indicates a breakout to higher price levels. The stock rises to an initial high at point A, which is followed by a counter-trend to point B. The price level A represents the 'breakout' price that the trader expects to either represent the high price point or a coming marker for higher prices. The point B is taken as the risk level or new level of support. After reaching point B, the stock will rise a little and show a slower uptrend along C, until it eventually reaches a new high at D. The trader will use point A as the guideline that can determine where to set a limit order to sell and take profits.

Trading Volume

Trading volume is an important indicator, as we mentioned earlier. One of the first things you will need to do when considering volume is to determine what the historical trading volume for a stock is. The word historical should be considered carefully, as historical doesn't necessarily mean you take the all-time average or go back 20 years ago. Historical trading volume that is more relevant is how it has been going recently. If you start to see a large increase in trading volume coupled with a trend reversal that could be a signal that more trend reversal is coming. Whenever you see other signals, such as candlestick indicators that are coupled with increased volume that should reinforce your confidence in a trading situation.

Retracements vs. Reversals

One of the most important things that new swing traders need to become conscious of are retracements. These are small counter trends that can look like trend reversals over the short term, but they are not real reversals. Rather, they are small random blips in the midst of a solid trend that is continuing one direction or the other. They key to recognizing a retracement as compared to a genuine reversal, and its not easy, is to look for the share price breaking through previous levels of support if we are looking for a new downward trend, or resistance if we are looking to identify a new upward trend. This chart showing SPY, which tracks the S & P 500, is a good example. For most of 2018 SPY showed a steady upward trend. Retracements are indicated by the dotted arrows. These were short term counter trends that were not interrupting the inexorable upward trend. Toward the end of the year, we see a massive downshift that broke levels of support. That is indicated by the dotted oval in the chart. This was followed by a genuine downward trend. Note the rise in trading volume indicated by the vertical bars at the bottom of the chart.

You will notice that another signal is present toward the right side of the chart. While SPY seemed to enter a sideways area for a time, there is another red candle with an extremely large body, which of course was followed by plummeting share prices.

Even professional traders have difficulty distinguishing between a retracement and a real change in trend that would qualify as a reversal, but you should spend time studying charts so that you can begin to recognize retracements more often than not.

Pin bars and price rejection

One thing to look for at (what may be) the peak of upward trends or (what may be) the bottom of a downward trend is a pin bar. This is a narrow bodied candlestick with a long wick sticking out in one direction or the other. When a candlestick has a long wick that means either the low or high price was way out of proportion to the open and closing prices – and so was rejected. A high price that is rejected at the top of an upturn can indicate a coming reversal. In the snapshot below, the green or bullish candle in the middle has a high price that went well above the closing price, and you can see this was followed by two bearish candlesticks (two days of declining prices). This could be taken as a sell signal, or a buy signal if you were shorting the stock.

At the bottom of an uptrend, when you see a low price that was rejected, that is the candle ended up with a much higher closing price, it could be a buy signal for bullish investors. Of course, you should always protect yourself by utilizing a stop loss order. In the event that you are wrong, you can put the stop loss order at slightly below the most recent low, to prevent your trade from being caught up in a renewed downward trend.

Inside Bars

Another price action strategy is to look for inside bars. This is when a long bar is followed by a smaller bar that would completely fit inside the previous bar, but it's the opposite type. So its kind of like the reverse of an engulfing patter. Forex traders in particular like trading inside bars. They can represent a coming breakout.

In the image above, on the left we have a bullish bar followed by a smaller bearish candlestick, while on the right side we see the opposite situation, a bearish bar followed by a smaller bullish bar. If either of these are seen in part of a trending market, they can be taken as a signal of a coming breakout. When occurring in or near a level of support or resistance, the pattern can indicate a coming trend reversal. You should confirm this type of signal with other indicators.

Chapter 9 Breakout & Breakdown trading

Break out trading and breakdown trading is typically what most traders look to trade when starting out. With this type of trading, one needs to be super disciplined in the approach you are taking. Having exact breakout and breakdown levels so you know when you need to get out of the trade and stops even if the stop is a mental one will keep you on the profitable side of trading. With this type of trading, taking quick profits is the name of the game and going in with a larger than average size will help the profits add up quickly. Although most beginners look to this type of trading starting out, most if not all traders eventually blow up accounts trading this strategy for a very simple reason: No discipline. This type of trading can be very profitable if the discipline is there. Having the exact entry and exit points are key in determining if you are going to be a profitable trader. This strategy typically works best if you have done your homework and are comfortable with the subject of support and resistance areas and are quick in reading the chart in determining which way the stock is going. Being reactionary works best with this trading style, let the area of support or resistance break before you buy or sell short and immediately have an area in which you get out to protect your account. Typically, if a breakout does not work you will know immediately. A few steps to help you stay on the right side of the trade

Step 1 – Identify why you think the stock/ticker will break out (Find the catalyst).

Step 2 – Draw support and resistance areas on the chart (Premarket information should be enabled on your platform).

Step 3 – Determine which way the stock/ticker is trending. If trending up you are looking at a previous area on the chart for resistance to break and a series of higher lows and higher highs into that break out point. The more times the breakout area is reached and not broken the better, the follow through on the trade once the area has broken will be more substantial. If trending down you are looking at a support area to break and a series of lower lows and lower highs into that break point. The same thing applies here as well in terms of how many times the support area is touched but not broken.

Step 4 – Identify your stop points for the trade. This is one of the most important steps here. Not identifying your stop points will ensure your trading career is short. Having a plan when trading is crucial towards your profitability as a trader and will give you the discipline needed to succeed. No plan, no success – simple as that.

Step 5 – Once you have identified the general direction of the stock/ticker, figured out your stop points next it is time to decide the position size of the trade based on how much you are willing to risk.

Step 6 – After all these things have been identified, next is to enter the trade based on the trend of the stock.

I know it may seem like a lot of things you have to consider before you enter a trade, this is to make sure that you enter the trade with an entry plan as well as an exit plan to protect your account in case there is the breakout fails to follow through.

Now that we went over the reasons for getting into a trade and how to judge and what to do when getting into a trade, let's go over the specific things when looking for breakouts and breakdowns.

Breakouts

When I am trading breakouts I am looking for specific types of resistance levels here. The resistance levels that I am looking for are levels that have been tested more than once and seen some significant retrace of the current up move. Once that level has been tested a few times I follow the steps above to determine where I need to get in and how much I am willing to risk based on the stop area. See the Chart below – KONE as of 7/21/2016.

Breakdowns

Some of my favorite trades here, when trading breakdowns the move typically happens quickly because of human psychology. Fear is a stronger emotion than greed, so when you are trading to the downside you need to be extremely disciplined because if the breakdown doesn't happen the ticker will turn around almost immediately and you'll be down 25 or 30 cents within a second. Identifying your stop out area first here is crucial. When the support area is identified, take a step back and look at the overall trend to make sure you see the pattern that you are seeing instead of an intermediate low in an uptrend, which is what newbie traders tend to do and have large losses in trading the downside. Trading the downside is harder than trading the upside or breakout. To be on the safe side let the support area break here and then let it retest the area and continue in the downtrend you were anticipating. See the example below.

In the above chart you can see the areas that you need to pay attention to when trading to the downside. You see the first highs around the $4.70s range this is the initial high here. Then the low was put in and the previous high was broken. The low area is where a lot of traders tend to get trapped thinking that it's off its highs it needs to go back down. This is what we call consolidation. The smart money is taking profits and churning individuals in and out of the stock while getting ready for the next leg up. Typically if you are looking at the 1 minute chart there is some confusion on this time frame, try looking at the 5 minute to see what is going on there this will typically give you a better idea of what the stock/ticker is currently doing. Churning individuals in and out of the stock is not an uncommon thing. The smart money is trying to get everyone going in the same direction before pushing it the other way, this also holds for breakouts as well. The lower high here is the confirmation of the trend that you are looking for to the downside. This is the type of picture perfect high, low, lower high you are looking for. If you look at the chart you can see a huge resistance area that kept pushing the stock/ticker down and the support area that needed to break was the New Low identified on the chart or the lower low. Once you have the lower high and the lower low breaks you are in a confirmed downtrend and you can hold the trade. The area we identified as the entry point was on the lower high, out stop was tight here and we know what we were looking for in terms of the actual break here. The reason I identified this area as entry is because of the resistance area right above and how the stock/ticker backed off every single time. The entry that you should take would be the break of the "New Low" identified on the chart.

Trading is one of the most difficult things that I have undertaken, but it has also been the most rewarding. There is an enormous amount of freedom when trading, you get the feeling that you are on top of the world. Trading can bring you tons of great opportunities to see more things in life and to participate in what is really happening in the market.

Your financial IQ will definitely increase because of the amount of detail that is needed to trade successfully. Although this may seem like a hard thing to do, I definitely think anyone with the discipline to follow directions and their own rules can make it trading. The 90% individuals that do not make it trading do not follow rules, do not have a set of rules to follow and are extremely undisciplined traders. The most important part of trading is to understand that losses are just the cost of doing business and they will happen. The successful trader knows this and welcomes small losses in search of the large gains. The best thing to do in trading is to continue to learn, take small losses so you are protecting your principal which will give you more time in the market and give you the opportunity to take advantage of the big trades that will increase your account along the way.

If you have any questions, feel free to email me at *traderjasper@gmail.com*.

Chapter 10 Predicting the Market

Indicators and charts are one of the most important components when we talk about technical analysis. In addition to experience, coldness, and psychology, a good analyst cannot disregard a thorough knowledge of the graphs. The latter can represent different information and may appear in different forms.

In graphical analysis, the graphs deserve particular attention because they represent the price dynamics of a given financial instrument and in a given period.

In the technical analysis, the most commonly used type of graph is certainly the candlestick chart, better known under the name of a Japanese candlestick chart. Before moving on to a detailed description of the candlestick chart, however, I would like to say a few words about two other charts, less used than candlestick charts, but which may be useful as they can help you understand the Japanese candlestick chart.

The price chart is shown on a Cartesian plane where, on the abscissa axis, that is the vertical axis the time is reported, while on the horizontal axis the price is reported.

Given this premise, we can still say that the graphs refer to different time periods whether they are fractions of minutes, hours and days, if not even weeks, months or even years indicating different sizes of opening or closing, of maximums and minima.

On the axis of the abscissas, we find a space called histogram of the volume, which represents the quantity of instruments exchanged during the period under examination.

In graphic analysis in the specific and more generally in the technical analysis, various types of graph are used.

Features of a good chart

With the above, I do not mean that you will need a chart that contains a myriad of information or detailed information in detail, but I would like to emphasize that the best successful traders on the market, use very few indicators. Yes, you understood correctly. Only a few indicators. You will, therefore, think that what has been described up to now is only a chat, but it is not so, as these extrapolate the most important information directly from the graph. The charts obviously can only be provided by the brokers, which as for the forex market, here too we advise you always to choose the best binary options brokers. So it is not true that the graphics are all the same, it will be the good broker to extrapolate all the information that interests him from the various detailed charts. And from here we recognize the best brokers.

The reason for this extrapolation is very simple: since the indicators express only the past in a graphic form, they can provide a very approximate vision of the future. So too many indicators in a chart can sometimes create confusion instead of aid.

Therefore, we consider it very important to keep the following points in mind:

1. Good graphic program.

With this, in fact, you should always be able to look far enough in the past, to plan the future and identify relevant barriers and gather a satisfactory overview. In the binary options charts of the different brokers, this time frame is too narrow to draw reliable conclusions.

1. Good quality graphs always indicate different time intervals.

These range from a few minutes to a max. of a month.

1. Never set just a common linear chart.
This fact would not be very useful for technical analysis purposes. On the other hand, candle or beam charts are used, which we will explain briefly.

What is chart analysis?

The analysis of the graphs is above all the search for particular shapes, also called graphic structures, configurations, figures.

They are figures that emerge from the price movement, and that can signal its future trend. They are tracked by analysts joining points in the price graph of a financial security or the performance of an indicator.

The purpose of the graphic analysis will, therefore, be to identify the most typical price patterns for forecasting purposes.

These graphic formations can be classified into different categories. The main categories of classes can assume inversion or continuation or consolidation characteristics. Fundamental feature will also be the dynamics of the volumes, which we will explain under each figure.

This is why it takes technique, experience, strategies, if not the analyst's ability to see these forms in the movement of a graph. These are the fundamental elements of this type of analysis. The concept of trendline, support and resistance are also part of this aspect of technical analysis.

Below we will list the most used graphs for graphic analysis and explain the operation. Before doing this, however, we must explain another very important and used concept: the figure of Continuation. These have common characteristics in all the graphs, they represent a pause in the prevailing trend in progress and are a prelude to a continuation of the trend in the direction of the direction previously underway. For this reason, they are also known as consolidation figures.

The main difference between the continuation and the inversion figures concerns the extension.

The continuation figures are often accompanied by a decrease in the volumes traded.

One of the first figures we are going to examine is the wedge.

Wedge

This too is a continuation figure on explained and is very similar to the triangle for 2 reasons:

- for the form;
- for the time it takes to form. This differs from the triangle that we will see below because the shape that forms is characterized by a strongly bullish or bearish inclination opposite to that of the current trend.

This means that:

this chart consists of two convergent trend lines and takes about one to three months to develop;

in an uptrend, a falling wedge or "a descending wedge" can be encountered;

while in a bearish tendency a rising wedge or "an ascending wedge" can develop.

As with the pennant and flag figures, the wedge can be found in the middle of a movement, thus allowing to calculate minimum targets.

The dynamics of the volumes see a decrease in the course of the formation of the pattern and it should go to be reduced for all the period of formation of the figure. On the contrary, they increase significantly when the trend line is broken, which is a typical feature of the wedge.

Pennant

This figure is also quite common in chart analysis.

This figure together with the figure of the flag, which we will see immediately after the flag appears after an almost vertical movement and represents a pause in the trend.

Its characteristic is that it is presented as a symmetrical triangle which, however, has a maximum extension of 3 weeks. Most often, in bearish actions, the refinement time of the figure is even lower and is equal to one or maximum two weeks. The pennant is halfway to the bullish or bearish movement, with the obvious implications in calculating the minimum targets for the movement's arrival.

It will, therefore, be obvious that the volume decreases during the formation of the figure and should be low throughout the period of formation of the pattern. On the contrary, instead, they increase significantly when the trendline breaks, which identifies the pennant. These are accompanied by a similar trend in the range within which prices move.

Pennants, most often coincide with a contraction phase, which does not necessarily have an opposite inclination with respect to the basic trend.

Both this figure and the next develop within a rather short time frame.

The third figure that we examine as announced is the Flag.

Flag

Flag formation, or flag, is a very common pattern of continuation in graphic analysis.

This form tends to appear close to the temporary exhaustion of a trend, which represents a brief pause in the market after strongly accentuated movements, are almost vertical and known as flagpole.

The flag has a shape similar to a parallelepiped, almost to represent a rectangle, bounded by two parallel trendlines but opposed to the prevailing trend.

in other words, it can be seen as a flag that is tilted downward in an uptrend and upward in a bearish trend.

His training ends within a medium period, that is between one and three weeks. It usually appears halfway to complete movement.

It must also be said that if it is in a bearish movement the perfection time is less and the figure is usually completed in one or two weeks. Precisely because it is in the middle of the bullish or bearish movement, the figure is important for identifying price targets. From here we will then calculate the width of the movement preceding the flag and report this distance after the break of the trend line delineating the figure.

The volume should also decrease during the formation of the figure and then increase again when the trend line is broken.

So let's see how to use Flag and Pennant.

The targets that can be identified in relation to these figures are two:

- The first is determined by projecting the width of the base from the breakout point; here this target assumes less importance if

587

we consider the reduced dimensions of the figure.

- The second can instead be obtained by projecting, from the breakout point, a distance equivalent to that covered by the movement that preceded the formation of the pennant.
- This means that these figures often materialize around half of the overall movement, giving a fair advantage at the operational level.

The temporary phase of price weakness can be exploited to enter the stock or even just to increase the position taken earlier, again using a stop-loss much lower than the potential take-profit.

The rectangle will represent the fourth figure that we will explain.

Rectangle

The rectangle is the simplest among the figures proposed by the technical analysis.

It identifies a phase of price congestion. In Technical Analysis, with this term, we mean a graphic formation in correspondence with which prices oscillate within a narrow range of values. This process takes place when the market moves sideways.

The pattern represents a break zone of the current trend in which prices move sideways. This also gives rise to the name of trading range or congestion area, a figure that represents a period of consolidation of the current trend that is resolved in the direction of the trend that preceded it. This represents a fundamental figure, to correctly identify the continuation pattern if not also the observation of the volumes.

Also, for this bullish figure, the rebounds must be accompanied by high volumes, with the corrections characterized by decreasing volumes. In the opposite case, instead, in the bearish rectangle, are the corrections to have more accentuated volumes.

Many investors, take advantage of the oscillations, selling to the top of the figure and buying at the minimum. However, those who use this approach risk not exploiting the breaking of the pattern.

The figure in question usually takes from one to three months to improve, and the minimum target is represented by the translation of the height of the rectangle when the price breaks the figure.

Prices move within a fixed band identified by a support and resistance as better shown in the figure below.

first target 1

The rectangles can also be configured as inversion figures, depending on the context in which they are formed. It is therefore evident how the congestion phases identify a moment in which the market expresses considerable uncertainty and awaits new information to decide the future trend. Unlike the contraction phases (in which the continuous reduction in volatility identifies in an increasingly precise manner the moment in which the market will receive the information that awaits) a figure of congestion like the rectangle does not allow to identify sufficiently in advance the moment in which the breakout will take place.

The operational cues that this figure can provide are basically of two types:

- The first requires waiting for the exit of prices from the congestion zone initially identified. This exit must necessarily be classified as a breakout and therefore must be characterized by an increase in volumes and volatility.

- The second operational step derives from the possibility of exploiting the lateral movement of prices to buy close to the identified support and sell when the values are near the top of the figure again.

Support and Resistance

Let me now explain briefly what are the supports and the resistance.

Support is defined as that price level at which there is, an arrest of the downward trend in prices. An excessive concentration of purchases that occurs in the vicinity of the same will cause a block in the downward trend in prices.

A level of support is defined as reliable when it shows resistance to repeated "attacks" without a bearish breakdown.

The Resistance is defined instead as that level of price where the growth of the same stops. In the case of the Resistance, the high concentration of sales prevents the continuation of the increase.

A resistance level, on the contrary, is stronger and more reliable as it resists repeated "attacks" without an upward failure.

Surely a historical minimum or maximum represents a level of Support or Strategic Resistance.

Consequently, the penetration or breaking of support levels or even resistance can be caused by:

- important changes in the fundamental values of a company (increase in profits, changes in management, etc.);
- from simple forecasts based on price trends in recent times;
- both, both levels of support and resistance can also arise from motivations exclusively of an emotional nature. Supports and resistances represent with great simplicity the encounter/clash between supply and demand.

From the above it is clear that in practice, a breakout, or an event in which the price comes out of a trend, breaking a support or resistance or a channel, above a level of resistance evidence an increase in demand, arising from more buyers, who are willing to buy at higher prices than the current ones.

In the opposite case, instead, the breakdown of a support shows an increase in the sellers, and therefore in the offer, as more sellers are willing to sell even at lower prices than the current ones.

If a level of support is broken, it automatically turns into a resistance level, just as if a resistance level is broken, it becomes a level of support. This process is known as pullback, which is a time when a trending market takes a break.

The support and resistance lines can be drawn horizontally and then we will talk about static support, where the support corresponds to a precise and constant point in time; both obliquely and in this case, we will talk about dynamic support, where a trend line is drawn with the variation of prices and with the passage of time.

The fifth figure, object of study concerns the triangle.

Triangle

In technical analysis, that of the triangle is a consolidation figure and is used to verify the continuation of the main trend. This is a pattern that lasts a few months when there is a pause in the current trend with prices that oscillate in an increasingly narrow area.

The figure has the following characteristics:

The triangle must have a minimum of four reaction points; two superiors, and two inferior; the first ones necessary to trace the upper trend line, the seconds necessary to draw the lower trend line.

A time limit for its resolution characterizes the triangle. Usually, the prices break the triangle at a point between two thirds and three quarters of the depth of the triangle.

The volumes in the formation phase of the triangle waves, lose strength and then explode when the trend line that delimits the figure breaks.

The minimum target for price trends is calculated by projecting the maximum height of the triangle.

The figure in question can present itself according to three different structures:

symmetrical triangle which has the trend lines that delimit it that are convergent.

Prices tend to move in a range that gradually becomes narrower with the passing of the sessions, due to a constant reduction of the maximums, and also due to a constant reduction of the minimums.

descending triangle characterized by a flat demarcation line, the lower one, and by a bearish trend line, the upper one.

In this figure, there will be a greater conviction on the part of the bearish and is often found during a downward trend.

The reduction in the range within which prices move, occurs only thanks to an increase in the minimum, while the maximums remain almost unchanged.

Just such behavior makes evident the greater pressure of the buyers with respect to the sellers and attributes to this figure a bullish value.

descending triangle

The figure represents a symmetrical structure, which makes it difficult to interpret. In the third case, on the other hand, we speak of an ascending triangle, characterized by an upper line of flat demarcation and a line, the lower, ascending line. This pattern indicates a greater strength of the uptrend and is often found during an uptrend

Regardless of the configuration, whether symmetrical, ascending or descending, it is possible to calculate the target of the figure, i.e. the level that prices should reach in the phase following the breakout.

This is calculated by projecting, from the breaking point, the "base" of the triangle, i.e. the maximum width that the figure recorded during its formation.

The sixth figure in question concerns the formation of broadening.

Broadening

This represents a rather rare figure, classified as a variant of the triangle but which presents a contrary opening, with divergent trend lines. It is a figure that occurs at the end of a trend, usually bullish.

The dynamics of the volumes are different from that of the triangles, as the volume gradually expands together with the increase in price oscillation.

The seventh figure that we are going to examine concerns the diamond.

Diamond

Also, the diamond as an inversion figure is one of the rarest and one of the least simple to detect. Graphically the diamond is formed by a double-figure composed of a first half that recalls the shape of a broadening from a second half that resembles a symmetrical triangle.

A diamond can present itself in two circumstances:

- at the end of an uptrend;
- at the end of a bearish trend;

In the first case, it takes the name of "Diamond Top," vice versa we would be facing a "Diamond Bottom."

The figure does not always develop symmetrically. Often, the second half is prolonged in time more than the first one did.

By its nature, the diamond needs very dynamic market phases. The figure of the Diamond can also occur during simple breaks of the trend.

For this reason, it is easier to find the diamond at the peak of an upward trend before a bearish reversal rather than the other way around. diamond

The dynamics of volumes go hand in hand with that of prices. That is, if volumes increase, prices increase, in the second half. However, prices fall and consequently also volumes.

There are 4 basic elements to identify the training:

an initial phase of price expansion;

a maximum;

a minimum;

a phase of price contraction;

The pattern is only complete when the support or resistance line breaks and a pullback to the violated trend line does not always occur.

The minimum price target is equal to the maximum vertical distance between the two extreme parts of the figure projected at the bottom (or at the top) with respect to the breaking point of the support or resistance.

It is possible, even for the diamond, to calculate a target price.

It is sufficient to project the maximum width of the figure and project it starting from the point where the breakout occurred.

In the event that it is configured as a continuation figure, it is also possible to derive a second target, projecting the width of the movement that preceded the beginning of the diamond, from the point of the final breakout. diamond breaking points

The eighth figure we examine will be a figure difficult enough to examine and represents the rounding and spike.

Rounding and Spike

This represents one of the many figures of inversions, which presents itself as a slow and gradual movement on the lows that will first have a slight downward, then lateral and then shows a growing movement.

The pattern is one of the slowest of all the graphic analysis and is usually identifiable on longer-term charts.

It is really difficult to establish the precise moment in which the figure can be considered complete, if not after the first substantial rises. More difficult, it will be to identify upward targets.

Spike is also very special. The figures in question show, without any transition period, a sudden reversal of the quotations. An inversion accompanied by an explosion of volumes.

Due to its characteristics, the figure in question is difficult to identify in advance.

Double Top and Double Bottom

Also, this falls into the categories of the inversion figures, which we remember are particular graphic figures that announce an inversion of the current trend. The figure in question turns out to be a very common figure in graphic analysis and together with other figures, the double bottom and double top figures are among the most common and recognizable formations.

We explain briefly in two essential steps, its operation;

1. The double minimum is at the peak of a bearish trend and is configured as a minimum, a subsequent rebound and a subsequent fallback to the level of the

previous minimum. The ascent that follows, if it breaks on the upside and with volumes, the previous maximum, leads to the completion of the figure. The pattern, due to its shape, is also called a formation in W. Volumes are growing during the formation of the first minimum, down in the following rebound, and then increase again during the upward movement that completes the figure.

Basically, therefore, the double minimum is realized, following a clear bearish trend, in which prices test twice a price threshold, but without being able to overcome it. This determines the realization of two minimums slightly spaced over time. Double minimum and double maximum.

1. Also, the characteristics of the double maximum are the same, but the pattern has a secularly opposite development. The double top is at the height of an uptrend and is configured as a maximum, a consequent fall and a subsequent rebound towards the previous maximum.

The double maximum is achieved when, following a sharp uptrend, prices test twice a price threshold, but without being able to overcome it, determining the formation of two maximums. Volumes are growing at the formation of the first rise, remaining lower in the formation of the second maximum and then increasing conspicuously at the time of the piercing of the traceable line starting from the previous minimum.

In both figures, it is possible to observe a return of prices to the level of completion of the pattern, in a pullback similar to that of the head and shoulders that we will see later, before the definitive start of the new trend, bullish in the double minimum and bearish in the double maximum. Small volumes accompany this pullback.

The measurement of the minimum upward (or downward) target is calculated by calculating the distance between the line joining the two minima (or the two maxima) and the first maximum (or minimum) relative and projecting this value from the upward drilling point or downward.

Chapter 11 Having the Right Mindset for Trading

Before you proceed with learning the technical elements for how you can successfully swing trade with options, I want to pause for a moment to provide you with some crucial mindset tips for making your trades successful. When it comes to trading, your mindset can either be the weapon you use to win or the weapon you point against yourself in a battle of self-sabotage.

People who are not in the right frame of mind when trading has a tendency to let fear and frustration rule their judgment, which can lead to them making poor trade moves that ultimately result in losses. If you want to hedge yourself against risk, you need to hedge yourself against your emotions too and learn how to trade logically, rationally, and objectively.

Although there are many different mindset strategies you can use to help you improve your trade skills and make better quality trades, the following five are the most important for beginners. Please take these tips seriously, as they can make or break you in the stock market and you always want everything working in favor of your success.

Beginners are especially at risk of making emotional trades based on the fact that there is a large amount of excitement and uncertainty swirling around when you are new to trading. If you get caught in this emotional state, however, your earliest experiences making trades may not be positive and could even put you off of the idea of trading altogether, solely because your mind was not in the right place.

Stay Committed, Be Persistent

You must be committed to your trades and stay persistent in your desire to win if you are going to be successful with trading any form of stocks.

Without commitment and persistence, you are going to find yourself struggling, as you will be unwilling to stay focused on what it takes to succeed.

Those who are not committed and persistent fall behind on their research and conduct low-quality tech analysis readings which can result in low-quality trades that lead to excessive losses. In the options market specifically, you might also find profitable options expiring before you act on them because you have not remained consistent in your approach to your trades.

A great way for you to stay committed and persistent in your trades is through setting a goal for yourself which will clearly outline the reason for why you have begun trading in the first place.

When you have a goal, you know what you are set to achieve and you have a strong reason for why you need to stay committed and persistent so that you can reach that goal.

I strongly encourage you to outline a goal for yourself before you get started so that you can leverage your goal to help you stay committed and focused throughout your trades.

Some great examples of goals include:

- Pay off debt and accumulate a nest egg for yourself/your family
- Set aside funds for your children to go to college
- Afford to travel and enjoy the world
- Replace your salary with profits from trades so you can quit your day job

- Buy a house or investment property with your profits

Pick a goal that is relevant to what you want for yourself and your life so that you are motivated by it, as this is an important step in making your goal worth going for.

Be Aware of Your Emotions

Self-awareness, particularly around your emotions, is a strong asset for you to have when it comes to trading. When you are trading, you need to be aware of your emotions surrounding your trades so that you can avoid letting fear, frustration, anger, or uncertainty rule your trades. People who trade fearfully or with frustration tend to make decisions that are not founded in logic, which can result in massive and unnecessary losses incurred. As a result, they may grow even more fearful or frustrated with trading because they are not seeing the results they desire, which makes it even more challenging for them to make successful trades going forward.

Rather than starting that cycle, it is better to become aware of your emotions and practice staying aware of them during every trade you make.

The way that I manage my emotions and stress during trades comes in the form of a quick and simple self-check which I make periodically throughout the trading process. Generally, whenever I conduct tech analysis, choose my position, execute a trade, and complete a trade, I engage in an emotional check to see how I am doing. If I discover that I am feeling fearful or uncertain, or even frustrated, I manage my emotions first. Then, once I am feeling more balanced, I make my trade decision. This way, I can guarantee that every decision I make is founded in logic and reasoning, not fear and frustration.

Always Make Decisions Founded in Logic

Elaborating on my previous point, it is crucial that every decision you make is always founded in logic and reasoning. It can be surprisingly easy to engage in trades based off of how your emotions are feeling, or even based off of what you are hearing out in the world around the topic of trades. You might find yourself noticing that whenever you hear about the market in the news or in trade circles that you spend time in that you feel persuaded to change your mind based off of what you are hearing from other people.

While it is important to take their information into consideration and use it to help you educate yourself, it is important that you never make a decision based off of what someone else has told you, or based off of your emotions. Instead, always conduct *your own* research to validate this information to ensure that you are making your decisions based off on logic and reasoning.

In today's society, it can be easy to get swept away by what other people are telling you. When I was brand new to trading, I tended to doubt myself and trust others' judgment anytime I was engaged in groups where people who had more experience than me were trading. I assumed that because they had been trading longer, they had greater experience, and therefore, what they said must ultimately be true, which lead to me making some trade moves that I did not validate with my own research.

Most of those fell through with losses, which made me realize the importance of this. Make sure that you hedge yourself against this risk by always validating everything with thorough research and tech analysis to ensure that you are always making the best decisions possible.

Stay Humble

Regardless of how and where you trade, the stock market is a place where you need to stay humble. Just like fear and uncertainty can push you to make poor trade deals, being overconfident can also lead to you making poor trade deals. People who are overconfident in the market tend to lose respect for how volatile the market can be and forget that just like you can profit plenty, you can also lose plenty. This can lead to terrible decisions and cocky trading, which may ultimately lead to potentially devastating losses in your trade deals.

Staying humble is not just to protect your pride, it is also to protect your trade deals to ensure that you are always hedging yourself against possible risks and losses.

You must always thoroughly conduct every step of tech analysis and trade research before getting involved, even if you have been on a winning streak. Do not roll the dice or gamble with your trades or assume that you know exactly how to win every single time just because you have won a few trades in a row or earned yourself massive profits. Stay humble, or the market will humble you.

Be Open to Learning

The final mindset note I will leave you with is that you need to be open to learning. As you get involved with trading, you will find a strategy that works for you and that you will want to stick with that strategy because it is familiar and comfortable. That is great, and everyone should be on the lookout for finding a way that works for them. After all, this is a strong way to ensure that you feel confident in the decisions that you are making so that you can make strong deals.

With that being said, you should always be open to learning and evolving your strategy so that you can do even better over time.

Continually learning is not just about improving your strategy either, but it is also about staying up with general trader trends. Trader trends are different from market trends in that we are not discussing what direction the market is moving in, but rather the strategies that traders are using to trade on the market itself.

Keeping up with these trends ensures that you are always trading similarly to how other successful traders are trading, which improves your chances at generating success with your trades.

Chapter 12 The Secret of Profitable Trading

The most important thing in trading, what professionals traders call the "secret" is not having the ability to recognize when a trade is going bad , most if not all traders know when they should exit the trade, the getting out part is what is hard for the 90% of traders who fail. The key here is having the discipline to cut a trade off when it is not working. It is that simple. Developing the habit (which can be found here on how to develop successful habits: click the link *HABITS: How to Build any Habit and Make it Stick*)of getting out of trades when you are told to by the stock is easy, listening to that advice is the key. If the trade is not doing what you expect, get out immediately. Trying to make the trade work is not going to help you and only reinforces horrible trading habits. This is what separates successful traders from traders that never make it. This goes back to anticipating what you think the trade is going to do and reacting (putting the trade on) once it starts doing what you anticipated.

This type of trading will save you from being in trades and not knowing what to do. We are all about preserving capital to take advantage of the large moves in the market. We want to be a part of the moves not trying to anticipate the moves and making sure we are trading when everything is in our favor.

Trading is not a race, it is not a marathon either. I would consider it more of high intensity interval training (HIIT), there will be times when you lay at rest waiting for the opportune time to take advantage of a situation and then there will be times why you will need laser focus on a specific trade and you will have to give it everything you have to extract the most profit from that trade. This focus is necessary for it to work.

Smaller Account Trading vs. Large Account Trading

Small Account Trading

Working with a smaller account, there is extreme risk. You cannot afford to take multiple large losses in a row. Your main objective is to take the losses when they come, small losses do not hurt your account here. They will actually start to give you a sort of discipline and allow you to stay in the market longer when a trade will come your way that will make up for the losses you sustained. When taking a trade with a smaller account you are looking for a trade that will give you more than you are risking. Risk: Reward, so for a trade that is 1:3 this would be a great trade, you can make the money you loss on three trades back with one trade. *Working with a smaller account doesn't provide you with a lot of flexibility but it teaches you more about the discipline of trading than anything else.* This is why I recommend day trading with the minimum $500 that SureTrader allows. You will definitely learn discipline this way. When you are disciplined as a trader making profits with a smaller account or larger account is the same, the difference is the size of the position. Small account trading doesn't necessarily mean you have to trade a small position. With certain brokers, the leverage sometimes goes up to 1:6 which means, depending on the size of your account you can get into some pretty large trades relative to the equity in your account. When trading a smaller account the issue you run into is being able to take enough size on the ticker you are trading to make a decent profit to cover commissions. This typically means that you need to take all of your size on the first entry, which means that you need to be right more often that you are wrong. With this type of trading, discipline is the main factor to success and being able to identify the proper setups. Trading with smaller accounts vs. larger accounts means you need to be reactive instead of anticipating. We will go over reactive trading vs anticipatory trading later. For example, let's say you are starting with a trading account of approximately $3,000 and with the broker that I am trading with, that will give you approximately $18,000 in trading capital. Below are the break downs on the levels of stocks that I typically trade and the money that can be made on the 1st base through home run scenarios:

Large Account Trading

The strategies remain the same, the major difference is the larger account trading and the smaller account trading is the size of positions you can trade and the amount of trades you can put on at once and the size of position you can put on at once. Trading a larger account gives you the flexibility to make more money faster and also allows you to make more mistakes along the way. When trading with a larger account, you can make larger mistakes but I strongly advise against trading with the total size of an account. I would trade or restrict your trading to a smaller portion of your account until you learn how to trade with the discipline you need to make the money you want. As an example let's say you have $10,000 in your account and you are using the same broker as before, let's look at the chart to see what the profit potential can be:

As you can see the profits are multiplied 6 fold as well as the amount of money you can lose. We all know that trading goes both ways here. The money you stand to make is also the money you can lose depending on what your risk level is and where you place your stops when reviewing the charts. This is why stops are so important. With large account trading there is also an added benefit, you can size into a position as it gyrates in the direction you expect it to go. There is obviously more flexibility when trading a larger account, the ability to absorb losses is huge here. Still the discipline remains the same, or you will be back to trading a smaller account very soon.

Mental Stops vs. System Order Stops

I have tried both approaches and there are drawbacks to both. Mental stops are at your mercy and you need extreme discipline to make these work. I have used mental stops before and have had great success and failure with them. One of the biggest failures I have had with mental stops is not getting out when I was supposed to and letting the stock run more than it should. The success that I have had with them is being able to put on a trade and knowing exactly how much I am risking on a trade and letting the trade work. This approach has given me the greatest amount of profit. Actually placing stops in the system is a great thing, if the stop actually triggered when it was supposed to. The issue I have had in the past is the stop didn't trigger and the stock ran right through the stop, which the purpose of the stop was to stop this from happening. There are all sorts of reasons, if you are going to use a mental stop, I warn against it if you are just starting out. I would suggest using a system stop (Stop Limit) to make sure you get out close to the price that you want and nothing else. This will give you more comfort in knowing that you have predetermined your risk tolerance for that specific trade and in doing so, you know how much money you are risking. Once the trade starts working in your favor you should start moving your stop down according to how the stock is acting. Depending on the activity of the stock, I would move it down it 10 to 12 cent increments to lock in some profit on the trade. This will help you build your account and also help you take profit once the stock has a bounce which they will inevitably do. This will also get you out of stocks that have more downside, so use this method with caution. For example if you have not locked in any profit at the 1st base level, consider selling some and allowing the stock to bounce before moving your stop down to that level, once it moves to that level and beyond, place your stop at the 1st base mark and allow the trade to work in your favor for the rest of your position.

Chapter 13 Commandments of Swing Trading

Some of the most experienced swing traders of 2019 like to focus on what has become known as the 11 commandments of swing trading. Popular trader, Melvin Pasternak, developed this list and discusses it after his trading classes.

1. Make Sure to Have Long Strengths and Short Weaknesses

There are two periods that you should be looking for when you are taking on a trade. The first period is known as bull and the second period is known as bear. You need to be able to identify these periods when you get into the market because this will let you know what the market conditions are like for that time.

When you look at the bull market condition, you are looking at an increasing market. The stock trends are on an upward trend, which they have been on for a good period of time. This proves that the levels of the economy are high and you should spend your time looking for longer trades.

When the market's condition is focused on bearishness, this means that the stocks are on a downward trend. The prices of stocks are dropping and many traders believe that this is the spiral that they will see in some stocks for a period of time. Bear conditions happen when the economy isn't doing very well. This is normally during points of economic recession and when unemployment is high. When you notice the bear conditions, you will want to focus on short trades as this will limit your risk of loss, especially if the downward trend continues.

2. The Overall Direction of the Market and Your Trade Should be Aligned

This is one reason research is important. You not only want to research when you are starting your swing trade profession, but you also want to continue your research. In fact, every day that you sit down in front of your desk, is a day that you will be doing research. One of these reasons is because you have to make sure to research and analyze every stock. This will help you determine whether you should purchase the stock or not.

When you are focusing on your research for a particular stock, one of the main focuses should be does the stock match the overall direction of the market? When it comes to the stock market, you will find that it's either on an upward or downward spiral. You will want to match your trade with this direction.

3. Always Look at the Long-Term Charts

One of the biggest mistakes that beginner traders often make is that they will only focus on the short-term charts when they are looking into a stock. Many experienced traders feel that this is the wrong course of action as you should have a better idea of what the trend of the stock has done over at least a six-month period. Of course, you can always go longer than six months.

You should start with the chart that will give you a couple of weeks. From there, you will want to make sure you go over the chart and notice every single detail. There is nothing that you should miss during the analysis of your chart. After you have looked at the first couple of weeks, then you can dive more into a long-term chart, such as the six-month chart. Again, follow the same microscopic process you did with the previous chart. Do your best not to miss anything. In fact, some traders will often create an excel spreadsheet where they can list everything they have to view in the chart and even write down information. This is a great piece of advice for any beginner.

4. Do Your Best Not to Enter Near the End of the Trade

Once you start to get into the stock market, you will notice a trend when it comes to traders. You will find that the stock market is busy within the first hour because there are so many traders who are buying new stocks for the day. You will then notice that the stock market begins to get quiet around the 11:00 hour because people are either holding on to their stocks or closed out for the day. However, about the last hour, which starts around 3:00 pm, you will notice the stock market picks up again as people, especially day traders, sell all their stocks and close out.

As a swing trader, you might not buy and sell stocks every day. Unlike day traders, you can hold your stocks for a few days to about a week or two. However, there are a few traders that are not allowed to do this as it would cause them too much loss.

Another reason people enter into trades earlier rather than later is because this can give you the most profit, especially if you find a stock that is hitting an upward trend. On top of this, you will have less risk to worry about if you enter a trade early. Doing your best to cut down on risk is always something traders focus on, even if they don't mind taking risks.

5. Track a Consistent Group of Stocks

Just like every trader is different, every stock is different. This is why it is important to not focus on jumping from one stock to the next. Instead, as you are learning the tricks and strategies of swing trading, you will want to start getting an idea of what kind of stocks you like. Every stock has its own personality and once you catch on to that specific personality, trading will become easier if you stick to groups of stocks that are similar.

One reason for this is because you will most likely be able to use the same strategy for all of your stocks. This can help you when it comes to learning techniques and strategies. It is easier to stick to one strategy because there are so many tiny details about swing trading you need to remember, the human brain can only hold so much information.

Another reason for this is because this allows you to be able to manage a certain amount of stocks consistently. If you are a full-time swing trader, you will find this system will give you less stress, keep your focus, and increase confidence in your abilities. Of course, all this will help you keep your right state of mind as a trader.

6. Always Have a Clear Plan

Whenever you enter a trade, you will want to make sure that you have a clear plan of action. This plan will most likely be your trading plan; however, this is known to change from time to time as traders start to learn and grow with their profession. While this is great as it means you are becoming a more successful trader, you will also want to make sure that you continue to update and adjust your plan as you need to.

Before you enter any trade, it is best to go through your plan and make sure that it will work with that stock. If you find it won't, then you will need to either adjust your trading plan or choose a stock that will fit your trading plan better.

You will want to make sure that everything is including in this plan from your entry to your exit. You will want to make sure that you have all the key points and details down. On top of this, you will also want to make sure that you have a stop-loss strategy in place so you can quickly let go of that stock through a trade and walk away from losing a large amount of money. Remember, when you decide the stop-loss strategy is the best course of action, it will happen quickly. In fact, trading is a very faced-paced business, which is another reason making sure you always have a clear plan of action is a commandment.

7. Always Integrate Fundamentals into Your Technical Analysis

While I will discuss technical analysis later in this book, one of the 11 commandments of swing trading is to make sure that you integrate fundamentals into your analysis. If you have looked into day trading, you will know a bit about fundamentals and more about technical analysis. However, when it comes to swing trading, fundamentals becomes just as important as technical analysis. The main reason for this is because you hold your stocks longer than a few minutes to a few hours.

8. Make Sure to Master the Psychological side of Swing Trading

As you will see later in this book, there is a lot of psychology that goes into swing trading. In fact, psychology goes into any type of trading, but it is more crucial when it comes to swing traders. While part of this is about keeping the right mindset, the other part comes from the overall experience of swing trading. There are a lot of factors, such as making mistakes, learning, and losing that can affect your psyche throughout your day. For example, if you take a loss you might find that you feel like a failure after you have closed out your day. This can affect your personal life as well as your working life. It is extremely important to make sure that you have a healthy frame of mind and not just the right mindset when you are a trader.

9. Try Putting the Odds in Your Favor

Sometimes you will look at a trade and wonder if you will be able to make a profit on it. This is why it is important to use technical analysis with every trade. However, even if you feel that you might not be able to make a profit, this doesn't mean that you walk away from the trade. In fact, you can take this time to work on putting the odds in your favor. While this means you might end up risking a profit, trading is always full of risks. In fact, you will never be able to fully eliminate risks. Therefore, there are times where you have to take the leap and use certain techniques in order to try to work the trade into your favor.

One way to do this is by having a target price, which should always be a part of your target plan. This price will tell you when you should quickly turn to sell or trade the stock and when you should hold on to it for a bit longer. No matter what the market conditions are, you always want to stick to your target price. Therefore, you want to make sure that you complete your technical analysis to the best of your abilities before you go forward with your trading plan.

Furthermore, it is important to not only assess the chart once but also to reassess the chart. This means that you don't just analyze the chart before you take on the trade as you will continue to look at the chart and see what the stock's trend is doing in real-time. This means that you will notice the stock price increase and decreasing throughout the time you are analyzing.

10. Trade in Harmony with the Trend Time Frames

When it comes to the stock market, there are three types of trend time frames. The longest time frame is a year. The intermediate time frame is about three months. The shortest time frame is less than a month. When you are a swing trader, you will typically focus on the intermediate and short-term time frames. However, there are traders who have stated that they have looked at trends as far back as six months. Typically, swing traders don't have to focus on the longer time frame because they are considered to be short-term traders. At the same time, swing traders need to do more than just look at the short-term trend lines.

In fact, many expert swing traders will tell beginners that if they only focus on the short-term time frame, they are more likely to make mistakes. While you can always get a good sense of what the stock is doing with the short-term time frame, this can also limit you. The stock market is a very unpredictable place. This means that the further you look back, the better your idea will be about the type of trend that goes with the stock. The key is to heavily focus on the short-term trends and then do an analysis of the intermediate trends.

11. Make Sure to Use Multiple Indicators and Not Create Isolation

Sometimes traders will often feel that they only need to use one tool to give them an idea of what stock will give them a profitable trade and what stock won't. You should never do this. You always want to make sure that you use multiple tools and that these tools give you consistent results. For example, you might use a strategy, candlestick chart, volume, and other tools in order to find out that your trade will be profitable.

One of the reasons this is important is because it helps you limit your risks. The more tools you have that give you consistent results, the more likely you are to be able to make a profit.

Chapter 14 The Top Mistakes That Beginners Make

As a beginner, there are a lot of things that you need to learn to do well with swing trading. Learning all the strategies, learning how to read the charts and making smart decisions when it comes to picking out stocks to work with can be a challenge. As you are getting used to the whole process, it can take some time and effort, and you are likely to make some mistakes along the way.

These mistakes are pretty normal when you are a beginner, but no beginner wants to deal with them. They want to be able to make as much money as possible, without losing a lot of money as they start to learn how things work. This chapter focuses on some of the top mistakes that a lot of beginners make and some of the things that you can do to avoid these common mistakes.

Let the emotions get in the way

One mistake that almost all beginners will make is that they let their emotions get in the way of their decision making. They see that they are about to lose out on a trade or they see that the profits will keep reaching a higher value, and they want to stay in the market longer, despite what all their research and their strategy told them before. This will end up disastrous and is one of the leading reasons that beginners lose so much money and end up having to stop at day trading.

You need to learn how to keep the emotions out of the game. If you are a highly emotional person, swing trading is not going to be the best option for you to try out because things can change in an instant. The good news is that there are a few techniques that you can use to help keep the emotions out of the game so you can reduce your risk and increase your chances of profit.

First, make sure that you use stop points and that you stick with them. These stop points will ensure that you enter and exit the trade at the right times to either limit your losses or to help limit the risk that you have while gaining a profit. They aren't always full proof, but if you stick with them, you are less likely to have issues later on. Picking a good strategy, asking for advice, and really doing your research before you begin are all good ways to ensure you can keep the emotions out of your trading.

Forget to use stop points

The stop points will be so important when you start out as a swing trader. These points will tell you when to get out of the market, whether the market is going up or down and can reduce your risk. You need to have a stop loss point, which is the point you will get out of the market if you lose so much money, and you need a stop profit point, which is where you will get out of the market once you earn a certain profit.

Both of these are important to ensure you cut down on your risk and that you make as much money as possible in the process. For the stop loss point, you are figuring out how much money you are comfortable with losing in the market. Once the market goes down to this point, you need to get out. It is highly likely that the market will keep going down and if you don't get out at your stop loss point, you will potentially lose a lot of money in the process. This takes the emotions out of the game. You simply see that the stop point was reached and cut your losses until the next trade.

You also need to have a stop point for the profits that you want to earn. This may seem silly because you want to earn as much profit as you possibly can with each trade. But emotions can come into play here again too. Without the stop point, you may end up staying in the market too long, and make some costly mistakes. The market can turn around just as quickly as it went up, and if you are still in the market, you may lose all your earnings instead of gaining anything.

For this stop point, figure out what you can realistically make on the trade. Where do you think the market for your stock will go over the next few days based on the trend that you are setting? Put the stop point there and then as soon as the market reaches that point, you will take your earnings and withdraw from the market.

Putting in more money than you can afford to lose

With any investment that you work with, you need to be careful about the losses that you are dealing with. If you take on too much risk, you will end up losing all your money and never getting a chance to give it another try. Coming up with a good risk to reward ratio will help to limit your losses, but you also must make sure that you never put in more than you are willing to lose.

A good place to start is to put some savings behind for your swing trades. Never use money that you would need for rent, food, and other necessities. The second you do this, you bring the emotions into the game, and you are more likely to lose it all. Starting a savings account right now with the money you can use for swing trading allows you to have a little cushion without having to eat up all the money you need for other things.

When you are using the extra money, rather than money that you really need elsewhere, you are ensuring that you will spend it wisely. You won't stay in a trade too long in the hopes of recovering that money. No one wants to lose money along the way when they are trading, but it is much easier to cut your losses when it was just a little savings rather than if that money was your rent payment for the month.

Not understanding your strategy

If you do not understand the strategy that you are using, it can be impossible for you to get results when you get started with swing trading. Your strategy will outline exactly how you will behave in each trade situation. It will tell you how to look at the charts, how to pick out the stocks, when to enter the market, and when to exit the market. Each strategy has the potential to be successful, but you need to understand the strategy and use it properly.

When you get started in swing trading, it is always best to start with a simple strategy. Yes, there are some more complex ones that may sound fun, but since you are already learning about the market and how it works, why add in more complications with a hard strategy. There are a lot of great strategies that are simple, and some even designed for the beginner, that will make you just as much money as the more complex strategies, without all the work.

Picking a strategy is really important when it comes to doing well in swing trading. Before you pick out one, make sure to read through them all and fully understand what you will need to do to make it successful. You want one that is effective and easy to follow, as well as one that you will not want to switch out of in the middle of the trade. There is nothing wrong with trying out different strategies to see which one you like the best in between your trades, but if you switch strategies while in the same trade, you are setting yourself up for failure.

Not having the right tools

As a trader, you need to have some of your own tools in place if you would like to get started with swing trading. This can be a very difficult method when it comes to investing, and without the right tools, you will miss out on some important information that can help you see trends and make smart decisions along the way.

The first place to go for some tools is to talk to your broker. Often the broker will have a variety of unique tools that they can give to you as part of their fees. If you don't know how to use some of these tools, make sure to ask questions and learn how to make it all work or you will miss out.

You can also bring in some of your own tools to the game as well. Find charts about the market, look online, and ask questions. Remember, the best way to notice a trend is when the same information starts to show up on more than one chart or tool so always strive to have as many of these tools available as possible.

Following others rather than learning your own way

When you first get started, it can be tempting to find a mentor or a group and then just follow along exactly with what they do each time. This is really tempting if you see that they are making a lot of money and you want to join and make that money as well. But in the long run, no one knows the trading style that you like, and there are times when even an advanced mentor will get things wrong.

Instead of following along blindly with what someone else tell you, it is better to learn your own way. There is nothing wrong with talking to a mentor and others who have been in the market for some time, but you need to learn your own methods, your own strategies, and how you want to behave in the market. This will help you to stay on track with your trades and will ensure that you don't get misled by others who may not have your best interests at heart.

Not cutting your losses

Even the best swing traders will make mistakes at times. They will misread the market, they will try out a new strategy that doesn't work for them, or the market just doesn't behave in the manner that they had hoped. And when this happens, the trader will lose out on their money. As a beginner, it is more likely that you will earn a loss at some point. The important thing is to learn how to cut your losses, rather than staying too long in the market.

Some beginners will see that they are losing money on one of their trades and so they will try to regain that money. Even with the market going down, and no signs of reversal, they will stay in the market and hope that things will reverse. This is dangerous because it results in you staying in the market way too long and you will lose out on way too much money in the process.

Instead of sticking with a market that is not working in your favor, it is much better to learn how to cut your losses. Pick out an amount that you are comfortable with losing if the market does not go the way that you would like, put a stop point there, and then withdraw from the market as soon as you reach that point. This will help you to limit your losses and can give you more opportunities to try another trade in the future.

Conclusion

Congratulations for making it to the end of this book! I know it was a lot of information for you to take in, so this is really an accomplishment in your swing trading career!

One of the goals of this book was to give you a start on your swing trading career. Not only did I want to explain the key concepts of financial trading. Because this is considered to be a foundation when it comes to trading, I didn't want to leave this information out of the book. On top of this, it was important to explain to you the difference between trading and investing. There are a lot of people who get into trading when they believed they were going to be investing money instead of trading stocks in order to gain a profit. Because these two topics are different, it is important to make sure you want to be a trader and not an investor before you go too far into your research for swing trading.

Another major point of this book was to give you a concise beginner's guide about swing trading which touched on a variety of topics. Instead of you having to read dozens more articles and a few books about swing trading, I wanted to give you a way that you can place one book in your device to turn to when you need a refresher about swing trading. On top of this, I wanted you to be able to bring this book to your friends who are interested in swing trading and show them this beginner's guide, so they can get all the information required before opening their account with a broker.

As you have realized by this point, swing trading is not the easiest career; however, when it comes to the stock market, there is no easy career. It doesn't matter if you decide on swing trading, become a buy and hold investor, or get into day trading you will find that each one of these areas have their own challenges. However, you will soon come to find that they each have their own advantages as well. You should already to be able to pick out a few advantages to becoming a swing trader. For example, you could one day be able to trade without the assistance of a broker. On top of this, you have been able to get a sneak peak of the many online communities for swing traders. Once you decide to join an online community or two, you will realize how enjoyable swing trading is.

You should also understand what simulation trading is and how important it is to make sure you complete this type of trading before you start trading for money. You should also not only understand risks which are associated in swing trading but also have an idea on how to decrease these risks once you start swing trading. Of course, this is one reason you want to make sure to practice simulation trading at first. As stated before, simulation trading will help you make sure that you understand the risks and the strategies which are associated with swing trading.

By now you should not only clearly understand what swing trading is, but also what the average time fame is for a swing trader. You should be able to remember the 11 commandments of swing trading, techniques, what the right mindset is when you are trading, know a variety of tips to help you get on your way, and also understand the many mistakes that other swing traders have made.

Furthermore, you should be able to explain how a day will go for a full-time swing trader, be able to explain the two different types of stock market conditions, and the art of short selling.

On top of all the information you need to know about being a swing trader, you also know how to get started with researching as much information as possible. On top of this, you have learned tips to help you become a better researcher, so you can gain the most out of your research time. It is important to keep these tips in mind as you will need to used them throughout your career. On top of this, you can also add your own tips, which will become useful when you begin to help other beginner swing traders in the next few years.

Thank you for not only purchasing this book but also reading it. I hope that you found it helpful in your swing trading journey. I wish you the best of luck! If you would be so kind, please take a minute to leave a review about my book. Thank you!